Caroline Hillier and John Mosley are the author and photographer of three topographical books, *A Journey to the Heart of England* (The Western Midlands), *The Bulwark Shore* (Thanet and the Cinque Ports) and, most recently, *Images of the Downs*. Caroline Hillier is also the author of two novels, *The Flood* and *Dialogue on an Island*.

Together they researched and completed this book on the Western Midlands while living and working in the area in the 1970s. Recently, they have travelled back, and their impressions of the area a decade later are recorded in a new Foreword to this edition of the book.

CAROLINE HILLIER

A Journey to the Heart of England

with photographs by John Mosley

PALADIN
GRAFTON BOOKS
A Division of the Collins Publishing Group

LONDON GLASGOW
TORONTO SYDNEY AUCKLAND

914.248

Paladin
Grafton Books
A Division of the Collins Publishing Group
8 Grafton Street, London W1X 3LA

Published in Paladin Books 1978
Reprinted 1987

First published in Great Britain by
Victor Gollancz Ltd 1976

ISBN 0-586-08291-3

Printed and bound in Great Britain by
Collins, Glasgow

Set in Monotype Ehrhardt

Acknowledgements

We should like particularly to thank all the people who, often at very short notice, have talked to us about themselves and their work. They are too numerous to list, but it is their friendliness and generosity which have helped to shape the text, and we shall remember them long after this book is published.

For their advice and unstinting information I would like to thank Keith Brace, Literary Editor of the *Birmingham Post*; Lyndon Jenkins, Press and Public Relations Officer of the National Exhibition Centre; Peter Neeld, Keeper of Local and Industrial History in Wolverhampton; and many others, again too many to list. (None of them have read proofs of this book; if errors there be, they are not theirs.) I should also like to thank Jon Raven for kindly allowing me to quote from his collections of traditional songs: 'Nine Times A Night' and 'Brave Collier Lads' from *Kate of Coalbrookdale*; 'The Tommy Note' from *Canal Songs*; 'Black the Name' from *Folk Lore and Songs of the Black Country and the West Midlands*. Extracts from 'Parta Quies' and *The Shropshire Lad* by A. E. Housman are reproduced by kind permission of The Society of Authors, literary representative of the Estate of A. E. Housman, and of Jonathan Cape Ltd; the quotation from 'The Death of Simon Fugue' from *Tales of the Five Towns* by Arnold Bennett is by kind permission of Mrs Cheston Bennett and Chatto and Windus Ltd; extracts from *Precious Bane* by Mary Webb by kind permission of the Executors of the Mary Webb Estate, and of Jonathan Cape Ltd; extracts from Elgar's letters by kind permission of the Trustees of the Elgar Birthplace Trust; extracts from *Potbank* by Mervyn Jones by kind permission of Curtis Brown Ltd; extracts from the *History of Birmingham*, Volume II, by Asa Briggs, by kind permission of Birmingham Corporation and the Oxford University Press Ltd. The introductory quotations are from *English Cities and Small Towns* by John Betjeman (Britain in Pictures series, Collins, 1943); *Walks in the Black Country and its Green Border-Land* by Elihu Burritt (London, 1868); and *Chilterns to Black*

Country(About Britain no. 5) by W. G. Hoskins (Collins, 1951).

Finally, we are deeply grateful to Kevin Crossley-Holland, our editor, and to Giles Gordon, our agent, both of whom made this book possible.

Swan Bank,   C.H.
Penn
1975

Contents

Foreword   8
Introduction   15
1. Hampton in Arden; Meriden; Packington Hall; Bickenhill   19
2. Coventry   34
3. Wolverhampton; Bilston   45
4. The Black Country   67
5. Birmingham   89
6. Bridgnorth, Ironbridge, Telford New Town, Wellington; Wroxeter; Newport, Tong   108
7. Stafford, Stone; Shugborough and Cannock   124
8. Lichfield, Wall and Tamworth   137
9. Burton-upon-Trent; Tutbury, Rolleston; Uttoxeter; Dovedale and the Manifold Valley   147
10. Stoke-on-Trent: the Potteries   161
11. Kidderminster, Stourport-on-Severn, Bewdley   176
12. Worcester, Droitwich, Leominster   183
13. Clun, Offa's Dyke, the Welsh Marches   193
14. Shrewsbury, Ludlow, Much Wenlock, the Long Mynd   204
15. Oswestry, Ellesmere, Wem; Whitchurch; Llangollen   221
16. Chester; Wrexham, Nantwich, Market Drayton   234
Notes   243
Select Bibliography   248
Index   253

Foreword

The first edition of this book was dedicated to all those who have never made the journey to England's heartland, in the hope that they would do so. Now, a decade later, the wish is repeated. We are a divided nation, but in the Western Midlands, there is hope, and determination.

Will this or that scheme, enterprise, technological development or 'greening' of wasteland be an improvement? The answer was summed up for me in the Black Country, making no bones about it: 'It's got to be better, hasn't it.'

1986. Midwinter. We are travelling back, to an area where we no longer live, an event which as everyone knows can be a mistake. The known and loved region will have shrunk in size and attractions. But not so in the West Midlands. Despite the economic body blow, the area is bracing – sometimes astringently so; its buildings well built, streets well kept, spirit alive; its green border-land characteristically beautiful; its people still friendly, ready with smiles or a straight answer, still walking briskly without overcoats on a bright winter day. The welcome still there.

Approaching from the more somnolent – and more complacent – South, by train: still the impression of the countryside opening out, beyond that old watershed of Watford, of skies becoming wider, as the space of the land takes over. Factories – a few with chimneys still smoking – scrapyards, allotments, dumped cars, the accompanying criss-crossing canal, tall lines of poplars, longboats, boys fishing. 'Stone and Webster House' at Milton Keynes, all glass, and the man-made cows grazing. The gnarled oaks of Northamptonshire and Warwickshire. Rugby – only one smoking chimney there. Coventry – its small rows of houses freshly decorated with green, pink or yellow drainpipes (by the newly unemployed?). The West Midlands Sports Centre for the Disabled. Cattle with longer coats at a pond, their breath freezing in the already colder air. The National Exhibition Centre, now crowning its successes with plans to double in size, and the adjoining Birmingham International Airport, to which in 1986 tour operators flew thousands of American visitors.

How *has* industrial decline hit this area? The answer is, suddenly and drastically. Since 1981 alone, more than 10,000 firms have gone to the wall; unemployment is now running at over 16% in the West Midlands Metropolitan County area, slightly less in the region as a whole. Famous names such as Alfred Herbert Ltd, and the Round Oak Steelworks, are no more. The Meriden Motorcycle Co-operative's stubbornly brave venture ended in 1983. The workforce at the then British Leyland was slashed; GKN and TI 'slimmed' down.

We visited the site of the British Steel works in Bilston. Nothing remains of all that heat and power, the miles of track, the 212-foot-high blast furnace Elisabeth. The area, like a hole in the middle of the Black Country, is greened over with scrub and grass, and the churches of Coseley and Sedgley and Dudley Castle on its hill, look down on desolation. The view is like a kick in the solar plexus. (John worked there for close on two years; what must it be like for those who worked there for 40 years?)

But Bilston, people will tell you, has been dying for a long time. Has it all gone then? Is this West Midlands area of a proud skilled workforce changed beyond recall? Has the plug, as Sid Platt of NALGO neatly put it, 'gone out of the bath', while 'people with cups try to fill it'? Will enough investment ever be made in British industry to enable firms to instal the new technology and new plant for their new products?

The spirit is still alive. Red-brick housing may have encroached on the Black Country's wasteland where wildflowers blew, a saver-centre may have landed on Oldbury, and professional people – not speaking the dialect – have bought up many of the little houses of Gornal, but you still see men walking their bull-terriers, a man in a car trying to tow a lorry and shouting 'Yo buggers' to the traffic tailback, and men in pub bars assessing the situation with dignity. The Old Swan at Netherton, where we spent such a memorable New Year's Eve, is refurbished after a fire, but still stands, having defeated more than one demolition order, still brews its own beer. Mrs Pardoe died a few years ago, but her photograph watches over her bar with kind authority, and the beer still tastes as it should.

Wolverhampton, which looks towards the green border-land of Shropshire and towards the people of the countryside as well as of the Black Country, has still its 'one fair church' and more. (Sainsbury's are building offices within the restored shell of St George's Church to adjoin their new store, a singularly 1980s juxtaposition of God and Mammon.) The town has lost its Queen's Ballroom but the Art Gallery and Museum will have from 1987 an outstanding new Local History Department overseen by Peter Neeld, who is of an inspired antiquarian, rather than mobcaps and mead, turn of mind, giving to Wulfrunians, and outsiders, the true taste of the town and a sense of place.

For the past can be not just a dusty answer, but a pointer towards the future.

So, not for nothing, is the motto of the country's Second City, Birmingham, 'Forward'. Totally undiminished by its bid for the 1992 Olympics, Brum's self-esteem is soaring. Businessmen (and business travel brings in 450 million pounds a year to the 25-mile area round the NEC), between talk of targets and telephoning from the middle lane, and of visits to Croydon and 'the Smoke', say 'Brum really *is* a city'. And Japanese businessmen (who find it 'quiet') are in Birmingham for *training*. Learning, perhaps, from the burgeoning Science Parks at Aston and at Warwick University, but if so, what a compliment.

Birmingham has finely restored its Great Western Arcade, and St Paul's Square; is restoring, to open in 1987, its Snow Hill station (a busy renewal of infrastructure one would like to see elsewhere); has new concert halls, and Simon Rattle with the CBSO reaching new heights of international prestige; will have by 1991 an International Convention Centre that has won a massive grant from the European Regional Development Fund. What other British city would have the nerve to rival Monaco with a Super Prix road-race, and despite pouring rain promise to repeat the occasion? (Generally it has now been at last admitted that it was a planning mistake to banish pedestrians rather than the traffic to underpasses). Why, finally, are imaginatively converted offices standing empty? What is wrong with London firms that they don't leap at the chance to re-locate here? Birmingham is warm, friendly, enterprising; 'service' is not a dirty word here, one feels.

If the service sector is one way forward, tourism is another, and this region's sites will not quickly become stale or overtrodden. The Ironbridge Gorge Museum, the Potteries, the Cathedral cities, the varied countryside, the hills towards the Welsh border. Much of it lonely, difficult of access and requiring a determined assault by the tourist, and none the worse for that.

Employment? The old industries? The saddest change: the scale of the human tragedy is evident. Pockets of the unemployed, as in other urban areas, create their own sub-cultures, not necessarily negative, not always short-fused. Overall there is no whining or whingeing; again and again we were told, 'We don't ask for handouts.' The old days of heavy metal-bashing are past; the machines I described 'pounding away' are silent. But in Birmingham, the City of Twelve Hundred Trades, the Jewellery Quarter flourishes (the British Jeweller's Association celebrating its centenary in 1987); up narrow flights of stairs, a skilled jeweller can still alter a ring in minutes, measuring it perfectly by eye; new shops at Hockley, even if accused of selling 'hollow chain made in Italy', bring in the visitors (while the ghost of Joseph Chamberlain calls again for tariffs).

In Digbeth, a circle of craftsmen work at 100-year-old industries: brass, steel, iron. Here at Corley Welding, Mike Dennis showed us the steel horses by Kevin Atherton which he was completing, which will stand along the railway line between Birmingham and Wolverhampton, the view stamped on Auden's heart.

Craftsmanship, quality. West Midlanders have always excelled at these. Gunmaking, Jaguar cars, silverware, symphonies, enamels, precision tools, town halls. Worthy of emulation. (And another way forward for the country as a whole?)

The view by the tracks is crowded now with new housing, waits for its promised green trees. (And for the outcome of new 'hi-tech' plans for regeneration over which local authorities show a healthy propensity to argue with Central Government 'planners'. 'We don't want the place greened up. We want jobs.' A Chief Executive quoted in *The Independent*.)

Leaving Wolverhampton late, towards the shortest day of the year: one thin chimney sending red smoke across the red horizon; two spires challenging the tall square of the Mander shopping centre; then the mixture of pylons and houses and poplars and works and canal and the silver pools of water on derelict land; the small castle of Dudley on its hill; the past and the future; the changes half hidden by darkness; the myriad lights from homes. The human landscape, vital to us all.

'It's got to be better, hasn't it.'

1986   C.H.

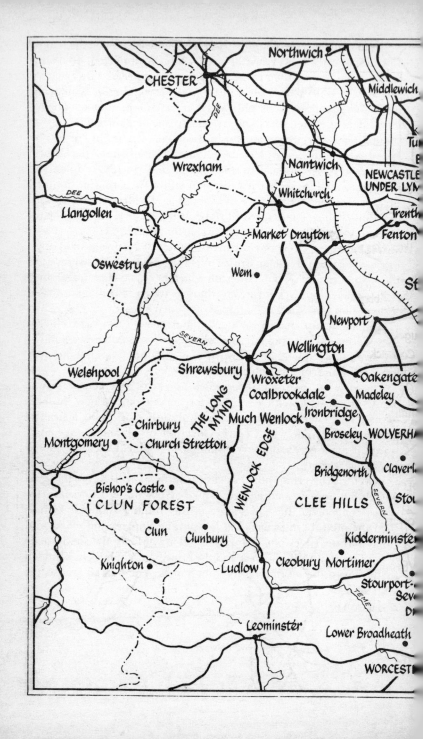

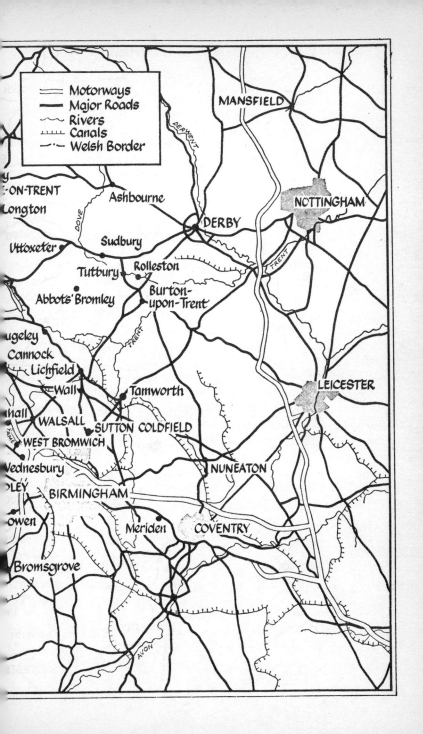

To someone who likes people as well as buildings, the industrial towns are the hope and the life of England.

John Betjeman

Within this *arrondissement* of the industries and ingenuities of nature and man, may be found in remarkable juxta-position the best that either has produced . . . the Black Country is beautifully framed by a Green Border-Land.

Elihu Burritt

There is no dull uniformity about the Midland countryside: it is essentially English countryside, the very heart of it all . . .

W. G. Hoskins

Introduction

There is an unshakeable conviction, which has often been remarked on, and which even today is held by many Londoners and people from the south of England, that civilization ends at St Albans, or some point a little farther north. Those people, from the part of the country which John (adapting Winston Churchill's famous phrase) calls the soft underbelly of England, sometimes do not even know where Birmingham – let alone the Black Country – is. Is Birmingham farther north than Leeds, I was asked by one who knows Europe and America like the back of her hand. I was equally ignorant, having voyaged to Greek islands in storm-tossed boats, crossed the hot plains to Toledo, footed it along the Côte d'Azur, junketed down the Rhine – but never having been to Birmingham, or Meriden.

This is very sad, not for superficial reasons of tourism, but because the process is largely reciprocal, with the result that South and Midlands – and possibly North, East and Midlands also – do not know each other well enough to draw benefit from their differences, and often remain in an attitude of suspicious antagonism or dogged indifference, region to region, culture to culture, man to man. It is difficult to see how England can cope with changing patterns in employment, or economic crises, or preserve an 'offshore island's' much-trodden heritage, unless there is a greater glimmer of understanding of the components which make up the whole. As a linguist, I have always felt myself a European; it seems to me that one of the most hopeful aspects of the consolidated EEC is that membership of a larger community may make this country look more squarely at what it has to offer, and realize that each region has an equal right to shape the general pattern, to be heard. A Frenchman or German may be delightfully ignorant of where St Albans is; but he may well have been to Birmingham. His machines may be pounding away in the Black Country. Travelling through the cities and green fields of the Western Midlands – of Warwickshire or Staffordshire or Shropshire – he will see the landscape from which the wealth was wrested that made Britain a powerful nation, and the 'green fields in the past of English history'. The durable, changing centre. For those who still love England, there is a need to find, re-find its heart again. An exploration to the centre is part of that journey.

John Betjeman has pointed out that a good way to approach a place is by train, 'for from the railway line you get an impression of the surrounding country, undisturbed by the adjuncts of a main road'.[1] I first saw the West Midlands in this way, and was amazed at what I saw, at the different features of the scene as we sped northwards. The faces in the train already seemed different to some extent – heavier, with less worry in the eyes and more kindness about the mouth, an added solidity, and lack of fashionableness; with less cleverness but more shrewdness.

We sped on; Berkhamsted, Bletchley. The air grew colder. Pale, greyish bricks and stone cottages, somnolent trees and a flat pale sky, rows of fruit trees, calm wheatfields and white-brown soil gave way to large red-brick farmhouses, stumpy oaks, a timberyard, wide fields of black-legged sheep, tussocky watermeadows where a solitary figure walked under wheeling gulls; a feeling of space, where the eye could range without seeing a house. The Grand Union Canal, running beside the railway and road, charts an older route, and everywhere small churches chart an older map still – the countless small churches of an island not much torn by internal wars, the metal pennants on their weathervanes like flags, which still catch the eye among pylons, semis or caravans, still tug at the heartstrings, are still, indefinably, our country. Frail grey spires give way to sturdy red sandstone towers, a more weathered element. A mill, painted barges; pylons, man's poor attempt at trees, which are nevertheless part of a working landscape, human effort; well-kept allotments.

Wolverton, Rugby; Midland Red buses, cranes, gasworks, the old English Electric works; rounded ironwork windows; factory chimneys with streamers of smoke, homely, homelike houses. Coventry; small tower blocks, spires, well-painted windowframes, British Leyland, cars and cars. Then farms, rivers, a packhorse bridge, scrap dumps, black-and-white cattle, and the startling rows of poplars of the Midlands. An airfield; prefabricated houses, tyres, warehouses like scalloped opera houses and old corrugated iron warehouses like mills; wind-bent trees. Birmingham; an island of tower blocks; the GPO tower; depots, factories, scrap iron, vans, soot in the nostrils, grime, factories, chimneys, Typhoo Tea, Dunlop, posters of Kent 'Get Away from it All', red-brick toy houses, swirling, exhilarating concrete, ugly shoes, pink-cheeked girls. A railway guard whistling cheerfully. And on – railway, canal, railway, derelict houses, small church towers, iron and steel, car dumps, scrap, columbine and pink willowherb, the motorway; the Chance glass works, rubble, a castle against the wide sky, clouds reflected in water, ragwort, slag-heaps, baskets of flowers swinging outside Victorian pubs, a horse grazing, the green wastes of the Black Country, a human landscape.

By the reverse process, if you return to the South, everything seems paler, more bloodless. The colour ebbs from the scenery; there is more cynicism in weary, intelligent faces. You feel you are leaving a hub, a more dramatic and infinitely more rude and rough region.

The West Midlands is at the centre of the country's communications network. Geographically it is the centre, and historically it has been a stronghold against invaders. It is the industrial centre, producing an estimated forty per cent of our exports. Are its industrial problems, its social patterns today the same as those of the country as a whole, or not? The answer becomes clear as you get to know the region.

I can only write as an outsider, having lived in the West Midlands for three years. Knowing it would be very different from the South, one hoped to find something that if not lost in the South, is in danger of becoming so. Had the Midlands people kept a sense of involvement, of pride in achievements, without losing attributes of kindness, unsophisticated values? (There was certainly no risk of being in an enclave of the retired – the industrial cities are nothing if not places of work.) I must plead that, on the credit side, an outsider may perhaps get a vivid picture of what is new to him.

The area of the book is defined by what seemed to comprise a distinct, integral region, with the strong characteristics of this heartland. Farther south in the Western Midlands, in parts of Warwickshire, such as Stratford, in the Vale of Evesham or the Cotswolds, there are closer links and similarities with the South. It was a temptation to include the Shakespeare country, but that would have needed a book in itself.

I hope the Welsh will forgive me for crossing the border occasionally.

Our journey has been together; our explorations often apart. A traveller on his own often has a heightened sense of discovery, of being in tune with a landscape as yet uncharted by him. The typewriter and camera demand different speeds, and in this no one should imagine that the writer's is the more difficult undertaking. With some paper and a ball-point, or typewriter, a writer can work. A photographer has always to be at a specific place at a specific time, catch it in a certain light. Having driven miles, he may find a car parked in the square he has come to photograph, or, if in Birmingham to photograph among other things the statue of Boulton, Murdock and Watt, discover at second glance that Boulton and Watt have unreachable Coca-Cola bottles in their hands.

For both of us, our hope is that our book will awaken a desire to visit the places we have attempted to portray; and for those who know them already, that we may have added the occasional fresh angle.

I shall doubtless be accused by many of painting too rosy a view of the West Midlands. One can only follow one's bent, and mine is to travel hopefully. It seems to me also that the topographical books or traveller's accounts – or those having a strong flavour of the countryside – which last the longest, and which I would emulate if I could, are those expressing enthusiasm, even euphoria for a place, for life. Kilvert, Izaak Walton, Elihu Burritt – all saw life through nothing if not tinted lenses. And if I have talked to more poets than politicians, that is not only from personal preference. Poets have a knack of giving a place substance, of being able to express in words the non-ephemeral. They do not need to take the Westminster eye view. They may look farther into the past, or the future.

The West Midlands has an important past. What of its future? Since we have been here the region has plummeted from one that had confidence in its past record and achievements, to a crisis area, one of the most hard hit by economic distress and unemployment. But whatever it is, the region is not static. The elements of which it is composed make for change, and indomitableness, and so even in dire straits, for hope. Its future is England's.

1   Hampton in Arden; Meriden; Packington Hall; Bickenhill

> Hath not old custom made this life more sweet
> Than that of painted pomp? Are not these woods
> More free from peril than the envious court?
>
> I would not change it.
>
> *As You Like It*

In the heart of England lies Arden. Here are Shakespeare's mossy oaks and holly, his greenwood tree. Warwickshire is not densely wooded now, as it once was. Then, the southern part of the county below Stratford and the Avon was the arable Feldon, the northern part the woodland of Arden, a forest which covered a large part of the Midlands in the Middle Ages. Its oaks spread as far north as Staffordshire, and their descendants can still be seen around Atherstone and in Sutton Park, and in small woods and copses all over this central plateau to the east of Birmingham. For this, unlike Shropshire, is flat land, although not dull.

Green-belt land wedged uncomfortably between the sprawls of Birmingham and Coventry. At the centre of the country's communications links; bisected by the M6, soon to be joined by the M42. Cut through by railway and canal, with power stations, sewage-treatment plants, an airport, mining-spoil heaps, converging oil pipe lines. What is left of Arden?

I got off the train at Hampton in Arden, a commuter village for Birmingham and Coventry. Hawthorn was in blossom by the side of the station, and daffodils. The ticket office was shut.

'It's a leisure place,' smiled a pensioner at the top of the steps, as he droned happily in the sun with the bees.

I began to breathe more freely; a sense of apprehension left me.

The sky was unclouded, and it was spring. Lorries thundered up the road.

'Two hundred and twelve lorries and vans in an hour,' I was told by duffle-coated children on a school project.

Nevertheless, there by the road are 'Rose Bank' and 'Beech House', pretty, small houses and larger ones with gables and orbed gateways; the

Midland Bank in a pint-sized cottage with flowerbeds; the Women's Institute, Victorian and tile-hung. Willow trees droop greenly by new semis. It is very English, with some of that indefinable taste at which the English are so adept – one up from gnomes: gables and rhododendrons; laburnums and labradors; pink-cheeked girls in anoraks; daffodils and dormers. Memories of green-belt land in other counties came flooding back to me.

In the Hampton post office it is 'Hullo, Glad' and 'ta, love'. In the pub the Shakespearean face of a farm hand bends over the peas he is shovelling up. The White Lion, unmodernized, crammed with beams and gumboots, farmers in knitted hats, jokes and purposeful munching. Across the road, cleaners' mops lean against the church tower, and under a window to a niece of Shelley, bright with stained-glass poets, the vicar tells me with inconsequential charm that he calls the rugged, medieval stone head on a sill his great-uncle. Neither he nor I can recognize the verses on a minutely worked sampler of crucifixion crosses sewn by a child in Hampton in 1800.

While working on this book I have not had to play the game of 'dodging the vicar', to which Sir Nikolaus Pevsner, pressed for time in his mammoth task of recording *The Buildings of England*, says he sometimes has to take recourse. Clergymen are marvellous exponents of their flocks and parishes. The strange details of the past which they remember, or occasionally forget, give history a quirky and human aura. At worst, if you stand and take it on the jaw, you will glean kernels of information after half an hour of digression. I sometimes think clergymen are the only died-in-the-wool Englishmen left – full of vague bonhomie, educated, the classics tripping off their tongues, whether booted on foot, in small cars or on mopeds, totally regardless of fashions – although often snobbish – and endlessly benevolent.

(Sir Nikolaus has other tactics, which I was relieved to hear I was not alone in using, of knocking on house doors, or even prowling round domains – he was once nearly taken for a burglar. As he says, if you write for permission to visit, you may be told to come back at 8.30 on Wednesday the tenth of next month, when you will be many miles away.)

The vicar of Hampton in Arden is up-to-date about the position of the village in its changing environment. The new motorway (the M42) would, he said, relieve them of much of the traffic. Elsewhere I was told that there had been a great increase in traffic in the last two years. Not surprisingly: the National Exhibition Centre at Bickenhill is only two miles away, bringing with it not only its own lorries, but also construction work for hotels in the surrounding area. Yet here the people seem amazingly relaxed. I had expected horror at the commercial giant on their doorstep. 'It will have to be open for a while before we can tell,' was the strongest criticism I heard.

The place is amazingly unspoilt. Some cottages by Nesfield, in Late-Victorian style, have white pargetting – a flowered band of plasterwork like icing pricked out by a child – and the lodge of the manor house opposite is decorated with a single large innocent daisy. Up the hill are a Providence Chapel, and the library, sleepily open two days a week, in a charity school building of 1782, with the names of the trustees on iron boards in large, clear script. Would the education ministers of today be so proudly profligate of their names?

I walked on past the sixteenth-century Moat House, and then back in the other direction, towards the marsh where a packhorse bridge crosses the Blythe. Heartened by the White Lion's bitter, I stopped by a farm to eat my sandwiches. The warm smell of cottage flowers drifted up; there were beehives; a farm garden with run-to-seed sprouts and dock-leaves; celandine and groundsel, and nettles and wood chips under the trees; mossy trunks. Although I could hear planes in the distance, nothing disturbed me here but a white horse. A helicopter buzzed over like a dragonfly. The birds were singing fit to burst their throats. Horses stood peacefully under the elm trees. Fields stretched to the skyline, and on the horizon was a blue haze of oak trees – etched, inky, both sharp and cloud-like, like a dream sitting on the fringe of this twentieth-century landscape. Seeing a view such as this, your eyes smart, and you realize achingly that it isn't only the bright sunlight that is bothering you.

There is still something of Arden left, and, as in an ageing face, the lines and spoliations make it unbearably fragile; one can still see what it was.

*

I was arguing recently with a cosmopolitan West Indian, who knows England rather better than I do, as to why I should never want to live anywhere else for long. It was nothing to do with the brotherhood of man. Obviously one might be as happy among Eskimos as among Englishmen. I tried to analyse my feelings. I said: 'It's the hedges.' I played in them as a child, when cow parsley still grew higher than oneself, and campion was not as rare as plovers' eggs. Which were not so rare then either.

Also in Hampton in Arden is a manor house, which Pevsner and Alexandra Wedgwood in their *Warwickshire* disarmingly describe as 'rather dull.'[1] It is now a home for handicapped girls, with their own crafts shop. Up the drive I found dilapidated greenhouses, and a disused walled garden with shields on the gateway. Through the arch two sleek blackbirds were sitting with their golden beaks in profile in the shining grass – armorial bearings. I remembered climbing as a child along such walls with the girl owner of a great house in Dorset, who stole peaches from her own gardeners to eat with us. We also stole plovers' eggs, and pheasants' eggs, which we ate roasted over fires in the woods. A heinous crime, I can see now. They tasted delicious.

Manor houses have many fates in England today. Homes for the blind and disabled seem some of the most apt, the least ossified. Armorials which breathe.

*

It was a cold day when we went to Meriden. This village is bleaker, but again surprisingly unspoilt, if you can disregard the caravans on the outskirts. A cross, headless, marks the centrepoint of England, the point farthest from the sea in all directions.

'It's been headless as long as I can remember . . . I've been here sixteen years,' a girl in the village shop told me.

There is also a bigger pillar 'In Remembrance of those Cyclists who gave their lives in World War II', and a tree planted by friends of the Cyclists' Touring Club. John, who often bicycles to work, noticed that there was a seat to the memory of Wayfarer (W. M. Robinson) who was devoted to cycling.

Bicycling always strikes me as a very English pastime, although I am sure just as many or more Frenchmen or Americans (certainly more Dutchmen) own bicycles. Perhaps it is the way Englishmen bicycle: inadequately and carelessly dressed, looping head erect, necks stiff under their caps, through the traffic. At all events it is appropriate that the bicycle, which made this region prosperous, is remembered here.

Up a hill from the village stands St Lawrence Church, its tower sturdy beneath jutting gargoyles and a golden weathercock. Across the road is a moathouse, now a farmhouse, dated 1609 but largely older.

Rain beat against our faces; lambs bleated, calves lowed, motorways roared, aeroplanes thundered, daffodils were growing and the sun appeared fitfully. Red plough, stretched away towards Birmingham on the skyline in one direction, and Hams Hall cooling towers to the right. John was busy taking photographs, and I pondered on Lady Godiva who founded this church. The lady of the farm and her dog got out of their large car, looked tolerantly at us. English country life was alive and kicking.

Down the road flags were flying over the Meriden Triumph works, a large Union Jack in the centre. Signboards proclaimed 'REMEMBER TRIUMPH STAYS AT MERIDEN WHERE THE LEGEND WAS MADE'.

Since we came to the West Midlands three years ago, we have followed the saga of the Meriden works with fascination and trepidation. The factory was taken over by workers in November 1973, in response to being made redundant when Norton Villiers Triumph decided to concentrate production of Triumph motor-cycles at Small Heath, Birmingham. They formed their co-operative, and until March 1975 there was a continual see-saw of probability as to whether Tony Wedgwood Benn would finally grant the co-operative government aid. At several points, as when the workers at NVT Wolverhampton became apprehensive, fearing for their own jobs, the prospect seemed unlikely. Opponents classed the project as woolly and blamed it for the troubles at the Wolverhampton and Small Heath NVT works. But would they have proved successful without Meriden? Despite all this, the co-operative caught the imagination. The tradition of independence and self-employment is strong in the West Midlands, as is that of dogged stubbornness. Something might come of it.

'For heaven's sake,' John said, 'approach them through the union.'

Bill Lapworth of the Transport and General Workers' Union and a member of the co-operative was very friendly. 'Tell them you've spoken to me...'

The factory had been open a few weeks, backed by the government's £5 million, when I went there. It was a high point; an optimistic beginning. The first sit-in in recent years to result in workers gaining ownership of their factory.

'It got a bit desperate ... for people with kids,' Mrs Wilson in reception told me, speaking of the eighteen months' picketing. 'We lost a few hundred pounds, but it was worth it.'

'Reception' was informal, humming. Mrs Wilson prefers working on wheel construction, 'lacing' of the spokes, but jobs were being run on an interchangeable basis. Her son-in-law had died recently; his one wish had been to see the co-operative in action before he died. It was clear that their factory mattered, intensely.

It took a bit of time to track down Denis Johnson, the chairman. In fact cries of 'I've found so-and-so – he's down the boiler house' or 'Where's Den . . . get Stan to talk to him', 'Get down there, mate', rang down the telephones. Everybody calls everybody by their Christian names, and there is complete equality between men and women. It seemed like an ant-hill in turmoil.

'In normal circumstances it would have been difficult to make it work,' Denis Johnson told me. 'There was the loyalty to the product, and the spirit was "To hell with it, we'll make a go of the co-operative".' He explained that the eighteen months of equality, of picketing, had welded the team together. They started with 800, which as people dropped out became 280. They had worked through it together; it was not a scheme that had been imposed on them. 'It took so long; this would deter others. The most difficult thing was coming back from talks with the government and having nothing new to report . . . The bailiffs never came although they threatened it . . . The most difficult thing in life is bringing about change.'

A red-haired tornado burst into the room. 'Money's in the bank,' he said. John Grattan, who had been the man who chained the gates at the beginning of the sit-in: 'Management out, we're chaining the gates.'

'How much are we going to pay for those bloody wrappings?' (Bloody is so usual a word in the region that it has about as much effect as a comma.) Conversation seemed spunky. 'Ring the gatehouse . . .' 'As long as he kept me bloody waiting this morning, tell the bastard . . .' 'See if you can get something definite . . . don't leave it floating about . . .'

'The whole thing was Trade-Union organized,' Denis Johnson told me. Yes, smiling a little embarrassedly, there were one or two Conservatives among them. And they had been approached by extremists who had wanted to use them as a platform. (I imagine Grattan saw to those.)

There used to be four different canteens, he told me, four car parks and four 'toilets'. There was a sign 'Women' on the brickwork, and five paces farther on a notice 'Lady Staff'. I forgot to ask him how the label now reads, but the women are obviously more than pulling their weight, and a woman company secretary has since been appointed. This, again, is typical of the West Midlands. There is really no need for Women's Liberation here, since women have been used to working alongside men for so long. In the old days in the Black Country, women nailmakers worked with the men in the yards of their little one-up-one-down houses, and a small window was built looking into the kitchen, so that they could glance into the house from time to time to see the children were not falling in the fire. Old customs, old loyalties. Brenda Price, the company secretary, has moved back to Meriden after beginning work there as a junior twenty-five years ago.

The workforce is flexible in the jobs they do, with safety the only limiting factor. 'The track is soul-destroying.' There is a two-tier system, with eight on the supervisory board. There are three trustees, who represent and vote according to the decisions of the beneficiaries. Everyone who was there on day one of production in the co-operative is a beneficiary (with an equal salary also). Others must wait a year after joining. And the product? (There has been much gloom in the press about the death of the large motor-bike market.) 'We've checked the market. We've met 400 dealers from the US and they say give us your bikes for the next five years and we can sell them. After two or three years we may alter the model. There's got to be a purpose, and our purpose is to be successful ... Yes, there are snags,' Denis Johnson said with quiet feeling. He clearly has immense patience. When all are equal, there is no privacy in your office, and you are on call all the time.

I hoped intensely that they would be successful.

The product itself is worthy. The bikes stood in their wrappings like racehorses in blankets. 750 c.c. twin-cylinder Bonnevilles. Cherokee red for the US market, Chuck Knight who showed me round told me, as he lovingly pointed out their lines. 'There's real craftsmanship in that.' He pointed out the skill that is needed to regulate the tension of the spokes – craftsmanship no less delicate and precise than that of a pottery worker.

He has been there twenty-five years and during the eighteen months they were not allowed to take bikes out he did 11,500 miles round the car park with 92,000 gear changes, testing. He does overtime (unpaid) if a job needs doing. 'I worked over the weekend to get the rear disc sorted out.'

Cyril Miller has been at the factory since it moved there from Coventry. He remembers the old factory being bombed during the war when he was a boy, and how the army made smokescreens over Coventry, and how people wheeled their possessions out in prams, and drove out of the town to sleep in their cars and then back to the factories to work next day.

And these are the sons of those men. It seems there are still cinders of memory burning. As if the Canute-like gesture at Meriden could help to turn the tide of ailing industry, even if it becomes part of a painful scouring of the old structures.

*

To the north of Meriden across the M6 is the small village of Astley, which has only been given electricity and running water within the last twenty-five years, and where there are still no main sewers. There are privies, but also pylons, the worst of both worlds. Some of the villagers feel Astley is dying for lack of improvements; others 'don't want 1980 designs round here'. The council are considering more housing within the green belt as a special case.

Shustoke, where William Dugdale, the Warwickshire historian, was born, is to the west, and on the Nuneaton road from Astley lies Arbury Hall, rebuilt in the late eighteenth century by Sir Roger Newdigate, and one of the finest examples of the Gothic Revival in England. This was George Eliot's Cheverel Manor, 'the castellated house of grey-tinted stone, with the flickering sunbeams sending dashes of golden light across the many-shaped panes in the mullioned windows'.[2]

South Farm on the Arbury Estate was the birthplace of Mary Ann Cross – George Eliot. Her father, a shrewd countryman of iron integrity, managed the estate, and although she has been accused by some of too much intellectuality in her writing, this great novelist shows very clearly the reverse of the coin, those down-to-earth, sensible qualities, which make her very English, from the English countryside. In the closing lines of *Middlemarch* she movingly spells it out – 'the growing good of the world is partly dependent on unhistoric acts, and that things are not so ill with you and me as they might have been is half owing to the number who lived faithfully a hidden life and rest in unvisited tombs'. Far from passionless, able to adopt free-thinking religious views and live in Victorian society with a man who wasn't her husband, George Eliot's strength of character, her environment kept her feet tethered safely to the ground. And she can depict the monotonous and deadening side of provincial life, or a Mrs Cadwallader, 'active as phosphorus', frank but interfering, the archetypal county female.

In *The Mill on the Floss* she writes most brilliantly of her childhood countryside:

Life did change for Tom and Maggie; and yet they were not wrong in believing that the thoughts and loves of these first years would always make part of their lives. We could never have loved the earth so well if we had had no childhood in it . . . These familiar flowers, these well-remembered bird-notes, this sky with its fitful brightness, these furrowed and grassy fields, each with a sort of personality given to it by the capricious hedgerows – such things are the mother tongue of our imagination.

To see the countryside as it must have looked in George Eliot's day, one has only to go to Little Packington – a hamlet which consists of a gabled farm-house and a little Victorian church with a wooden bell-roof, standing among water meadows. The scene, only a few miles from Birmingham, seems incredible.

Farther on, the river winds into a broad ford, leading to one of the entrances to Packington Park. Another drive, across the park, runs past Great Packington church to Packington Hall. A herd of moth-like black fallow deer browse and run beneath the broad oak trees.

The church, by Joseph Bonomi, is coolly and rather grandly late eighteenth century inside, square and Byzantine outside. From it there is a magnificent view of Packington Hall and from the library of the Hall there is an even more delectable view, of the lake and grounds laid out by Capability Brown, who here as elsewhere attempted and succeeded in the Icarus-like task of improving on nature, making a more naturally beautiful landscape than the environment itself achieves. A typographer poet in trees.

The Fourth Earl of Aylesford added two wings to the house. A member of the Royal Academy and patron of music, he had an organ designed by Handel installed in Packington Hall; it is now in the church. The Fourth Earl also introduced the Chinese cock pheasant into England in 1770, which has bred with the old English black-coloured pheasant to produce the lighter, ring-necked strain.

'And now we're breeding out the ring,' said the present Earl, the Eleventh Earl of Aylesford. Lord Lieutenant of the West Midlands, Master of the Rolls and Commissioner of the Peace, Lord Warden of the Woodmen of Arden (who pull their longbows at the Forest Hall in the park), his roles are legion, but possibly first and foremost he is a devoted advocate of the countryside, sportsman and conservationist (a visit to Packington shows that this is not a contradiction in terms). As representative for the Queen in the area, he is responsible for all royal visits, and for presenting British Empire Medals and Police Medals, Duke of Edinburgh awards and the Queen's Award to Industry, among other things. In an area where the Lord Lieutenant is more active than in others he has at present twelve deputies instead of the prescribed ninety-six. This will be altered, but meanwhile he missed seeing a sea-eagle which dropped in on the park, because he hadn't time to watch for it.

He had with great kindness allowed us to see the house, which is not open to the public. A horde of creamy labrador puppies were his out-runners.

'Do you want one?' He has a very engaging smile under a not particularly military moustache, although he fought with the Black Watch regiment and was wounded in Sicily. Then, with the perfect, gentle manners which will probably die out if the aristocracy ever does, said, 'How can I help you?'

Sufficiently of the old guard to speak unblinkingly of his tenants referring to him as 'my lord' ('None of our men would dream of not coming up and talking to me . . .') he is, equally, forward looking enough to be a great believer in decentralization and delegation. He would like to see the government give more power to the central West Midlands Council, who would then not need to indulge in the present tussle with city or town councils, or as he put it 'they wouldn't need to grab from below'. On royal visits he insists that the visitor in question is introduced down the scale, so that for instance an education officer might say his bit and then hand over to a schoolmaster, who will talk about what is after all his province. After presenting a Queen's Award, he goes round the factory. He shot a sneakingly envious glance at me when I said I had been to the Meriden co-operative – over-controversial for a Lord Lieutenant to visit.

His views on industry are unstuffy. 'Twenty years ago looking at America we decided that bigger and bigger things are not necessarily economic. Great size comes into conflict with human nature . . . One of the worst things we ever invented, my father used to say, was the phrase "Safety first" . . . We can't pay drones . . .'

Will the estate survive? In spite of the fact that he does not, as some of his more commercially-minded rivals have suggested he ought, drip candle wax on the floor by the window at which Jennie, Lady Randolph Churchill, stood with her lover holding a candle. 'I'm told the way to avoid capital transfer tax is that my son marries his daughter-in-law and I marry my daughter.'

In fact in earlier days 'Sporting Joe', the Seventh Earl, nearly ruined himself in extravagant preparations for a visit from his friend the Prince of Wales, later Edward VII, by building a ballroom over the south terrace. The Earl, known as the Cowboy Earl in later life, was a 'great sportsman and a bit of a daredevil'. When Lady Aylesford and Blandford 'got together, he threatened to divorce her, which was not done, and to fight a duel, which was illegal'. To prevent him, the Churchill family threatened to publish letters *their* wives had had from the Prince of Wales ('I have the Crown of England in my pocket,' said Lord Randolph Churchill), and with truly quixotic gallantry, Joe prevented a scandal by emigrating. 'Poor Joe, he felt desperately affronted and went to Big Springs in Texas. The story goes that he arrived on the train and went to the hotel and said, "I want your best room." It was not free, so he asked how much they thought the hotel was worth and wrote a cheque for it and said, "Now, I want the best room". But he gave the hotel bac provided they kept the room for him, and there he died.' The true facts were rather diminished, Lord Aylesford feels, by the fact that Joe arrived with a special train and 200 retainers. The Prince of Wales gave Joe a cigarette case in the shape of a log cabin . . . 'I've since discovered it was plated,' said Lord Aylesford.

The present Earl's survival obviously dates from the day when he said to his father, 'You know, Dad, [or words to that effect] if you look out of the windows upstairs you can see tower blocks going up in Birmingham. And some people live at the top of those, and at some point they'll want to come out . . .' To give them space he opened the grounds instead of throwing open his house with its beautiful ceilings, fine tapestries 100 years older than Goya which have foxed the V. and A., and letters from George III. It remains a private house (although he shows parties round a few times a year), as the well-deserved reward for the imaginative scope the grounds offer – a trout fishery (20,000 rod visits last year on a subscriber or season ticket system), a clay pigeon shoot (day, or annual member), the independently run Heart of England Wildfowlers, a golf-driving range and practice course, with an eighteen-hole course to come. There will possibly be a shop for produce if the estate becomes self-sufficient. 'We hope to dig a channel with the golf-course bulldozers and put the birdwatchers in a cage so the birds can see them.' 'Unselfish birdwatchers' are allowed in free if they will watch a particular area for some of the 128 species of birds (originally there were 67). 'There are buzzards. You can't run an ecological area without predators. As man isn't God he always makes a mess of it . . . We don't shoot anything unless we have to. We put the maximum of pheasants on the ground and the farmers were swearing, so we shot a cock out of season and its crop had 280 wireworms in it. Now they agree with me.'

His attitude seems totally un-ego-oriented. When John asked if he could photograph him, Lord Aylesford looked in brief nervousness at his Sunday pullover and then smiled heartily and said, 'I don't suppose it will hurt me . . . more likely to hurt your camera.'

His way of running Packington seems a very fair type of compromise, a way of preserving a bit of Arden, and without overdue advertising, making it available to the second largest conurbation in the country.

I hope the sea-eagle will be back and that he has time to spot it.

*

'Three years ago you in the Midlands saw the opportunity and grasped it . . . You have demonstrated how quickly progress can be made, today as much as in the past.' Mr Edward Heath, 1973.

'That is why the nation will need so crucially the shop window which will be provided by this exhibition centre.' Mr Wilson, April 1974.

'Say, it's inneresting – you plonk it down there in the middle of nowhere. It will be inneresting to see if anyone comes to it.' American in train to Coventry.

'We didn't want it to stick out like a sore thumb.' Edward D. Mills, architect.

'The world will arrive on Birmingham's doorstep.' John Slim, in *Birmingham Post* supplement, *Welcome*.

'Where is Birmingham?' Londoner.

The National Exhibition Centre at Bickenhill should teach many more Londoners where to find Birmingham . . . that civilization doesn't end in Hertfordshire, or Bucks, or even Stratford. It may help a little to bridge the gap between South and Midlands. But equally importantly it is an arrival point for Europe, and it is ready to meet Europeans on their own terms. Nearly 400 acres in size (roughly the size of Hyde Park), it has an exhibition area bigger than Frankfurt's, about the same size as Düsseldorf's. The million square feet of exhibition halls are the size of Olympia and Earls Court put together. Its great advantage is that the complex has been designed as a whole, with easy access from the railway and motorways, and with hotels among trees, so that there is every chance that visiting the exhibitions may not be a gruelling experience. The special heating and ventilating units came from the States at a cost of £14,000 each for 101 units; with the man-made lake, 25,000 young birch trees in the car park, and the cork-like aggregate for the finish of concrete walls, the place has inbuilt coolness. There are plenty of restaurant facilities, and a ramp to the central piazza for invalid chairs.

Nor has the surrounding area been slow to grasp its chances. Showing the alacrity to seize opportunity of the West Midlander, hoteliers and entrepreneurs have increased hotel rooms within a twenty-mile radius from 6,000 to 14,000 within two years. In a region bare of late-evening eating places, restaurants have opened. With a rush of civic pride to the head, councillors have made unguarded statements as to providing those used to Milan or Denmark with what they will expect – all but saying 'We must have brothels'. Such unlikely headlines as '*Brennpunkt der britischen Industrie*' and '*L'industria nella città del futuro*' have burgeoned.[3] But sobriety has prevailed, everything seems in very good taste, and as

Mr Lyndon Jenkins, Press and Public Relations officer for the NEC, said as he showed me round the site, the basic need for someone on a business visit is a comfortable room and a place to eat out. Remembering enervating visits to the Frankfurt book fair, I agreed.

This was before the centre opened. There was a security gate like something in a Hitchcock movie, and clouds of red building-dust. Mr Jenkins showed intense enthusiasm and a dazzling head for figures. If all promoters of Britain were like him, we would not be in such a sorry state. (He also writes some music reviews for the *Birmingham Post*, which gives a fair idea of his relaxed versatility. And charm – he told me over the telephone that he hadn't the heart to criticize a particular promenade concert because people had *enjoyed* it so much.)

The Prime Minister was to visit the site that Friday, and BBC helicopters were already descending on their prey, with technicians burrowing in the unique system of tunnels (bringing services such as electricity and waste disposal to stands) under the halls. Mr Jenkins seemed content to let them play there, and showed me the hall where Mr Wilson would be given a cup of tea. There would be tile carpets put down for him; we agreed he was unlikely to come in his gumboots. 'I think I ought to get rid of that shed, he might think it's a privy,' said Lyndon Jenkins frowning. I said I didn't think Mr Wilson would let that worry him. 'I could put up a notice saying "Not a Toilet",' continued Lyndon Jenkins, on a note of inspiration. He swept me on to other, vaster vistas.

He also introduced me to Edward D. Mills, CBE, architect, with his partners, for the exhibition buildings.

Edward D. Mills was made a Churchill Research Fellow in 1969 and is a consultant to UNESCO, author and broadcaster. The partnership designed part of the Festival of Britain South Bank Exhibition in 1951 and the British Industries Pavilion for the 1958 Brussels World Fair. It would be hard to meet a man of achievement who is more unassuming. Funnily enough, having written those words, when I next met Edward Mills, he used the same words about Mies van der Rohe. 'An extraordinary person, the most unassuming person you could possibly meet.'

'I've just written that about you –'

'Perhaps some of it rubs off. The first time I met Mies he greeted me like a long-lost son. He always sent any information I asked for by return of post. This is the sign of a great man anyway ... it's those ones one can never get at I'm suspicious of.'

Edward Mills worked under Gropius for a year, and speaks of that time with due reverence. Mills is a Londoner, with a florid, kind, very English face, which can be burly and jolly and yet sensitive. Typically, he seemed more anxious to wish me success with our book than to speak of his own successes. He is far from the clinical, faddy type of architect (I once knew an architect who put felt shoes on all his chairs, and who could smell a mothball two floors away). I asked what his favourite buildings had been, what, to date, he would like to be remembered for. A cathedral he designed in Mbale, Uganda. And of course the NEC. 'God and Mammon, if one can put it like that.' He smiled. He has the kind of eyes which mean what they say. 'The cathedral was built entirely with African labour and using African materials . . . the whole site was cleared by local people who came to clear the trees. It was *their* building.'

The same concern for people runs through his book *The Changing Workplace* (George Godwin, 1974)[4] in which he suggests with startling clarity that much of work in industry and commerce in a technological age is tedious and monotonous 'almost beyond bearing point', and also the theme that modern factories need not be isolated and dirty, but with gardens and rest areas (and canteens and sports facilities open to non-employees) could form a more integrated part of city life, of life in fact. He spoke of this in a BBC Third Programme talk over fifteen years ago.

This insight has been applied to the National Exhibition Centre. The colours have been selected so that the buildings won't be obtrusive in the landscape – which they are not. Tinted glass lets in the daylight and picks up cloud reflections. There were birches there, so they have planted more birches. The steel-sheet cladding is brown so that it won't need cleaning (no tear-streaked concrete). Inside, the halls are uncluttered so as not to detract from exhibits. The design separates pedestrians and traffic. In the central area, shops have had to get the architect's agreement to decorations and furniture.

'The chaps are beginning to feel it's all worth while,' he said of the building team. 'There has been a tremendous amount of interest, visits. We had trouble on the South Bank Exhibition site. Then we had an open day and the people working there brought their wives and families on a Saturday to meet the designers. This made an enormous difference. To be personally involved, not always working for some faceless developer, or unknown group. Midlanders? One thing that strikes me is that they're very parochial . . . like one big village. It's very difficult to break into the circle. But once you get to know them you're part of the family. Here, from the chairman downwards everyone uses Christian names. You've been admitted to the family, so you're all right. You've got the same objectives . . . you can get a team spirit . . . We've got to push industry and get this country back in a state to sell itself again.'

Edward Mills previously worked on a study considering a new exhibition centre on the Crystal Palace site, which proved impracticable. 'There is no exhibition site in the world with the facilities we've got at Bickenhill.' And, strangely enough, the first permanent exhibition centre ever built in England, in 1850, the oldest exhibition building in the world, is not far off at Bingley Hall, in Birmingham.

The Exhibition Centre has succeeded by opening on time, by being fully booked for its first year, by catering for simultaneous smaller exhibitions, and by providing a showplace for things as varied as the 1977 World Table Tennis Championships, and international machine tools (planned for 1978). The Centre has been highly praised by foreign exhibitors and buyers. Its larger successes remain in the future. The Motor Show will be held there in 1978. Its place in this region from which forty per cent of the country's exports come is more than symbolical. Mammon is here certainly, but also other driving forces which have made the area what it is, and which have at times in the past changed the nation's fate. Things, as ever, are happening in the West Midlands.

2 Coventry

> The woman of a thousand summers back
>> she took the tax away
> And built herself an everlasting name.
>> 'Godiva' by Alfred, Lord Tennyson

'I think it's common.' The woman in the bookshop dismissed present-day Coventry. 'The Coventry people used to be very proud of their town before the war. It's got no character. There used to be lovely old houses – now there are ghettoes. Thirty people to a house.' She flicked her books with a duster distastefully. 'The pavements would make you sick. Immigrants. And students. We get trouble with the students and they get huge grants.' Direly: 'No young girl would go out alone at night here . . . But fancy me telling you this and you come from Wolverhampton.' She looked at me pityingly.

It could be any city. But in Coventry, 'before the war' has more than usual significance. With its war industries the town suffered more than most, and the three major raids on 14–15 November 1940 and 8 and 10 April 1941 left devastation of tragic proportions. On the morning of 15 November the Cathedral of St Michael's was a gutted ruin, nearly seventy-five per cent of the city's industry had been damaged, and 46,000 houses, 2,000 of which were uninhabitable. It is difficult now to find people who witnessed the raid. If you do, they are likely to say, 'It was terrible . . . but we never think about it now.' It was clearly a time when the town saw human greatness; the voluntary and civil defence services doing their utmost; men such as the Vicar of Holy Trinity sleeping in his church every night, having installed extra taps and a telephone system to fire-watchers, or the Provost with three others fire fighting on the cathedral roof until 'we realized with intense consternation and horror that nothing could now save the roofs of the cathedral nor any of the interior wood-work . . . the whole interior was a seething mass of flame';[1] or Bill Lewis who commandeered a double-decker bus to drive casualties through the

34

burning city; or Gilbert Griffiths who returned through the raids to his post at the switchboard at the top of the General Post Office to keep communications open; men digging in the rubble with their hands to free survivors.

And reactions to the disaster – rapid, and human. The Queen sending blankets and children's sweaters with her letter through a lady-in-waiting, but with less ceremony HMS *Coventry* telegraphing 'assure them that the ship will endeavour to repay'.[2]

On 18 November, under a headline 'Coventry for Courage', the *Daily Express* published this story. 'An old man who had lost his entire family of wife, daughter, son-in-law and grandchildren came to a canteen for a hot meal. He dug in his pocket, found just sevenpence and said "How much do I owe you?" The man who told me the story – a cynic – said "I wept".'

*

But the phoenix has risen from the ashes.

I was glad to visit Coventry in Easter week. The twisted burnt cross in the ruin of the old cathedral contains it all: Christianity and the war, sombre overtones of a twisted swastika of evil, humanity and frailty and resurrection. Behind the altar the words 'Father Forgive'. In the empty windows bent strips of lead, fragile and torn against the sky.

Among the plaques and benches presented by different nations, and Epstein's sturdy *Ecce Homo*, twenty-year-olds were fooling aggressively. A member of the war generation chased them roundly away. German and Japanese cameras clicked by the altar. Easter music was being played in the new cathedral. The sky was blue and clear. *Ecce homo*. Father forgive.

*

I saw Basil Spence's new cathedral again on another day, when it was snowing, and I have to admit that the exterior was bleakly uninviting. If a church doesn't invite, what hope is there for it? But he wanted a casket for jewels, and some jewels he has got: Ralph Beyer's incised lettering; much of the stained glass; the Chapel of Unity with its mosaics by Einar Forseth and circular shape which Spence designed to represent a crusader's tent 'always ready for the next move', as Mr Rose, Secretary to the Joint Council of the Cathedral Christian Service Centre explained to me. But not jewel-like, emphatically, are the choir stalls, topped by what Pevsner aptly calls 'the Mercedes trade mark'.[3] (On a burning hot day, and seen from the bus station side, the cathedral does have the sculpted, Mediterranean look of twentieth-century churches which inspired Spence – but how rare the Mediterranean sky is in Britain.)

Whatever it is visually, the cathedral works. In the Chapel of Unity, different races and denominations meet, Baptists and Roman Catholics uniting in hilarity over unfamiliar hymns. 'Some people were shocked when the Bishop had people dancing before the altar,' Mr Rose told me. But corduroys and guitars are more run-of-the-mill. I saw an exhibition of paintings by children from the Cathedral Centre for Young People round the walls, and there are strong links with the special social services of the local Council of Churches. As Provost R. T. Howard wrote, 'Primarily a church is not a building, but people ...'

I listened to a 'Mass for Four Voices' by Byrd – one of the regular lunch-time concerts. Above the apron-like knees of Graham Sutherland's tapestry Christ the face was compelling, with eyes which seemed alive – stern, wounded and melting. Then I became aware of the hands, delicate and fluted as dove's wings. *Kyrie ... Gloria ... Agnus Dei ...*

We all flocked into the crypt for the weekly cheap lunch – rolls and cheese and soup and flan for tenpence and very good value as the young man from the council next to me said. He eats there every week. 'It wasn't all razed in the raids. *My* house was standing,' a plump woman in a red velour hat said. 'Luckily I was out of Coventry at the time.' She bit into her cheese flan with strong white non-National-Health teeth.

The new cathedral was a long time being built – 'eleven years of toil, frustration, hope and ecstasy' Basil Spence wrote, in *Phoenix in Coventry*.[4] People then were not ready for united services. Unity began via marriage guidance, clubs. And the new spirit of the times went out into the town on a bicycle in the shape of Bishop Neville Gorton, a legend in his own lifetime, who wanted the church to be part of people's daily lives; who, dressed in old overcoat, heavy woollen stockings on his spindly legs and deerstalker spiked with flies, could talk informally to trade-union leaders and shop-stewards. He laid the foundations of industrial chaplaincy, and campaigned for a major Institute of Technology in Coventry.

He is only one in a line of men and women who have worked for the people of Coventry – a tradition comprising figures such as Alice Arnold, who became the first woman mayor of the city, in 1937. The daughter of a blacksmith who kept the family in food by poaching in Stoneleigh Park, she herself left school at eleven to work in a factory. Figures who have given the town a Labour bent – Philip Noel-Baker, Richard Crossman, Elaine Burton. A tradition going back through Friendly Societies and Freemen and interest-free loans to apprentices to start their own businesses, through trading guilds and charity schools and common grazing lands (meadows which impeded expansion and thus one reason for Coventry missing the industrial revolution), to the distant days of the woman of a thousand summers back – the Lady Godgifu or Godiva.

*

Some authorities hold that the famous ride never took place, or that Godiva was merely 'naked' of her jewels, or that in her an old folk-myth rode on. The story was not written down until over a century after the event was said to have taken place, and Peeping Tom does not appear until formal processions began in the seventeenth century. But the legend has caught the imagination. ('Since Godiva,' as John pointed out the other night, 'streaking has become rather a bore.') Godiva rode in a frilled petticoat in Victorian days, and she rides in a body stocking today. As can be seen in the Herbert Museum and Art Gallery in Coventry, she rides pink-fleshed on a Landseer horse, breastily in a fourteenth-century German lithograph, boyishly on the Hon. John Collier's Pre-Raphaelite canvas. She was, Ingulphus of Croyland tells us, 'the most beauteous of all the women of her time'.[5]

Her husband was Earl Leofric of Mercia, a just man, despite Tennyson's poem where he strides along, 'His beard a foot before him, and his hair A yard behind', then 'fillip'd at the diamond in her ear' in a Victorianly lascivious manner. She is described by the chronicles as noble, pious and worthy, with hair long enough to cover her legs, which were fair and white (*candissimus*).[6] She had a daughter who married a king of North Wales and later Harold of Wessex, and a son Aelfgar; legend gives her another son, Hereward the Wake.

Leofric and Godiva lie buried in the church ruins of the Benedictine monastery they founded at Coventry in 1043, just along the cobbled streets leading from the cathedral, which give this part of the town a mellow peacefulness. The Earl of Mercia and his wife owned land in Warwickshire, Gloucestershire, Shropshire, Staffordshire, Northamptonshire, among other places (including Penn, where we live), and their foundations were many. They gave land and endowments to Burton Abbey, Evesham, St Mary Stow, Leominster nunnery, and restored two churches at Chester, those of St Werburgh and St John. They also gave gifts to Worcester, which had been sacked in earlier days – before he married Godiva – by Leofric himself. Godiva owned Coventry, and seems to have had a special affection for the place. The tax from which she saved the citizens was the oppressive *Heregeld*, used to maintain the king's *housecarles.*[7] The monastery later drew wealth to the town, and when it was dissolved, the population fell from 15,000 to 3,000. But in Godiva's day, or within twenty years of her death, there were only sixty-nine families in her part of the town (as distinct from the monastery and its surroundings) – fifty villeins or free peasants, twelve bordars or cottage dwellers and seven serfs, or men who were not free. They had farm houses and cattle sheds, and there is evidence that the surrounding countryside was a hive of farming activity – clearing the forest, cultivating virgin land.

There are still many old buildings of later centuries standing in Coventry, and the three delicate spires – St Michael's, Christchurch (Greyfriars) and Holy Trinity – hold the eye inescapably as you approach the city; their pull following you everywhere as they taper through mist or heathaze, diminishing the tower blocks. Yet this is a modern town, the town in the West Midlands in which visitors from other European countries must I think feel most at home. It is one of the few places I know where unremarkable older buildings become an irritation spoiling the general scene, rather than vice versa. (It is also almost the only town in our area where on leaving the streamlined station one sees at first glance a restaurant open until 1 a.m.)

There have been mistakes, but this was partly owing to the fact that of the cities which had to rebuild their centres after the war, Coventry was the first to adopt a radically new plan, which encompassed a traffic-free precinct. This today is remarkably quiet, and although parts of it seem rather earnest and drab, much of the precinct is striking, and small luxury shops are creeping in to add brightness. Near by, the revolutionary – in more than one sense – Belgrade Theatre, looks like something from a Communist republic's travel brochure, but is brilliant compared with the Odeon-style Coventry Theatre rendered in two-tone mushroom – 'I can't think *why* the Germans didn't bomb it,' a citizen said desperately. The Leofric Hotel, however, has not the comfortable imposingness of Birmingham's old Midland, and at night the young of Coventry hang round its doors like lost souls in their heavy-wedged footgear, while the cold wind blows the litter of Lethe round murals and past fountains, past a plaque saying that Dame Ellen Terry was born here on 27 February 1847.

Architectural successes are dotted all over the town. Blocks of modern flats, the Lanchester Polytechnic and the city library have clean, uncluttered lines; shop fronts curve serpentinely, and there is much brown-tinted glass, as in the council offices. Some of these stand round a small courtyard, the old Palace Yard, where a statue of a thin naked girl sits in a willow-fringed pool, cool and unperturbed. The town swimming baths, by Arthur Ling, completed in 1965, are among the finest in the world, and to my eye the best modern building in the city. They are what modern architecture is about, at its best: without conflict, unobtrusive in the landscape, yet striking in line, the effect is of a sweep of cool glass melting into the trees that surround the structure. There is boardwork for sunbathing outside, and on a hot day when the cathedral is teeming, you can lie here in cathedral coolness under willow trees.

Of new housing estates, some have been more successful than others, architecturally and as communities. The Tile Hill estate won national acclaim as one of the first with a community centre, shops and school. As areas of comprehensive development, the old industrial villages of Hillfields and Spon End have been more recently re-developed. Both were severely damaged in the war. (The total of Coventry's damaged houses in the war was 3½ million.) In Spon Street some of the oldest houses in Coventry have been restored or have been moved there from other areas. The Windmill inn has an oil-painted windmill of 1897; there are old warehouses with poppies and ragwort growing on their roofs; a fourteenth-century house, once two workshops with curved braces on its front, was the first restoration undertaken by the city's Spon Street Town scheme, between 1969 and 1970, with the aid of gifts of material (in these lean years the scheme is hard pushed); farther on is one of the very few surviving three-storeyed jettied buildings, moved from Much Park Street, with curlicued window frames, now a fine art gallery. The whole street is exceptional, and both here and at Spon End new and old have been mixed to blend. One tries to forget the English bent to nostalgia, assess merits. Yes, underpasses are useful – but they can be squalid – I have even seen excrement in them in Coventry. The new flats look very good, but a girl at a corner shop told me tenants often don't stay long because of high rents. The old back-to-backs which come on the market are quickly snapped up. So it is possibly not only nostalgia that makes one lean towards the narrow alleyways with open workshops, still in use as small upholsterers or printers, the potato patches in the back, the jumble of old enamel pans in gardens. Down an arched alley I saw a tabby Beatrix Potter cat sitting on a wall in front of blazing irises; washing hung in the back-to-back gardens, lilac blew and birds sang. That such things compensate for hardship can be seen from an autobiography of the good, bad old days – that of Joseph Gutteridge, a Coventry ribbon-weaver caught in the depression of the

1860s (of 18,000 in the ribbon trade, only 2,500 were in work in 1861). Often he, his wife and two children had no food, and slept on the bare ground as they had sold their bed. Honest, hardworking and thoughtful, it was his passion for wild flowers and plants which kept him sane and led to a serene old age, and a clarity of thought that could be of today.

After a long period of what may be characterized as short-sightedness, if not of gross stupidity, on the part of the past generation, the citizens of modern Coventry appear to have realized their position, and to have braced themselves to meet the requirements of the new times, and are looking hopefully forward to the future.[8]

Hillfields was the centre of the silk-weaving industry in the early nineteenth century, and Spon End the centre of watch- and later bicycle-making. Silk-weaving and watch-making were the traditional trades, following the medieval wool trade, the trades with their manufacturing families and independent artisans whom in 1871 George Eliot described under the name of 'Middlemarch'. The house where George Eliot lived as a young woman still stands in what is now George Eliot Road. Then it was close to the Lammas and Michaelmas meadows which hemmed in the city. Beyond to the north was the ribbon-weaving area, including the cottage homes of the Cash workers. The watch-makers lived to the south and west; they had slightly easier lives and neat little gardens. Rich manufacturers later built in areas such as Stoke and Coundon Green, within 'carriage distance'.

Coventry has always been a working town, with skilled craftsmen, no large leisurely class. There are few quiet town houses now, I was told, as alternatives to flats. Nor is it an intellectual town, with keen readers. In 1970 it came bottom of the list of county boroughs for books in stock.[9] 'It's more philistine than Wolverhampton, if you can imagine that,' said someone who was at the University of Warwick there. The university has its own events, but is not closely linked to the town. 'One can sometimes go for weeks without having an interesting conversation,' a young executive told me, half ashamed to admit it. This absence of a visible upper-middle class is typical of the West Midlands conurbation. The area is not strewn with retired officers as is the south-west; shops do not ring with the high-pitched voices of high-bred wives. There is plenty of brass ('This is where the mooney is,' a Black Country diamond-setter said to me recently, waving receipts for rings, bought as the economy toppled further, under my nose). But while obtrusive brass can be as tiresome and certainly uglier than obtrusive class, it is marginally less arrogant, more human. The urban West Midlands often seem drab to a southerner's eye, to lack grace. 'Not *another* butcher's shop,' they will cry in despair, coming from the pretty pavilions of Brighton. But there is less artificiality, more strength, more to fall back on; and a visual quality that things have when they have been made with loving concern and a lack of aesthetic vanity – buildings as carefully shaped as watch mechanisms, streets as practical and homely as the lines of a hand. Some of this is perhaps what many Coventry people miss now in their buildings; you will find more of it still in Birmingham and the Black Country, or in Stoke-on-Trent.

Coventry was a city of guilds and apprentices, of trades. It was the guilds which performed the famous Coventry mystery plays on Corpus Christi Day. And if demands for one trade died out, for example when Swiss watches began to steal the market, the inventive craftsmen turned to other outlets. A large industrial expansion did not come until the late nineteenth century and the bicycle boom. Then in the first half of the twentieth century Coventry's population increased five times in size, with new industries, including war industries. Cycles, motor-cycles, cars, tractors, aircraft, buses. Legendary names such as Riley, George Singer, Harry Ferguson, Lord Rootes, Frederick Lanchester (after whom the Polytechnic is named), John Davenport Siddeley, Sir Frank Whittle. Legendary factories: the Meteor Works of the Rover Company, the Triumph factory in Priory Street, Daimler, Courtaulds, latterly the giant GEC making telecommunications equipment.

It is difficult to trace the early history of the car industry, because small firms were legion, not all making all parts of a car. Makers and firms mixed and merged; some cars were made in very small quantities or never actually materialized. To get an idea of the range one can visit the city's industrial motor store, or see models in the Herbert Museum – a delectable 1913 10 h.p. Arden, navy blue with coach lamps, fawn hood and mottled wood steering wheel, cylindrical petrol tank at the back; or a 1932 beetle-backed Alvis tourer in bottle green; a 1911 Daimler; a Singer 9 Le Mans special speed model; a 1926 Austin Swallow saloon. Countless others, and examples of 1897 flowered blue-glass candle-lamps, used before oil or acetylene gas headlamps.

The Herbert Museum and Art Gallery was named from the bequest given to the town by Sir Alfred Herbert, who founded the famous machine-tool firm. He also made the apprenticeship scheme in his firm a model for the city, and many Alfred Herbert apprentices are today running firms in Coventry and overseas. Coventry is fundamentally as much a place of machine tools and tools, and industrial engines, as a place of car manufacturing. The town was more prosperous than most between the wars, but it has had slumps in the past – in the 1860s for instance, or with the closure of aircraft factories in the 1960s. When watch-making became difficult one small firm specialized in watch jewels, and then moved on to industrial jewels, indispensable in the Second World War. There seems no reason to suppose that in the long term this practical ingenuity, promoted by schools and colleges which favour technical and technological education, should not emerge in other forms.

The position as I write is critical. Alfred Herbert are in trouble and machine tools themselves are threatened by transfer machines – automating a series of machines -- which are better made on the Continent. Factories such as Alvis, although swallowed up by the giant Leyland, do better because they are small and compact and have specialized in military vehicles and aero engines. The giant itself is in dire straits; and within it firms such as Jaguar, which used to be a fiercely loyal company, swearing at the boss Sir William Lyons, but working hard. (Jaguar always had a good profit except for one year in the war, and more than half the Jaguars ever made have been exported. That the Jaguar engineering and development sections are now to be kept separate within the group is seen as an excellent move.)

To say that the dire straits of West Midlands industry are merely heightened symptoms of our national malaise is not correct, as more people now realize. It is true that disaster strikes first in a densely manufacturing region, and in past slumps the West Midlands have been first to succumb but also first to recuperate. But in Britain as a whole more and more people are moving from jobs in agriculture, mining and manufacturing industries to service industries and offices. This trend is apparent in the Midlands too, but just over one in three jobs in the West Midlands are provided by the vehicle, engineering, electrical and metal industries – the industries which for a long time formed the core of Britain's industrial strength. A large proportion of those in the last three groups are producing components and materials for the motor industry. New growth industries such as chemicals and electronics have largely passed the area by. Unemployment in the West Midlands is rising faster than in any other region.

Because of the interlinking of countless small firms making components, if one group fails it affects a whole area, as has been highlighted by the closure of the Norton Villiers Triumph factory in Wolverhampton. If the giant car industry collapses world-wide, what will become of the West Midlands? Can it attract new industries? Can it adapt as the watch-makers did by switching to bicycles? Or by developing its service industries within the area? In the depressed days of silk weaving in Coventry, William Andrews, a weaver, was one who survived and prospered by learning new organizational expertise on the Continent, but on the whole the old-fashioned organizations of the industry could not hold their own with foreign competition which came with the signing of the Cobden Treaty of 1860 giving free trade between England and France. Today, the initiative seems likely to come from groups rather than individuals. It would be tragic if by the 1980s the West Midlands was one of the depressed areas of Europe as the West Midlands County Council's document 'A Time for Action' suggested, in 1974, was possible if present trends continued.

*

The car industry has in some ways been the bane of the area. Drunkenness figures are high in Coventry, because of fluctuating high wages and unemployment. Other areas are made discontented by the legendary high wages of car-workers 'for doing nothing'. The hard work is forgotten, the dreariness, the inventiveness such as that of a design team at British Leyland working on a 'micro Mini', or of Austin Morris at Longbridge winning a Design Council award for a device for reducing exhaust and costing only £1.

And what is it like to work for the giant? For instance if you are not a Worker but a worker, in a white collar. And as one such white collar worker said to me plaintively – 'On the Continent, I'm always impressed by the smartness of men driving lorries. Here, there is a built-in thing, they don't want to tidy up, so a canteen for everyone doesn't always work.'

I approached the new British Leyland headquarters, Leyland Coventry House, with an open mind. By the door of the high block was a stubbed-out cigar. On entry, or exit? It seemed portentous.

I thought in fact everyone looked remarkably healthy for a company narrowly missing receivership, but I was told with slight strain in the voice that a term 'execuplas' has been coined for those who may be succumbing to the system – 'we sometimes look round the room to see who is execuplas, and who are people...'

In the execuplas dining-room, iced water is drunk in efficient jugfuls.

I talked to people mainly on neutral topics – the rest has been much aired in the press, and when times are tricky it is unfair to ask people to stick their necks out. There is much to be proud of in the past. Jaguar and Daimler have distinguished histories. Daimler's original factory in Coventry was Britain's first volume-production factory for the industry, converted from an old cotton mill; its first catalogue came out in 1897, and shows the old plant. Great characters have been legion in the car industry – 'Dr Fred' Lanchester whose original car was the first petrol-driven four-wheeled car ever made in Britain, and which originally had a tiller for steering as he had previously constructed the first all-British motorboat; Sir John Black; Lawson – 'he tried to monopolize the whole of the British motor industry – a bit of a rotten chap'. In the present day, there is Sir Alec Issigonis, who had the idea of both the Morris Minor and the Mini and who is currently retained by British Leyland on research. Surely there must be a way out, in the long term.

At present it is felt that to have an eye on markets for every size of car is both practical and a way of hedging bets. The structure of the corporation on paper looks like one of those puzzles where you have to find your way out. There are about 80,000 employees in this area, and as one of them said, 'every individual prefers to work for a corporation of a size he can comprehend. Otherwise it's like trying to comprehend the universe.' To an outsider it would seem that the innovation of worker participation can only help, may help lead towards a healthier situation, at a critical moment.

Is the whole car industry toppling on shifting sands? Do we need more and more cars? One who would answer no, and whose story, and decision, I like, is a highly successful executive who was head-hunted for a top job in the car industry and threw it up to go and farm turkeys. 'Now I can make sure every hour I work is a useful one . . . I don't want a swimming pool in the front and back garden . . . A lot of my colleagues were envious of me . . . They wanted to do a job of work but had to fight the old political battle to get to the top and keep their slates clean.' An old car enthusiast, he now runs a mini-tractor, a van, and a bicycle.

3 Wolverhampton; Bilston

'A handsome town, one fair church in it.

So wrote a diarist during the Civil War, when Wolverhampton was Prince Rupert's headquarters. The King stayed at Bushbury, 'a private sweet village . . .'. Now, beside the tall red sandstone tower of St Peter's Church, looms the square office block of the Mander shopping centre. But the tower, with its four expectant pinnacles, still dominates the high hill, as one approaches from the country or along the railway line.

> But let me say before it has to go,
> It's the most lovely country that I know;
> Clearer than Scafell Pike, my heart has stamped on
> The view from Birmingham to Wolverhampton.
>
> Tramlines and slagheaps, pieces of machinery,
> That was, and still is, my ideal scenery.

So Auden, in *Letter to Lord Byron*.[1] Despite changes, it is very easy to see what he meant, share his feeling. As you approach Wolverhampton, the capital of the Black Country, you are aware of the particular elements of the landscape in a heightened manner. For a start, as elsewhere in the West Midlands, you get the impression that the sky is larger here. I don't know why this should be, unless it is that you are often on the broad curve of a hill without near mountains to screen the distance. The weather is extremely variable, as on an island, so the sky is constantly changing, moving, dramatic; it dwarfs the land, reducing it to its proper vulnerable proportions, and however solid or slow or drab Black Countrymen might be, the vitality in the skies around them lends an air of eventfulness, promise to the scene. Old men walk upright here, without overcoats in the winter, careless of the wind; they fight the elements and keep their sinews.

Beside the railway line from Birmingham run canals, with narrow black-and-white iron bridges. There are poplars, rows of small old brick houses, thin church spires, factory chimneys of every size and shape; a piebald horse is reflected, beside the sun, in a canal; yellow ragwort, seas of willowherb, clumps of mustard; over on the horizon Dudley castle faintly outlined on its hill; everywhere the pricking ears of the small churches like little dogs baying at the sky. Nothing is static; everywhere, in the ugliness of scrapheaps, new warehouses, in the old bricks and bridges, in lights and canal intersections, you read the same dogged human script. In mist, with a white skyline, in the evening light, the scene becomes fragile, almost pathetic, as men's small efforts are dwarfed by the mellowing sun in the big sky. The thin factory chimneys, poplars and towers alone emerge from the smoky mist in the distance and the spires of St John's and St Peter's and the tower blocks of Wolverhampton take fire in the white sky.

*

The high hill on which Wolverhampton stands (the Saxons called the town, in the dative, *aet Heantune*, high town) is part of a ridge stretching from the Clent Hills and Dudley in the south, to Bushbury and on to Cannock in the north – a ridge which provided a good trackway through the forest in primitive times. Authorities of the more imaginative breed from the Rev. Stebbing Shaw in 1798 onwards have seen Staffordshire, and in particular key spots such as Cannock, Aldridge ('Druids Heath') and Wolverhampton as likely centres for the Druid cult, with oak woods and brass cutting-tools for lopping mistletoe. But in cooler moments these historians admit that the mounds they have found could have been small Roman camps.

The surprising thing about Wolverhampton is that it *has* a history. The churchyard of St Peter's Church – originally St Mary's – has been a Christian burial-ground for almost a thousand years. By the church is the oldest man-made object in the town, a Saxon pillar, the remains of a cross, that is the largest and most impressive of its kind in the country. 'There is nothing quite like it in England,' wrote Sir T. D. Kendrick in 1938. It is probably late eighth, or ninth, century. Luckily casts were taken of its carvings in 1877 and are now in the Victoria and Albert Museum, because recently atmospheric pollution has eroded the surface far more than the weather and grime of previous centuries. Between bands of decoration are zoomorphic designs, typically Saxon, showing beasts and birds. Most of them have their heads turned over their shoulders, as if in flight, which gives a great feeling of movement, and transience, to this durable monument. I have visited it twice in particular; once in the cold of winter when the churchyard was deserted; once in the spring with the grass busy with daffodils and benched pensioners, calling out helpfully to me that that was not the way out. On both occasions I have experienced the sensation which one tends to shy away from in fiction when the hero is irritatingly transported back into the past. It is difficult to describe; perhaps a filled silence, as if there were a silent beehive thrumming, violently but peacefully. The element which chiefly conjures it up must be the turned animal heads: wild, savage, but elegantly stylized, *civilized*, fleeing . . .

*

In the porch I met the church's 'resident tramp', who told me he was trapped underground for a day and a half after a mine explosion, and fought in two wars. He had not slept in a bed for many years, now the hostels were too expensive for him. His eyes were very blue. He told me his mother was the Countess of Assisi. But I believed him about the mine. He was immaculately clean. Possibly only in Wolverhampton would he be so clean, tolerated – and ignored. Wulfrunians are irreproachably clean. The brass in the public lavatories gleams. (The lavatory attendants at Bilston were recently invited to a political ball in token of their achievements in this line.) The houses in even the meanest streets are spotless, freshly painted, the net curtains washed on either side of the pot plant. The paint is brightly coloured. It is as if having escaped from the squalor of the Black Country to its 'capital', they are determined to wash it from their hearths for ever, and on any sunny day you can see women busily wielding cloth or paintbrush on their windows, who will smile laconically at their own activity. (It is reported that one woman spends hours a day washing graffiti from a subway wall.) Cleanness has even been heard to exonerate immigrants – those bugbears of the more tight-lipped matrons. 'But they're quite *clean*,' I have heard in a launderette, said with surprise. (Although this does not prevent one of our dearest friends, whose foible this is, running from carriage to carriage at Wolverhampton station, in search of one without figures in bright saris, children with smooth dusky cheeks – which is a difficult task in this town.) Equally, voices will take on a note of hushed horror – 'He hasn't got a *toilet*, you know.' And because we have a shower, I didn't realize at first the full commiseration extended to us – 'You've no *bathroom*, have you?'

The church tower is less clean, but the soot doesn't spoil its striking height, or colour. It rises to a height of 125 feet and is elaborately panelled on three sides, with jutting carved heads and strange clinging animals. Inside, the church encapsulates the history of the town, with its coats of arms and memorials and 'faire gallery' built in 1610 by the Worshipful Company of Merchant Taylors for the boys of the Free School, now the

Wolverhampton Grammar School. At the foot of the fifteenth-century sandstone pulpit, decorated with rosettes and vines, is a grotesque lion, which the verger and I agreed looks far more like a gryphon. It is said by choirboys to yawn if the sermon goes on for more than half an hour.

The verger remembers the days when he saw members of the rich town families queuing to reserve their pews at 5.45 a.m. for the 6.30 service. But those days are gone, and the rich families – and there are many rich families – now live outside the town.

By the church door is a slab which states that 'In the year of our Lord 994 and in the reign of Aethelred II the noble matron Wulfrun endowed the ancient Monastery of S. Mary at Hamtun with lands.' The Lady Wulfrun, or Wulfruna, was granted lands by King Alfred in 985 which subsequently formed part of her gift to the monastery, and it is she who gave the town its name – Wylfrome Hampton, Wulfruna's Hampton. Staffordshire was then mostly wasteland, the most backward part of the Mercian earldom. It was thinly populated, because of its high, wooded ground, having originally had British hamlets (Penn, Tunstall, the Lea) rather than Saxon villages.

The figure of Wulfruna captures the imagination, possibly because we know tantalizingly little about her. She was a person of consequence. When King Edmund overran Mercia in 942, he was attacked by Olaf the Dane, who had taken Tamworth by storm, and 'Wulfrun was taken captive in that raid'. The monk Florence of Worcester, and Ranulf Higden writing in the fourteenth century, both held the theory that through her son Aelfhelm, earldorman of Northumbria (her other son was Wulfric Spot who founded Burton Abbey), Wulfruna was the great-grandmother of King Harold Harefoot, son of King Canute and his mistress Aelgifu, daughter of Aelfhelm.

Great-grandmother of kings or not, Wulfruna was a pious woman, 'the noble matron and religious woman Wulfrun'. She probably lived at Dunstall, where there are Wulfrun's meadow, and Wulfruna's Well. The latter, so magical in name, is hard to find if you are looking for a pool of clear water. It is now a square, waterless stone at the roadside, wedged between the railway viaduct and Dunstall racecourse.

*

John Betjeman, writing of English provincial cities with their modernistic shop-fronts, enormous cinemas, asks, 'Why is it then that they are so attractive?' and concludes: 'Possibly it is because English people who live in towns retain the country talent for gardening . . . Possibly, too, the visitor finds himself sharing, unconsciously, the local pride in the place.'[2]

Wolverhampton is not yet a city. This is a vexed point, and one gets the impression that councillors hope that if it is made one, civic pride will soar. A start has now been made on the civic centre, an estimated £11½ million project, which has been on/off for the last few years, with heated antagonists on either side – for saving money, or long-term gain. Not to mention preservationists, although even ardent ones admit a good modern building could be a bonus. On the whole, though, as a race, we seem reluctant to admit that towns, like people or plants, may need change, lopping, to allow for growth and life.

Somehow Wolverhampton seems to have missed the point. With its situation, which historians noted as particularly 'salubrious', although the town only had four wells – Pudding Well, Horse Well, Washing Well and Meat Well – the town could be to Birmingham and the Black Country an elegant, almost spa-like neighbour, a retreat for visitors from the National Exhibition Centre for instance. It is healthily breezy, and one can be tempted to attribute the most frequent cause of death today in the area – heart disease – to such factors as drink and fast driving, in their turn perhaps partly attributable to frustration and boredom. (I should say here that drivers in the West Midlands, the home of the car, seem worse than elsewhere – nerveless and uncoordinated. Girls drive almost before they can walk; cars are expendable; young men make brakes squeal with a murderous, muddled show of virility.) The town has been renowned for pulling down good old buildings, but as a part consequence it has on the credit side a town centre that works, which can be a pleasure to be in – which cries out for pavement cafés, attractive focal points, dazzling architecture. Why is the nostalgically arcaded Queen's Ballroom not blooming with flower-baskets, wine and music? (It has recently evaded the threat of becoming a supermarket.)

Wulfrunians seem to lack confidence, to have an inferiority complex. They will drive to Birmingham to spend the evening, and in pubs in Wolverhampton one notices a gaucheness and self-consciousness about fashionably dressed Midland pacesetters and their girls, as though their clothes didn't fit their bodies, were new that day. Conversations are equally uneasy, defensive.

This year the town organized a Fiesta. This did not mean, in Wolverhampton, the music of sardanas in the streets, or oxen roast on a spit. Fiesta stood, one was told, for Festival of Industry, Entertainment, Sociology, Technology and Art. A councillor was quoted as saying, 'It is all set for a good commercial venture . . .' Wulfrunians were tired of their music-hall image, and this was their answer.

In fact the fiesta was successful. The stands showing local industries and planning were excellent. There was singing by the choral societies, and at the Art Gallery an exhibition, 'Going, Going, Gone', which showed buildings now demolished (churches, the Georgian St John's Square, the Hippodrome, the wholesale market) or threatened. (One that has escaped is the shop of W. T. M. Snape in Queen Street, selling tea and coffee, with black and gold caddies painted with dragons and flags, and scales and scissors suspended from the ceiling on pulleys.) As one woman said to me 'Wolverhampton used to be a lovely town. Not now. It's so common . . . but that's progress. Nice people won't come into the town now. All the old cafés are closed. It's two wars that have done it.' (And inevitably, being over forty, she added, 'And the immigrants.') It is the citizens that have done it.

It is said that if you put on a play in Wolverhampton and it is a success there, you know you are all right. Yet the Grand Theatre does well, and it has the advantage of having a pretty auditorium. One couldn't ask for a happier evening than seeing, for instance, *The Merry Widow* there, with singers responding to an appreciative audience, old men rubbing their wives' stiff backs in the stalls, and ice-creams being eaten. *Oh Calcutta!* would probably fare less well.

It is hard to know why the town should be more philistine than others. Perhaps it is partly that a conversation can run:

'Is he a nice man?'

'He's a rich man . . .'

The racecourse, well laid out (Tattersalls – £1.30, or the humbler Dunstall Enclosure – 35p, or from the hill overlooking it, free), is a venue of clean tweeded figures, who can yell wholeheartedly when the winner comes in. The Art Gallery, and those who run it, are active and put on inspiring exhibitions, beside the permanent collections of English watercolours – David Cox, Bonnington, Sandby, Turner – modern paintings and enamel-bright cottage interiors such as F. D. Hardy's 'Baby's Birthday'. Music is by no means neglected. There is West Park to walk in with its flowers and frilled ironwork bandstand. Slade has blasted the eardrums of a generation with its own type of shatteringly effective rock ('They go berserk, luv,' as a sound man said encouragingly before a concert). On days when the Wanderers are playing, girls in the streets burgeon with yellow-and-black rosettes, traffic becomes congested, and the buses, instead of their destination, proudly display the score in their windows – WOLVES 1. The whole community is fiercely proud of and involved with its football team, and a star such as Derek Dougan can move on to be in demand in other fields.

Perhaps what is lacking is a desire to get away from the materialism of suburban life – Wolverhampton is surely more suburban than the Black Country elsewhere – and lacking too is a lead from those who should know better. For instance the public library is excellent, but one who can afford it will say, 'I always use the London Library.' Others who live in the rich rancho outskirts will say, 'I never go into town', or, of the town's history, they may say: 'But what is there *here*?'

*

As in most towns, you can read the history of Wolverhampton in its houses, and street names. Perhaps less than in some, because most of the Tudor buildings were burnt down in 1696 when hay in a barn caught fire. But names such as Blossoms Fold, Mitre Fold and Farmer's Fold go back to the days when this was a thriving wool town, much of the wool coming from the Welsh Marches, the sheep being driven into yards before the wool went on to the Staple of Calais for the continental markets. W. G. Hoskins has pointed out that some of the large hundred-acre fields in the area date to this time, rather than to modern organization as one might think.[3]

Important families of this date were staplers, such as the Levesons who built their Great Hall on Snow Hill, or clothiers and drapers, of whom Richard Pipe of Bilston, Lord Mayor of London in 1587, was one. There had been a market since 1258, and the market cross later became the town hall where both Sarah Siddons and her brother John Philip Kemble made their first stage appearances. By that time the whole character of the town had changed with the discovery of coal, iron and other minerals. There had been iron furnaces in Roman days, and John Leveson was 'makinge yron' in 1563, but in the seventeenth century the great 'ironmasters' or 'ironmongers' as they were called, got into their stride – men such as Joseph Turton and William Wood; William Bache who fixed the first steam engine to raise any quantity of water at Wolverhampton; John Wilkinson who in 1756–7 built the first steam-powered blast furnace in Bilston and revolutionized the iron industry, later making an iron barge which dumbfounded the nation. Molineux House, the handsome building in whose grounds the Wolverhampton Wanderers have their head-quarters, is of this era, being built by the rich ironmonger Benjamin Molineux. In 1760 the town got the fine, uncluttered St John's Church;

and another eighteenth-century building, with its own chapel, is Giffard House, continually threatened by redevelopment. With its thriving trades, and the opening of the canals, there was a tremendous increase in traffic and population.

As a metal town, Wolverhampton was originally renowned for its locks (and still has Chubbs, with a characteristic, now superseded, factory). Then came buckle-making, setting the pattern for small businesses, until buckles went out of fashion, despite a petition by David Garrick to George III; then steel 'toys' such as brooches, studs, sword-hilts, ornaments and jewellery, the latter being decorated as time went on with marcasite and semi-precious stones. When quicker methods of making jewellery were developed, an offshoot of the enamel toy trade, japanning, rose to eminence, with japanned iron and papier-mâché trays, coal boxes and Victorian trinkets. (The firm founded by Benjamin and John Mander as a japanning works in 1773 is still renowned for its paints and varnishes.)

At the apogee of the Victorian era the old High Green was renamed Queen Square, and the Queen made her first public appearance after her prolonged retreat into mourning to unveil an equestrian statue of Albert. The sculptor was Thomas Thornycroft, and local myth has it that after the unveiling he realized the position of the horse's legs was anatomically impossible and became so depressed he committed suicide. Another artist of the Victorian era, the photographer Rejlander, father of art photography, was working in his studio in Darlington Street, Wolverhampton, during the years preceding this event. There he posed his famous group 'The Two Ways of Life' (of which Prince Albert was said to have a copy in his dressing-room at Balmoral), and other, less controversial but equally dramatic, compositions.

By the end of the nineteenth century Wolverhampton was in the steam age, the centre of the heavy iron trade, at one time producing more galvanized iron than any other place in the world. Motor-cars followed, with the Sunbeam, and Guy Motors, and today leading firms are Tarmac, BSC Bilston, BOC, Goodyear, the vexed Norton Villiers.

In School Street the firm of William Evans have above their shop a now disused brass workshop. It was closed for safety reasons. In the narrow room the old grinding and smoothing machines, drills, a little forge, are crammed with only inches in between, surrounded by neat rows of tools, lock fittings, taps, metal pieces. On a peg are two jackets and a cap, left there by the workmen when the factory closed; on a door are pinned their dirty seaside postcards, a holiday ritual. One can't help feeling that holidays were more than deserved. On a hot day the confined quarters, working cheek by jowl between two serried rows of windows, with the sun beating in on metal and whirling belts, must have been a sweaty if orderly bedlam. The good old days.

Modern times are not entirely removed from these conditions of incredible toughness. Now we have lived on the edge of the Black Country, we are continually struck by how unaware much of the country is of what is demanded of the people who are producing the raw products for manufacture, the grist for the entire industrial mill. An advertising executive in the country's capital may speak glibly of lack of productivity, or an MP of 'our friends in the Midlands'. Neither would last a day in a melting shop. That a steel-man, for instance, may come from generations of iron- or steel-men, be brought up to the life, does not alter the fact that until there is a wider understanding of his contribution, and of those like him, there can be no unity in the country, there will be well-founded bitterness. Whether or whether not to eat strawberries at Wimbledon, visit Ascot, hold royal garden parties, is merely the froth on the wave of a changing tide, the tip of the iceberg of a split society.

Visit a steelworks, or a foundry, and your understanding of the Black Country character, of a side of the English character, becomes clearer. The cruel jokes, the beer swilling, the toughness, even the occasional sheer bloody-minded stupidity. And when one considers what iron or steel-making must have been like before modern methods were introduced, the surprising thing is not that such character has kept its toughness, but that it has survived at all.

*

I put on my safety helmet and protective glasses. I had been given an excellent lunch at the Bilston Works of the British Steel Corporation, but had not had much stomach for it.

'Steel-making is like cooking,' I was told. It was a hot day.

The works is vast, has about twenty-seven miles of loco track for a start and a 212-foot-high blast furnace, Elisabeth. Red smoke belches into the sky at certain times, and day and night activity goes on in the huge hangar-like sheds, lit like giant smithies. Scrap spreads for acres round the site. Iron- then steel-making has been carried out here for at least 200 years – the first Black Country coke blast furnace being established at Bilston in 1766 and shortly afterwards a furnace being built on the present site. By 1860, 200 blast furnaces were operating in the Black Country. Now there is one, and by tradition, after relining, Elisabeth must be lit by a girl. The only time it was lit by a man, it went out.

'The girl has to be a virgin,' I was told in the dining-room, with much laughter and munching of spring onions among the reps. There are about four canteens. Some have beer and others 'serviettes'. Those employees who are neither shift workers nor managers get neither. 'The girls get younger and younger,' they said, pouring out gins and tonics. (To be fair, we were eating in the visitors' room in the staff canteen.)

Trainee workers are warned about accidents. There is about one fatal accident every three years. Newcomers are told that if they have a hang-over, or have had a row with the wife, they should on no account start work until they have checked with the medical centre. When the shift get a cast, they are given a beer ticket – a necessity rather than a luxury.

My guide, a metallurgist, and I, climbed ladders, jumped puddles, inched past hangar-high masses of moving plant, stood back from erupting slag. 'Slag burns are very nasty – they always turn septic, not like steel burns,' I was told. The heat was monstrous. I was wearing a plastic macintosh and as it burnt against my back, I felt sure it was melting on to my shirt. A snow of grey ash, metal, falls on to your face and hair, works into your clothes. The heat and dust get down into your throat and chest until they burn. To look at the mouths of the furnaces, or molten metal, you must hold a treated red shield in front of your eyes.

The noise was so thunderous that I could not hear much of the steel-making processes, but gleaned them from booklets afterwards. Bilston works on the open-hearth pinciple, with modernized furnaces which are oil fired with an oxygen-enriched air supply. In brief, a charge of iron ore, coke, slag, mill scale, steel turnings, limestone and scrap is smelted to form pig iron in the blast furnace (by-products are gas, used to heat the works, and slag, used for road-making). Steel scrap is then charged into one of the open-hearth furnaces, with limestone to form slag over the melting metal, and molten pig iron is added. Refining is carried out to produce a clean steel, with samples taken at regular intervals for analysis. When the required carbon is attained and a casting temperature of 1,600°C plus is reached, the taphole is opened and the metal runs into the casting ladle. Ferro alloys are added. Steel is then teemed into ingot moulds.

To the layman, it does look like cooking, with giant ladles of red-hot metal rising in the air. The slag bubbles like red-hot beer. All the steel-men are issued with flameproof clothing, with headgear like beekeepers' hats, wooden clogs. As one shift was throwing aluminium and other ingredients into the molten slag, a junior operative (the modern word for apprentice) danced close to the blinding heat without any protective clothing, with no eye shield and loose footgear. My guide smiled ruefully. 'He may mature,' he said doubtfully. The boy told me he didn't like the job and wouldn't stay. And pranced on. To mature and stay?

'No one comes into steel as a first choice,' I was told. It is difficult to find men now who are keen to hold molten metal with tongs. Looking down from the height of the furnace, it seems impossible that anyone can go so near the white heat, within yards. One tries to imagine it in the eighteenth century . . .

But there is room for great skill, initiative (a suggestion scheme, under which Jim Latham for instance initiated a hotter oil–plus–oxygen flame for cutting down melting time); there is the teamwork of shifts, which form your social life during the week – you may work with basically the same people for ten years. And the beer – a furnaceman may drink twenty pints a day.

Is there loyalty? I asked Gerald Fletcher, shift manager in the blast furnace, whose father and grandfather worked here, in the tradition of steel families which still exists. I had been told there were pockets of loyalty (as once there had been in greater measure to the old firm of Stewarts and Lloyds). 'It's not so much loyalty to the firm as to the country, at present, is it?' he said, with great sincerity. People still have the capacity for wisdom at Bilston. Most of them looked very cheerful, not at all soured. The top union official to whom I was introduced in the melting shop seemed full of charm, with a zany badge on his helmet and a shy smile, a highly skilled eye on his melting-shop furnace reports and charts. A nationalized industry, in spite of the obvious defects, is full of surprises. (Recently, when a national steel strike was threatened, Bilston blast-furnacemen followed the example of those at the Shelton Steel works at Stoke, voting to continue production.)

Bilston is part of the special steels division, supplying a wide range of steel for the engineering market and also for tubemakers. Free-cutting steels are also supplied, to the US for example. Thirty per cent of steel is exported, and of that, fifty per cent to the States. The assumption is that by 1980 British Steel will be making 35 million tonnes of steel a year on five large sites. Bilston would seem to stand a slim chance of adapting to trends and carrying on. If not, the last blast furnace in the Black Country will close.

The near-by Birchley works is closing, but the men are loath to leave the area. I was told the Birchley works was a 'happy works'. Redeployment becomes a particularly brutal answer in this area, even if the fault lies in the employees' reluctance to move. Bilston men also hate to leave their home patch; apprentices are even reluctant to go on holiday schemes. A typical Bilston man was in the merchant navy in the war, went round the world three times, and then came home and has never left Bilston since.

I myself was glad to leave that day, after half a day in a steelworks. I was white and shaking, and could have done with those twenty pints of beer.

*

Bilston is one of the old villages which have come to make up modern Wolverhampton. Among others are Penn, Tettenhall, Merridale, Wednesfield. They still have something of the compact, individual quality of villages. It would also be difficult to find any town of Wolverhampton's size so closely surrounded by the open country with its villages.

In Bilston, now merged into Wolverhampton, one is in the Black Country proper. There is a pleasing theory that the Black Country tends to be where one isn't – over there, the next town, not here. It deserves a chapter in itself, but Bilston, part of it, is closely linked to Wolverhampton, although it lies on lower ground, which means that it seems smokier, 'blacker'.

Bilston has its own museum, which is associated with the Wolverhampton Art Gallery and Museum. Peter Neeld, Keeper of Local and Industrial History, the curator at Bilston museum, has reorganized it to great effect. Bilston people, he says, are immensely proud of their history, although cynics label it 'the forgotten area'. There are iron relics from the site of John Wilkinson's blast furnace, trade tokens which were issued by manufacturers instead of coins to be spent in the 'Tommy shop', beautiful examples of japanning and enamels. The famous collection of Bilston enamels is housed here and at the Bantock House Museum, Wolverhampton. They provide the perfect answer to those who think of the area in terms of heavy iron goods, dreariness and lack of imagination. I can think of nothing in English arts or crafts which has a greater lightness of touch, jewel-like delicacy, brilliancy of colour. Navy blue patch-boxes starred with white or green, black-and-white striped candlesticks, flowers scattered over white grounds, eggs as glistening as Russian Easter eggs. It is a riddle which I have often pondered over, how men not noted for their sensitivity, in a region renowned for being slow, tough and unintellectual, shaped and decorated these small, inspired objects. One answer lies in this slowness perhaps. If you rush through life in a Concorde, you will not see the speedwell at the roadside, and the same can be applied to the objects men make.

Coming from the south, one notices a talent for building materials in what have been called the 'utilitarian' Midlands. Except for the pre-war villa growths, as ugly as elsewhere, visually – disregarding living standards – the buildings of whatever era have a well-made look about them. The bricks, often of red ironstone colour as here in Wolverhampton, look of better quality and more mellow; in the old buildings very often there are additional patterns of blue-black bricks, or lines of black-and-white bricks striping cottages like the filling of a cake or a ribbon round the neck of a tidy cat. Even some modern estates show promise of weathering into the landscape; many houses have details such as curved architraves to windows, which are local and traditional and yet adapted to the new shapes. Because they are made to be functional and practical, the buildings look unpretentious, have their own character. Even hideous ones are well cared for. Victorian ones such as the Wolverhampton Art Gallery are very fine, and perhaps there is something Victorian about the regard for objects which is obvious wherever you look.

In Bilston there are an unusual amount of small, unspoilt nineteenth-century houses, old shops. St Leonard's church is calm and peaceful in the dusty central area which has not yet got the re-development it needs, and which will be difficult to carry out well. The shabby streets are dotted with treasure trove.

In 1790 a visitor wrote 'it is one of the largest villages in England, containing more than 1,000 houses'. It is part of the South Staffordshire coalfields. Until the beginning of the eighteenth century coal was carried by pack-horses, and 'a load of coals' was 'a horse load', about two hundredweight, carried in baskets. In the early days this coal was surface coal, true mining being more recent. Below the topsoil lay the seams, and below that again the ironstone for which Bilston was also famous. In 1830 Bilston was said to have produced more iron in its various blast furnaces than the whole kingdom of Sweden. Two years later a terrible outbreak of cholera struck the town. In six weeks 742 people died out of a population of 14,500. 'The inhabitants went on their way as usual; held their cock-fights, their bull-baits, their drinking bouts . . . the sanitary condition of the town was deplorable.'[4] In 1847 there was another outbreak in which 730 people died. The epidemic also visited Wolverhampton. By the Penn Road is a dip in the ground which is said to be the quicklime pit into which corpses were flung. Ghosts of men and children have been heard wailing there.

*

Ghosts of another kind hover round Moseley Old Hall to the north of Wolverhampton. It was here that Charles II took refuge on his flight after the Battle of Worcester, after his stay in the oak tree at Boscobel to the west. From the oak-panelled rooms or cramped priests' holes, he could look out on the lane close by, which was then the main road to Cannock; he saw the bedraggled and footsore Highlanders of his own regiment as they passed, hunted by Cromwell's troops. The Elizabethan house is now owned by the National Trust. The gardens are laid out with formal walks, lopped trees. Looking past the gateway towards the bleak countryside, where cows munch in the rain, one can feel the despair and sadness of that moment come flooding back towards the sturdy English house, which has defied Cromwellian spies, mining subsidence, and tourists.

A peak in Charles's career perhaps ended here, before distrust and disillusionment set in, the lines deepened between nose and mouth on the later, dissolute face. At Worcester he had shown great courage, tried to rally his men, said, 'I had rather you would shoot me, than keep me alive to see the sad consequences of this fatal day'.[5] After the battle a price of £1,000 was put on his head (about £50,000 in today's currency), but not a soul betrayed him. Always able to charm, particularly women and children, he had the honest gentlemen and farmers of Shropshire and Staffordshire – Penderels, Whitgreaves, Giffards – working day and night to save him. It is clear that his charm didn't flag even during the rigours of flight; when William Carlis, who had held his head while he slept in the oak tree, offered him cold mutton, he firmly and without giving offence, fried some collops himself on a knife-point in butter; after the trek to Moseley Hall, the three loyal Penderels who had escorted him set off home unthanked, but, weary as he was, Charles turned back to thank them. After his stay at Moseley Hall he rode as Jane Lane's servant with her to Abbots Leigh near Bristol, afterwards sailing to France from Shoreham.

*

Penn lies on a high ridge to the west of Wolverhampton, along which the ancient Pen-way ran over Goldthorn Hill, which was also called Goldhoard. Beyond Penn Church, looking away to the west, the town suddenly drops away and there lies the rolling Shropshire countryside, and Wales. As the sun goes down, it catches the bricks of the tower, makes the distance wide and luminous, full of the spirits of the past. It is the perfect site for a church, and before the Conquest, when the population was too small for one, Leofric and his wife Godiva erected a preaching cross here, of which the stump still remains; on its eminence it must have been visible to travellers approaching across the fields, up the hill.

The Countess Godiva, among her many possessions and lands, owned Nether Penn, now Lower Penn, which still has an unspoilt village character. Her son Aelfgar owned Over Penn. The two manors were in densely wooded land, with a common which was jealously preserved; part of it today is the Penn Golf Club, and residents have recently been asserting their rights once more, against the golfers. A decision has been given in favour of the Commoners.

In Upper Penn, the population as late as 1700 was only about 200. Today the older cottages are crowded by more recent growth, but there are large gardens, pockets of green, poplars, tall trees.

To the east of Wolverhampton is Wednesfield (Woden's field). In 910 the great battle in which the Saxons defeated the Danes was fought either here, or at Tettenhall, possibly between the two. In the fighting two kings, two earls and many nobles were killed.

*

Tettenhall today also has much of the quality of a village within a town, with a central green, and late Victorian houses. But it is threatened by congested roads, and a new development on the disused airport at Perton, on the fringe of Wolverhampton's green belt – one more slice of the countryside gone, which will inevitably eat up some of the farmland round it.

> . . . through one window man beheld the spring
> And through another saw the summer glow,
> And through a third the fruited vines a-row . . .[6]

William Morris's *Earthly Paradise* is illustrated in stained glass by Kempe at Wightwick Manor, below Tettenhall. The house was designed by Edward Ould in 1887, the estate having been bought by Samuel Theodore Mander, an enlightened and public-spirited member of the manufacturing family. He was discriminating enough in his day to order his furnishings and wall-coverings from the showrooms of Morris and Company, in Oxford Street, where, ironically, Morris's designs for the people were sold as luxuries for the rich. The house, now a National Trust property, is a dazzling treasure trove of William Morris wallpapers and fabrics, Pre-Raphaelite paintings, stained glass, tiles, embroidery and friezes. The beautiful wallpapers have a more individual texture than Morris papers produced today, and the vegetable dyes have not faded, in spite of the fact that Morris deliberately used a lot of blue because it faded and was therefore more of a challenge. There are glowing tiles by de Morgan with a metallic lustre glaze; in the library stained-glass windows with a greeny-gold lily surround by Madox Brown and Burne-Jones, who married a daughter of a Wolverhampton methodist minister ('a little country violet', Ruskin called her). Burne-Jones's 'Love Among the Ruins' hangs in the Great Parlour. There are also several photographs of Rossetti's model and friend Janey Morris – Morris's wife – whom Rossetti first met when she was the daughter of a groom at the King's Arms, Holywell, Oxford. The dark prints show that she did have that Pre-Raphaelite mouth, strong neck, elongated jawline. Whether she was also Rossetti's mistress, and his wife's sad death, are mysteries touched on in *Portrait of Rossetti* by Rosalie Glynn Grylls, Lady Mander, an authority on the Pre-Raphaelites and on the Shelley period, who lives in the house.

The garden has beds of shrubs and plants from Kelmscott Manor, from Tennyson's garden at Farringford, Ruskin's garden at Brantwood.

*

In 1868, an American, Elihu Burritt, wrote a book called *Walks in the Black Country and its Green Border-Land*. 'Wolverhampton is the border-town of the district. On its western outskirt the scene changes with surprising and sudden contrast. In a few minutes you are in the Green Border-Land. All is quiet, rural and peaceful . . .' It is still true. There are the green fields of Staffordshire and Shropshire; Claverley, an unspoilt black-and-white village; Pattingham, with some of the tall red Midland Queen Anne houses which look so like dolls' houses; Badger; Beckbury, with its cockpit. The cockpit is at the top of a hillock behind the church; it is an open-air theatre, circular, with a stone stage in the centre and wrought-iron arcading at the entrances. It is as formal as a little bullring, surrounded by trees. It conjures up the dramatic fights to the death, the gruesome cock's spurs, the formal betting, a whole brutal religion in the setting of these peaceful fields. The past seems very near. Cockfighting was banned in 1849. It is said that illegal cock-fights are still held in the Black Country. Grey-white pigeons' feathers lie on the grass at Beckbury. A cuckoo calls through the summer woods.

*

Staffordshire has always been a tough, rough county, noted for its brawls and bull-fights, pugilists, heady ales. There were ritual brawls at fairs and markets, and later constant religious strife in such places as Wolverhampton which had many Roman Catholic families. Later still I see that during one of John Wesley's frequent preaching visits to the town, a locksmith named Moseley, a 'notorious drunkard, pugilist and gambler', flung a stone at the evangelist, striking him on the head. The memory of this dastardly act haunted Moseley and he was later converted to Methodism at the Noah's Ark Chapel and became a staunch preacher, dying at the age of ninety. (There seems to be a defiant streak in those whose name may be derived from Mollesley – the manor of Mollesley; in the early seventeenth century it was necessary for Mrs Margaret Moseley of Dunstall, 'a great and possibly fearsome lady', to receive a general pardon for all her civil misdeeds; she died 'full of virtue and full of years'.)[7]

With its central position, the county, once densely forested, and inaccessible because of its high range of hills, was always one of the last places in the country to be subdued by invaders, and equally, provided a refuge for those driven out elsewhere. Even before England was an island, the original inhabitants sought refuge from successive waves of marauders here. Although the Anglo-Saxons colonized the region, the Danes and the Romans had never succeeded in completely taming it. Pockets of resistance have survived through the ages. Phil Drabble in his book on *Staffordshire*[8] says that until fifty years ago there was a herd of wild cattle at Chartley Park said to be descended from the native cattle of prehistoric Britain; there are still descendants of a swarthy race of primitive farmers from about 2000 BC, with narrow skulls and delicate features (named the Windmill Hill folk from another settlement in Wiltshire), whose burial-places or lows are scattered throughout Staffordshire, particularly in the north; the Black Country dialect is one of the oldest and the most unadulterated in England. With Cheshire, the region was the last to hold out against William the Conqueror. It is not surprising that it is an area which is noted for being hostile to strangers, newcomers, fiercely loyal to those who have become friends. Outsiders can be offered a front of obstinate, slow obtuseness against which there are few weapons, except perhaps humour and a sense of shared tribulations. (And slowness is a general characteristic. You can see thoughts ticking over. It can drive southerners to a frenzy of impatience, but is often not a disadvantage. Things will be thought through, and thought through independently, without adopting superficial conclusions.)

Helpful, with time to smile, intensely practical, horrified at waste or unnecessary spending (yet lovers of comfort – I have heard a woman talk of *re-covering* her 'three piece suite' for £200), South Staffordshire people can be immensely kind. Their enjoyment of life is sometimes crude – Staffordshire men are great eaters and drinkers and if you have visited some of the workshops you will understand why, but it does not explain why they talk so much about food. 'The steyks were joost raight – *that* thick. The scampis melted in my mouth.' 'I must have my Friday pints.' 'Thoase boons are very good.' In a sales office I heard girls speak of nothing but buns, beer and slimming, an unhappy triangle. Equally, Black Country humour is traditionally cruel. A typical and often quoted Black Country joke is that in which a doctor tells a sick husband he can eat anything he likes now, explaining to the wife that there's no longer any hope. The man asks for some ham. His wife replies that he can't have ham because she's keeping it for the funeral. Always situation comedy, it makes no bones about the situation in question. You can hear 'hullo Chocolate Box' said to a Negro in an office, unblinkingly, or 'chocolate-coloured coon'. You have to admire the directness. They have known tough times, they know life is harsh, but they will survive. Jack, in our street, in his sixties, walks most of the way to work each day, with a gas mask case (the usual dinner bag) over his shoulder and a white scarf in his shirt neck. He was very good to his older brother who lived with him and who often walked the street in pyjamas and Van Gogh hat, had a phobia about dogs, and in the end had to dress and care for him. He was very cut up when he died. I said I missed him too.

'It's worse for me. I lived with him. He's up there. Waiting for me now. We've all got to go.'

'You're marvellous to keep cheerful, manage.'

'I've got to, han I?'

★

How much will change here in the future? In Wolverhampton, where in some ways people are twenty years behind – still chain-smoking cigarettes in every office, still able to smile, still warm-hearted, independent – and parochial. In the suburbs old men sun themselves in their doorways, choirs sing to full churches on Sunday evening, children are neatly dressed and couples save up to get married. How is this town going to react to the National Exhibition Centre, to the foreign visitors to trade fairs, to the solidified Common Market?

There have always been foreign workers in Wolverhampton. There are many Poles, Latvians, Jugoslavs. Some of them are willing to do gruelling work in tyre factories for instance, for which English workers have lost the taste (although it can't be said that people don't work here; the infant-mortality rate is very high, possibly because so many young married women, in a town with a large young population, continue working hard). But the bastion has not been truly breached, and, partly because of Enoch Powell's particular brand of brilliant, patriarchal, breathtakingly – and sadly – prejudiced eloquence, people tend to think of racial problems in connection with Wolverhampton.

I went to see Aaron Haynes while he was at the Wolverhampton Council for Community Relations, a leader who made the sparks fly in dealings with the town authorities. He said that racial violence had been much enlarged by the press, that Hell's Angels or other youths had felt duty bound to prove their virility by asserting themselves against coloured people, by doing their bit of Paki bashing. But as Wulfrunians were patently unable to distinguish between unwarlike Pakistanis and Sikhs, their victims often turned out to be opponents expertly armed with hockey-sticks and knives. The hospitals saw some nasty wounds and the attacks died out. But after the comparatively sheltered atmosphere of school, there were in fact job difficulties and discriminations, he said, a 'colour tax' on rented property, difficulties in getting mortgages. Equally it was only when they had gained confidence in their own milieu that people can integrate properly, have the confidence to integrate. Beside the basic difficulties, he explained, there are added difficulties of moving into a structured society, coming up against the class barriers in a town where those who have made it want to keep it that way. Wolverhampton had its interests strongly challenged in the late fifties and sixties, when large commercial groups from outside came to take over the little firms. There was a closing of the ranks. As Aaron Haynes eloquently put it: 'The degree of tension in any society reflects the inability of that society to cope with inadequacies within it.'

*

'For me, the areas where Indians, or West Indians, live, are one of the best things about Wolverhampton: brightly-painted houses . . . beautiful dress . . . but they are not liked generally.'

The speaker, Stephen Morris, a Birmingham-born poet who now lectures in creative writing at Wolverhampton Polytechnic. He explained that when he was a child it was the Birmingham Irish who were not liked. With Birmingham he now has a love-hate relationship; speaks eloquently of the different areas, the waves of new buildings which have continually worked outwards from the centre, so that you can see the rings 'like cutting through a tree'. 'The old library was really beautiful . . . people went up ladders to get the books.'

He admits that he doesn't much like Wolverhampton, although in the past when he was in the RAF at Bridgnorth and Cosford and used to come up to the Music Hall and Madame Clark's Pub which had sawdust on the floor, barrels to drink off, and tarts, it had more character. This is not surprising for one whose poetry (*The Revolutionary and Other Poems*, *The Kingfisher Catcher*)[9] is concerned with instants which, in the broadest sense, make a political comment (he has also written effectively simple, ballad-like poems as in *Penny Farthing Madness*[10] and designs visual poetry or caligrammes). 'I've got all these working-class things with me . . . My wife says *clarse* and I have to watch that I don't [he says it as in ass] . . . It used to be unusual to be working class . . . I suppose now to be black and working class is the unusual thing . . . or a woman and black and working class . . . or a homosexual and . . .'

He delved deeper into the matter of roots, of a class he has worked out of. 'I would defend the working-class thing – if not entirely respecting it.' He feels the working class is being creamed off educationally, even union leaders being cleverly led astray. 'They have seen the fruits of the capitalist society and want them. There should be ways of sharing the cake out for everyone.' He has worked in Cadbury's for a bit, knows what he is talking about – 'one could get mesmerized by the work'. Not rabidly revolutionary, 'Revolutions happen when a country is on an upward trend; idealism comes when a country is expanding, not depressed,' he sees things with a decisive clarity, and humour. 'The East Midlands [he has a house in Nottingham] are less materialistic than the West Midlands – there is less heavy industry, smaller industries . . . they have produced writers such as Lawrence, Sillitoe, Stan Barstow, Byron – not working class of course – . . . This hasn't happened in Birmingham.' But clearly he cares about an area where people are working to produce the basic things of life. 'You could cut London off and let it float away and still do without it . . .'

Typical of the thoughtful voices of a polytechnic, a university, perhaps. With a poet's clear insight into new class formations, strata, and longing for a wider humanity.

The 'working class' in general may now regard the middle classes as finished and ineffectual, but in a stronghold such as Wolverhampton the old cachets still carry weight. The other day I was hurrying to catch a train. I saw, with a Through-the-Looking-Glass sensation, a crowd of top-hatted figures at the station. In dresses to the ground, flimsy plastic cartwheels of hats, Wolverhampton was preparing to board the special train (coffee on sitting down, followed by lunch, and on the return journey, presumably, dinner) for Ascot. Teenagers in trouser-suits, and cartwheels, looked a little embarrassed, but were going nonetheless. Later in the week there was a flowering of matronly ringlets dressed for Ladies Day.

*

Staffordshire is basically a conservative region, Wolverhampton a very conservative town. Yet it has been able to change in the past. Phil Drabble has written that it was not obstinacy but pride in ancestry, and a sense of continuity with the past, that enabled the people of Staffordshire to wrest prosperity from the unpromising mixture of barren uplands and impenetrable forests. Wulfrunians have been independent, martial (during the Napoleonic wars their quota for the militia was filled by volunteers, not conscripts), loyal and resilient. In trade relations they were practical. In 1815, during the terrible economic distress after the Napoleonic Wars (a year later more than a quarter of the population was unemployed), Joseph Pearson in Wolverhampton called for support for the small manufacturers who were paying high rents. In 1974 leaders of West Midlands industry protested to the government about including Saturdays in a three-day-week rota, to the detriment of the small company, and the three-day week was amended on a national basis.

Visually, the town needs to evolve. I had not quite realized how attractive a town Wolverhampton once was until I saw the sketches by Noyes in the Salt Library at Stafford, of the streets with their old houses winding up to the central church. But that is the past. Now there is a serious housing shortage, because of the town's position in the West Midlands industrial core, aggravated by the successful polytechnic. There are few facilities for the young such as swimming pools or arts complexes, so that even when our garden fence was not allowed by vandals to stand for more than twelve hours, I had a glimmer of sympathy left, although John who spent two days building it naturally had not, and the young policeman to whom we reported it clearly had trouble protecting his own garden, let alone ours. There are sparks of light. Recently, with public participation, the new Valley Park along a disused railway line, by a canal, has been planned. A corner was perhaps turned when the council refused to let a supermarket be built in central Queen Square instead of the Queen's Ballroom – but why in Wolverhampton do the new troughs for plants have to be tombstone grey? To some extent our towns are ourselves.

I have a possibly unfounded feeling that Wolverhampton, which has so long been part of the Staffordshire stronghold against invaders, is poised on the brink of change, that the new influences of Europe, a wider horizon, could prove the catalyst, combined with the economic depression, which transforms the area into one of flux and expansiveness, as, in a different sense, it was during the Industrial Revolution. Or will the role be left to Birmingham? But with its vital position in the country's industry, as part of the conurbation, change, for good or ill, has to come. It is sink or swim for Wolverhampton now.

4 The Black Country

When Satan stood on Brierley Hill
And far around he gazed,
He said, 'I never shall again
At Hell's flames be amazed.'

Traditional ballad

What is the Black Country? Where is it? Only one thing is certain: it is not Birmingham. Southerners who imagine one solid, smoke-grimed, soulless mass, a vast conurbation lying leadenly at the centre of their country, are about as clear-eyed as ancients stubbornly thinking the world flat. Today there is often more smoke lying over central Birmingham than on the hills of the Black Country, and to many the secret of the area lies more in the word 'country' than 'black' – and one is not talking about grass, but people.

But where is it?

It lies on 'the southern part of the South Staffordshire coalfield', the Black Country Society will tell you, the earliest developments being in those areas where 'outcrop' coal lay at a very shallow level below the surface (Wednesbury, Darlaston, Willenhall, Bilston, Cosely, Tipton, Dudley, Brierley Hill and the adjacent villages). The society is bristlingly proud of the 'Black Country mon'. I mentioned to a member some books I had read, and admired, on the area. 'Absolute tosh,' he said. 'There is *no* book on the Black Country.' He was obviously determined to be the Black Country 'mon' *par excellence* – chippy, independent, proud, swilling his pint of beer and nostalgic for the days of narrow boats and cock-fights. Bull-baiting is illegal, but by God the fighting spirit isn't dead in the Black Country and there are no flies on we. This terrible belligerence can be boring or endearing, depending rather on one's stamina at the time.

Richard Traves, Keeper of Science and Industrial Archaeology at Dudley Museum who, sadly, died recently and had been organizing the new open-air Black Country Museum, which will open in stages from 1977 onwards, broadened the area. 'Coalseam? Rubbish. The Black Country must be regarded as an economic entity.' As the museum will cost more than a million this is obviously a wise definition. 'Iron, coal, limestone and clay/Has made the Black Country what it is today –' is the jingle he thought up for visiting schoolchildren, and he included several border districts in the outer area, such as Cannock Chase, Bromsgrove, Seisdon. And, 'Look,' he said, 'the Black Country man doesn't *have* to be working class. What about Lord Dudley – and the chairman of GKN, Sir Raymond Brookes, would be proud to acknowledge himself a Black Countryman.'

He was clearsighted about the region: 'Anglo-Saxon people have never been noted for perspicacity or aesthetic appreciation . . . The Black Country jokes and stories don't sound funny if told in drawing-room style.' (He had just recommended to me a book with the title *Adventures of a Black Country Nurse*.) But he also said, 'I am quite content to live and die here,' and his enthusiasm for the new museum, which will have complete models of everything from chain works, candle factories and boatyards to public houses and millponds, and which will demonstrate how industrial processes and innovations have had an effect on people in their daily lives, was quite free from museum dust. He worked in fields as varied as engineering and button making before his last fifteen years in museums, and as a child stayed with relations near Walsall. 'The smell and flowers of the Black Country became part of my existence . . . I can never forget the smell of the tanneries and the sound of the shunting yards.'

I suspect the same, or similar, could be said of most Black Country people. Walter Allen, in his evocative book *Black Country* (which *does* include Birmingham), beautifully describes the attraction of some of the area, while at the same time pointing out the strange, almost mythical confusion about its entity.

The Black Country is never where one lives oneself but begins a'ways at the next town . . .
. . . during my boyhood I would have been surprised, indeed indignant, if you had suggested that I lived in the Black Country. The Black Country, I would have told you, starts at the "boundary", meaning at West Bromwich or Smethwick. This was not snobbery. The Black Country had for me the fascination of what lies beyond the boundaries, the known limits. It was therefore romantic.[1]

As an outsider, one cannot hope to know the Black Country completely. How could one when someone from Wednesbury is a foreigner to someone at Sedgley, and the dialect of Upper Gornal probably incomprehensible to both, certainly to me. But you can feel its attraction, almost painfully at times, almost with a sense of recognition. You can also see the reverse of the coin; why even its inhabitants might want sometimes to disown it. If one could penetrate the secret of the Black Country character, one would be very close to the secret of the English character, to the Churchillian bulldog in his finest hour and, in less fine hours, to a terrier turning its back on the world.

> The Devil stood on Bradley Moor
> And heard the forges roar,
> Quoth he, 'I've heard a row in Hell,
> But none like this before.'
>
> The Devil ran through Sedgley
> Booted and spurred,
> With a scythe at his back
> As long as a swered,
> He staggered onto Dudley Woodside
> And there he laid him down and died.

It is New Year's Eve. Quite near Dudley Wood (oh how trippingly pastoral the street and place-names are here – Windmill Edge, Primrose-hill, Blackbrook Road, Mouse Sweet, Tippity Green, Bumble Hole) is the Old Swan Inn, Netherton. John and I had read about it in the *Birmingham Post*, as one of the last pubs selling home-brewed beer. For no longer is the Black Country unacknowledged or unsophisticated. The *Black Countryman* magazine is read at Harvard University, a television film showing faggots and peas was a sell-out in San Francisco, and the Old Swan Inn had in fact already been on television. Sadly, the mass media have indeed led to a more stereotyped, universal culture, with the dying of old idiosyncratic ways and a self-consciousness about customs still practised. Yet it is still sometimes possible to find a genuine affection for and expression of the old, handed-down habits. And Black Countrymen can laugh at their new image. 'Black Coontry Workers' said three of them with a mock bow as we photographed them, astride gleaming new motor-bicycles.

I don't quite know what we expected on New Year's Eve. Possibly something between a Netherton Knees Up Mother Brown and an Irish wedding. Everyone knows that Black Countrymen are colossal drinkers, eaters; great ones for a Monday off and a Tuesday off for the boss. But that is the legend.

The reality is heightened initially for us by the door being barred on the inside. We are surreptitiously let in. Other pubs in the neighbourhood have possibly no extension and the Old Swan doesn't want them rowdying up the place. *Their* place. You don't crawl from pub to pub; you have *your* boozer. Here it is Mrs Doris Pardoe's pub, and she has been there forty-three years, and licensee for twenty-three. She is very kind and dignified in a black dress, with curling white hair. Everyone is very dignified in fact, their knees well down.

The ceiling is enamelled iron, very pretty, with a swan painted on it. A great iron stove with long pipes gives off a steady heat. The brewery is at the back, has had £15,000 spent on it and does for two pubs. The beer is delicious (although on another day it seemed to me to have a strong whiff of raw pork about it). We all sit at our tables round the big room, while sounds of singing come from the Smoke. There are quiet middle-aged couples and hefty young men with open-necked shirts, also quiet.

John is feeling very British. 'We're intruders,' he says, eyeing the small saucers of raw onion by each glass. I don't feel like an intruder. It is warm and peaceful, and the courtesy of everyone to everyone seems very real. We all sip our home brew and ruminate, and exchange a few words. There are calendars and lists of the Netherton Homing Society and the Royal National Homing Union (pigeons – you see them everywhere in the area, spun into the sky like flashing handfuls of corn thrown by a sower). Where are the streamers and funny hats and dirty jokes and sequins? No one seems to be looking at the television screen.

Towards midnight, Mrs Pardoe comes from behind the bar and sits down by each of us and talks a bit, like the nicest hostess. She even lifts and rearranges chairs. Then, with no fuss, she calmly pours everyone an immense tot of free whisky, each to his capacity obviously, as the heftiest young man gets a half tumblerful, neat. At last the singing breaks out, but it is not some boozy ditty. They sing the words of a hymn to the tune of 'Ilkley Moor', with great feeling and fervour. Then we all get up and link arms in a circle and sing 'Auld Lang Syne'. Surprisingly, a whippet-faced man bounds forward and kisses me. The hefty young man kisses my hand. John looks even more British.

We leave then, because we don't want to spoil anyone's fun. It's not our pub.

Mrs Pardoe wishes us a Happy New Year. And good health. 'That's the most important, isn't it,' she says. I remember this because the next time I call in she is ill, and elsewhere I hear rumours of a demolition order. (Will our society, which feeds with its television maws on places such as the Old Swan, bulldoze it out of existence?)

So this is one face of the Black Country. Very polite, but not in the least suburban. With strong pockets of religion. The chapel is as important as the pub and the working men's clubs, and the Methodist Church has been strongly entrenched here for a long time, although congregations are petering out now, an Anglican clergyman told me – 'They've got, let me see, six buildings to our four, but the congregations are dwindling.' From a black land it is good to sing of a green land 'far, far away'; the little chapels stand between the hulks of factories; in the churchyards there are a mass of flowers on the graves. Death is important here.

> A handsome young man from London came down,
> To set up his trade in a small country town,
> Being asked his trade he answered downright,
> I belong to the family of nine times a night.
> With my Tudy I oo–dy I A. With my Tudy I oo–dy I, O.[2]

The sense of ownership, of closely-knit communities, is the essence of the Black Country. The region is 'country' in that it was originally, and still is to a great extent, a series of villages, each with its own trades and character. Its heyday, although that may not be the appropriate word, was from about 1750–1900, but the history of its mineral wealth goes back much earlier. Ironworking has been traced on Wychbury Hill in the first century BC and the Romans knew how to use ironstone and coal. There was coal mining in Sedgley in the thirteenth century. It is the combination of these two materials, with the lime for the flux in smelting the iron, that enabled the area to rise to prominence. As Elihu Burritt wrote: 'Nature did for the ironmasters of the Black Country all she could; indeed, everything except literally building the furnaces themselves.'

Dudley, the historical centre of the region, with its ancient castle possibly going back to the time of Dud or Dudo, a Saxon, lies on a seven-mile ridge of high land, running from Wolverhampton south-eastwards. This ridge is sometimes called the 'Dorsal Ridge of the Black Country'; it is part of the main watershed of England. Rain falling on the western side drains into a tributary valley of the Stour and on to the Severn and the Bristol Channel. On the eastern side the rain runs into the basin of the Tame and onwards to the North Sea. The castle is built on a great lime-stone crag, and the near-by hill of the Wren's Nest is pitted with the caves of lime quarries, which at the time they were worked had names such as The Bottle Cave and Cherry Hole. The whole Black Country, in fact, seems to be precariously undermined. I saw a headline on a newspaper hoarding the other day: 'Quarry Bank garden slips into 8oft hole', and Phil Drabble tells of an old man who once saw the ground open up and swallow two horses in a 'crowning in'.[3] Houses, and the Crooked House pub, are pulled awry by mining subsidence, and smoke issues forth in people's rosebeds from underground fires which can last years.

Originally, charcoal was used to smelt the iron, and Staffordshire's forests were rapidly depleted. In the seventeenth century, one of the most intriguing characters in the region's history, Dud Dudley, illegitimate son of Lord Dudley and a collier's daughter, spent his entire life trying to smelt iron with coal instead of charcoal. Sent for at twenty to come from Oxford to take over his father's ironworks, he invented a method of smelting iron with coal from local pits. But his career was dogged by misfortune. Floods swept away his equipment; rival ironmasters hired a mob to smash his bellows and wreck his works; he spent a considerable time in a debtor's prison and was unsupported by Charles II although he was a Royalist during the Civil War. He was said to be quarrelsome, haughty and tactless but his persistence redeems these faults, and it was he who first put a stop to the tremendous spoilage of woodland. It used to take thirty 'cordes' of wood (stacks eight feet by four feet by four feet) to make a ton of iron. He wrote a book *Metallum Martis* claiming his success, but his secret died with him. It was not until about 1750 that Abraham Darby reintroduced the use of coked coal into Staffordshire.

With the use of coke, the natural resources could be developed on a large scale. The total output of pig-iron between 1788 and 1830 was multiplied tenfold. The age of the fiery furnaces was beginning. Steam (with Newcomen's first successful pumping steam engine in 1712), John Wilkinson's Bradley blast furnace *c*. 1758, canals, and later the railways all played their part in the tremendous upsurge of growth. Cost of manufacture lessened, and iron goods were exported all over the world.

And the cost in human terms? An account, in 1850, of 'Alighting at a station in the heart of the Black Country':

It is mid November, on a cloudy but rainless day, when we alight at one of the stations on the Stour Valley Railway in the heart of the Black Country. The landscape, if landscape it can be called, on both sides of the iron road bristles with stunted towers capped with flame, and with tall black chimneys vomiting forth clouds of blacker smoke, which literally roofs in the whole region . . . We direct our steps towards a point in the distance where the chimneys appear clustered the closest. There is no road to walk on, but a wheel-track of deep ruts through a bed of mud. The whole surface of the land has been dug up and turned inside out . . . From this dreary scene we pass on a sudden into a crowd of busy forms, clustering like bees around a number of flaming hives, feeding the hungry furnaces . . . a little chapel of dingy brick . . . the foundations have sunk below their original bed, and a ghastly rent in the main wall of the building, gaping almost as wide as the doorway, gives a prophetic warning of what may be looked for when the next disturbance takes place in the mine beneath.

. . . Children with unwashed faces are dabbling in the mire, or noisily grouped on the doorsteps. A savoury odour issues from the doors and windows, and from lattice and lintel, wives, mothers and daughters project their yellow faces . . . The faces of the young, which should be fair and interesting, are haggard and un-lovely – there is a jaundiced hue even on the childish countenance – and the neck of many a growing lass is disfigured with an unsightly wen as big as a pigeon's crop.[4]

*

As I walked forth one summer's morn, all in the month of June,
The flowers they were springing and the birds were in full tune,
I overheard a lovely maid and this was all her theme,
'Success attend the collier lads, for they are lads of fame.'

'I am a collier lad,' he said as black as a sloe
'And all night long I'm working so very deep below.'
'Oh, I do love a collier lad as I do love my life
My father was a pitman all the days of his life.'[5]

All blackness? The region of Dickens's *Old Curiosity Shop* and Disraeli's *Sybil*? Of children from the mines falling into bed too tired to eat their supper and women with crushed hips from thirty years in the pits, of girls carrying seven tons of clay on their head during one day? The black side of the coin is all too clear, highlighted by the terrible cholera outbreaks of 1832 and 1847 and by the work of social reformers such as Sister Dora in Walsall, who did for civilian hospitals what Florence Nightingale did for military ones, working in a primitive accident hospital on the industrial injuries of the time – burns, scalds, eye injuries, limbs crushed in the mines. She was possibly a contributory inspiration to the novel *Middle-march* and a moving book on her by Jo Manton quotes her first triumph when a young mine-worker begged her to save an arm which the doctor had said must be amputated. 'Oh Sister! Save my arm for me, it's my right arm.' She treated it for three weeks without a whole night in bed herself.[6]

And the bright side? Wages rose. By the mid-nineteenth century they were fifty per cent higher than half a century before; by the turn of the century one hundred and fifty per cent higher with prices twenty-five per cent down. Conditions gradually improved with evils such as the tommy shop and 'butty' miners who contracted labour for the bosses eradicated, and with the recognition of the trade-union movement by about 1880 finally helping to ease the exploitation by employers. And there were other bonuses, surely, which one can still see today. An unusual amount of independence, the possibility for the small man to succeed, the one-man business to flourish; achievement and craftsmanship; and the character of the area, the landscape itself, the curious mixture of the man-made and natural.

Elihu Burritt, the American whose report for the Birmingham Consulate was published in 1868, writes with splendid rhetoric and contagious euphoria of the dramatic impact of the area. He conjures up a scene of titanic industry, roaring furnaces, neighing pit-horses, nuggets of coal, a stream of raw material 'like an ever-flowing river', and always the contrast of red and black, fire and moonlight, darkness and the 'green velvet binding' tapestried with historical scenes, that is the surprise element in the Black Country, its closeness, intermingling, with true country.

There was an embattled amphitheatre of twenty miles span ridged to the purple clouds . . . The canals twisting and crossing through the field of battle, showed by patches in the light like bleeding veins. There were no clouds except of smoke over the scene; but there were large strips of darkness floating with crimson fringes into the red sea, on which the white moon rode like an ermined angel of peace.

For all that glowing empire was peace. Peace has her battlefields as well as war . . .

You have to walk through the Black Country to feel its visual impact. For a start, some of its most fascinating places *have* no road: it is a region of continual surprises, hidden oddities, sudden, astonishing views.

People who have not seen it for themselves will imagine that I am being absurdly romantic to say that it can be indescribably beautiful. I find these words in my notebook, so they can stand; the sharp emotion I felt when I wrote them is still within my grasp. I can roll it over my tongue, savour it.

I had got up early to see chainmakers at work, at Quarry Bank, and from there I was looking downhill, over towards Stourbridge, and then across to Cradley and Halesowen with the sun coming up through the clouds. The sky was pale blue, and the sun softly lighting up orange-brown clouds, falling on trees, factory chimneys with white smoke, wreathed in white mist. It was layered, with grey, water-filled colours; spiked with the red of bricks, the thin dark spire of a church against the glowing skyline. I was reminded of paintings of Venice.

And not all for the eye. The air seemed very pure. Birds were singing from hawthorn bushes, overgrown churchyards, patches of green. Anvils – or they sounded like anvils – were clattering away. The world was resoundingly awake. It was a good place to be alive in.

And the chainmakers, some of them, had been awake and working in this morning world since 5 a.m. If you are a chainmaker you also make your own hours, the most usual being about seven till the lunch hour.

Then you knock off. Freedom. What then? I gathered you usually had a pint, then a couple of hours easy and the evening is your own.

At Noah Bloomer's chainshop you will see chains made in the traditional method from wrought iron, and that is almost the only place you will see this method, and you probably won't see it here for ever. Wrought iron is not as one might imagine all of that tricksily-worked stuff you see made into ranch-style gates – it is the material itself. It is very corrosion resistant and easily welded by hand, and is now made by a firm in Bolton. The supply is not inexhaustible.

About six red-hot furnaces are blazing away in the open shed. It is immensely exciting. This week I am lucky as there are two men working at one furnace, one of them a striker hitting the iron with a dolly, which is an unusual sight now.

I climb across piles of coke and iron bars and rusting chains in the yard, and then, more gingerly through an area where red-hot rings are being casually spinned out as if they are harmless as doughnuts. The heat is terrific, and everyone has his pasteurized milk bottle of tea, which seems to be the favourite drink – possibly even ousting the legendary beer? (Many chainmakers are teetotal.) The men are all in open shirts or vests, without even the traditional 'sweat cloth' round their necks; they look tremendously fit.

You can't hear yourself speak. They smile at me and shout incomprehensible words. A small man says, 'You come and sit here by me and I'll explain it.' 'Here' is a small wooden bench within a few feet of the red-hot iron being pounded, and burning sparks are showering out in a wide radius from every furnace as iron meets iron. Frankly I am terrified. The sparks sizzle past my gumboots and macintosh. What if a spark gets in your eyes? The men seem to wear no protective clothing at all.

My patient mentor is explaining the process to me. The tools; the arcing willow rods above the furnace from which hammers are suspended. That all chains are made to different sizes. The Black Country accent is beyond me, if I could hear, but I can't. He is explaining the proportions, a Pythagorean ratio between the width of iron, and inside measurement of chain. I repeat the words in desperation. Sparks alight on my rush basket and slowly burn out. I turn round and he is gone. I have been warned that Black Country people will let you know when they have had enough of you, and my stupidity must have exasperated him.

At another furnace Edward – 'they call me Ted' – is taking a brief break. He has been at the job forty years, and used to get up at four. Now it's seven o'clock, 'since I was in hospital'. He indicates his stomach. He has an extraordinarily sensitive face, over which varying emotions flicker like waves of light. His eyes are bright brown and his smile very sweet – apologetic – for me? his mates? for himself? for the world? Yet ready to light up at unexpected turns of luck. A face you don't forget.

He tells me about his five sons, all grown up and gone now. We both look out of the window holes in the walls (no glass) on to a green hillside with hawthorn bushes and bracken. Outside the birds must be singing. Summer will soon be here.

*

After such Herculean labours, home-brew, or takeaway home-made faggots and peas, which you can buy in small shops, seem the ideal thing. It all falls into place. And although the days when many cottages in Cradley and Cradley Heath had their own one-man chainshop at the end of the yard (there is only one example of this now) are past, because of legislation – 'you cor do this' – and the cost of keeping fires going, the men here are their own masters, they seem part of an organic whole with their work. You still see many men without ties, wearing a knot of white scarf at the neck for street wear, because at work they would have worn their sweat cloths. There are a lot of check and tartan shirts; wide leather belts with buckles, small leather knapsacks worn over one arm, flat caps. You see Stafford bull-terriers; wives walking them and girls giving them the best seat on a bus.

But even jobs such as chainmaking are threatened by the times. Mr Bob Bloomer who with his brother runs Noah Bloomer's, which has been in chains since about 1800, told us on another occasion that they can't get younger men. And he added: 'It's as if there was a death wish all over the country.'

Samuel Bloomer, another chainworker, said of young men – 'they've only got to smell this for one day and they're off'. He added, making a gesture to indicate a big, broad, man, 'That doesn't mean anything.' He is slightly built; sweat was running down his face. 'Yo don't start pulling and jerking that [the tools; they make all their own] – it's stronger than yo. It could break your wrist like lightning.' And smiling – 'Yo've got to have the work inside yo.'

I walked on. Small Victorian houses; higgledy-piggledy yards; modern semis. They all have the same untidy air. Even modern semi-detached rows in the Black Country are soon unmodern, as much of a jumble, as vital as the rest.

A cock startled me crowing from a garden. A game-cock? One or two are said to be kept still. In the old days they were cherished like one of the family and fed on egg and sherry cake before a fight. They were bred to fight, and their spurs ensured a clean kill, however beastly the sport may have been.

There are hills, factory clad, in all directions. But also green hills. The hills add to the surprise of the place. On one, above winter trees bushy as hedgehogs and looking over fields, was one of the tall, four-eared, expectant churches so common in this region. I couldn't pinpoint it on my map, but I had to walk to it. The place gets you like that. It is explorer's country; parts of it a child's adventure playground that nothing could rival – streams, canals, ruined buildings, mossy treetrunks, derelict spaces with gorse and willowherb to hide in all day.

Up Saltwells Road (Cradley had a brief spell as a spa), past Saltwell's Clay Field, Lodge Farm reservoir, and Brewins Bridge over the Dudley Canal, with the canal stretching silverly, past a small white cottage with neat cabbage rows. On up to the church, which was in fact Netherton Church standing bleak and windswept, looking over fields where white horses grazed, with brown smoke from the iron works and the Round Oak Steel Works beyond, and in the distance Dudley Castle on its hill, away to the west the Shropshire hills.

Some of the old stone graves were broken open, but most were heaped with bright flowers. A stone cross of lilies rose above the tomb of James Fulleylove, who died in 1878, and his wife Harriett. Their children James and Clara had died in infancy. There were Abrahams, and Noahs and Job, son of Job and Thamar Bird. Some of the stones were eroded by wind and smoke, but most inscribed with thin curling script. 'To the memory of Samuel Spittle, late of Darby End, who died February 3rd 1897 aged 70 years. His End was Peace. Also of Selina Spittle . . .'

Cars roared up narrow streets. Men were busy doing-it-themselves with bricks and mortar. (The Black Country, ever adaptable, is full of Do-It-Yourself shops.) Across Halesowen Road and down Northfield Road, past the Loving Lamb pub. Here are the old red-brick buildings of Samuel Lewis and Co, established 1750, beside the Dudley Canal. On the opposite side of the road is the Darby End Providence Methodist Chapel, which a museum hopes to buy, and Swindell and Co. Here tools are made – garden forks, spades, rakes. There is a similar atmosphere of thundering iron and flying sparks as at the chainmakers. One man is making spades in an age-old way, sitting on a chair suspended from an iron chain and banging out a square of thick iron about four inches across into a large shovel. 'They bend em oop after . . . they're finished by we, but then they go across there.' The floor trembles; great iron bars are cut with a heavy weight; helmet-shaped troughs are pressed into shape with a great helmet-shaped beater.

'Do you ever get bored?' I asked a man at a machine making holes in brackets.

'I only started today,' he grinned crisply. He was a pensioner of sixty-seven, looked fifty, and worked two days a week, although he'd been in the trade all his life. Someone else told me it was all right there, easy, not bad at all.

In the yards stacks of clean rakes and forks stood ready for use.

Everywhere you get the feeling of a satisfying product, even in great sheds open on to other roads where iron is being puddled. Small works are thick as leaves on the ground, and one suddenly sees a huge silver funnel standing at the roadside, or a lorry of valuable scrap iron scurries past. Even in the neat rows of new houses, you suddenly come across a slag heap or a lorry loaded with metal, with a man bending over its bonnet while his small son looks on, learning the trade.

From Northfield Road you can see across to Darby's Hill. The canal runs up to it and by the water the song of birds was positively deafening. At Bumble Hole, two waterways meet, and there are three black-and-white iron bridges. Then the entrance to the Netherton Tunnel. Nearby is the Dudley Tunnel, which reopened for pleasure boats in 1973. In the days of boat traffic, the boatmen would leg through some tunnels by lying on their backs and pushing on the roof of the tunnel. In the winter ice would sometimes block the tunnel, because boats couldn't get through to break it.

From Darby's Hill, the view over the Black Country and beyond is sweeping. After climbing it, I called in at the Royal Oak, a modernized pub, with 'panoramic' views from its windows. The sun was pouring in, the juke-box was blaring, a couple in hideous clothes (mini-skirts are still enthusiastically worn in the Midlands) were happily eating. Younger people then came in, the present-day generation who are still of their particular area but not visually so – the girls with hair tied back and in smart macintoshes, the men with pipes and spectacles.

The music blared; the sun grew hotter; the carpet was unbelievably ugly, but everyone in the place seemed content. I looked across at Netherton Church on its hill, and hoped Selina Spittle had had such sun-filled mornings as this.

You Boatsmen and colliers all, come listen to my ditty,
I'll sing you a song before its long, it is both new and pretty.
It is concerning Tommy shops, and the high field ruffian
He pays you with a tommy note, you must have that or nothing.[7]

The cult of the traditional, and the real. They sometimes intermingle here and elsewhere, where there is a genuine desire to get back to roots.

Jon Raven, the folk-singer, who came to live in Wolverhampton when he was ten, but who is much travelled, has been responsible for unearthing and promoting the traditional songs of the area. He has kindly allowed me to include some of them in this chapter. He is much published in books (*Songs of a Changing World*, Ginn and Co., 1972; *Turpin Hero*, OUP, 1974 and others) and on records, and has published works such as *Canal Songs* through a company owned by himself and his wife, who also runs the Mosaic boutique in Tettenhall. They got out *Canal Songs* in a fortnight in order to be ready for the opening of *The Canal Show*, a highly successful production showing the history of canals for which Jon Raven prepared the musical side, and sang. He has found that 'ordinary real people' are interested in local folk-songs, and has tried to introduce more folk-music into 'folk-clubs' where often not much singing goes on. He also gives concerts jointly with the Black Country Society, to which young as well as older people flock. Not surprisingly, as he has a very fine voice.

The Canal Show, *The Nailmakers*, *Up Spaghetti Junction*, have all been successful theatre. Poetry readings, with the poet Jim William-Jones and others often reading in Black Country dialect, flourish at the New Inn in Cosely. At Christmas we saw a 200-year-old Black Country Christmas play performed in the street by the Jubilee Theatre Group (who are trying to get their own community theatre in Sandwell), in dialect, with local and modern allusions thrown in. 'W'em come for a pocketful of money, And a skinful of beer.' The play used to be performed by a Wednesbury man and his three sons for their own family, and I found a mention of it last being performed in a bar parlour in 1879. It came across very well and the form adapts naturally to topical jokes. Naturalness, lack of affectation, is one aspect of the area.

We had read much about whippet racing, and after several weeks managed to locate the track, as it was always shifting time and place elusively (although the pub for boozing afterwards remains the same – the Swan with Two Nicks). Old timers regret that the 'ondler, who used to set the whippets off, is no more. But the atmosphere is utterly genuine still; a family occasion with children learning, and grandmothers loath to give up. Dogs don't change hands – you hang on to them and breed from them. The course is 160 yards and if they can do 160 yards in under nine seconds, 'they'm pretty good'. (Usually it is 150 in about eight and a half.) You join the club, and they will train your dog for you. One woman, racing a dog who'd seen better days against the champ, was running up the course and whistling and yelling encouragement as they all do before a race while the dogs strain in the traps. The dogs streak like lightning, and are led back by the children. 'She done well . . . she bloody did.' A much-dyed blonde with a pale face ran up the course screaming to her dog at the top of her lungs, totally unembarrassed and rapt. Suddenly, at the right time, there are shouts of 'he's open, hurry up', and they all disappear. Bloody marvellous morning.

*

The reverse of the coin strikes one just as clearly. No one who has seen parts of Tipton, Tividale, Dudley Port, for instance, can easily forget their dusty, noisy, soulless ugliness. A lunch break there can be little better than a spell in a prison yard. On another long walk I trudged down Cinder Bank, which is as it sounds, and thundering with traffic, and in Dudley Wood saw hideous new estates in streets with idyllic names such as Spring Meadow Road. But the barren areas are not extensive, and you come on pockets that are more rewarding quite suddenly.

Such as Mushroom Green. It has in fact been declared the only 'outstanding' conservation area in the West Midlands County, by the Department of the Environment, and has the nucleus of a Victorian village virtually intact, although encroached upon by new buildings. We had noted it in the newspaper as something we must see, filed the cutting away and forgotten the name. From Saltwells Road I suddenly saw, surrounded by housing-estate houses, a horse grazing in a field by what looked like a slightly derelict farmhouse. There was no road to it, only an oily, muddy track through brambles. I went down it, and immediately felt myself in the past – this is what it must have been like in Victorian times, I thought.

There were signs of self-sufficiency about the farmhouse and neighbouring houses; crates and packing-cases piled up as though someone had started a small trade in boxes. The other small houses in the cluster are lace-curtained, some very narrow like half a doll's house, or with trelliswork porches. A row of three small white ones is a Snow-White-Dwarfs' housing estate. The village was to be 'cleaned up' for Architectural Heritage Year, with cables laid underground and 'road improvements'. I hope they leave the muddy footpaths.

One of these leads to the old buildings of John Griffiths and Son, chainmakers, now Griff Chains, building a new works. Even older than the buildings is a chainmakers' shop beyond, with bars in the windows and a stable double-door, iron and tools lying where they were left. Chains at Griff Chains are made by the electro-welded method, from steel, not wrought iron. Mr Bennett showed John and I round, told us how reluctant the Admiralty had been to accept steel anchor chains, particularly after the steel chain of SS *Normandie* had broken on her maiden voyage. In a corner is an old 'Oliver', the foot-machine for hammering down with heavy tools, used for centuries. At present, chains are in demand for the North Sea oil rigs.

Mr Bennett crumbled some of the lime and ash mortar from between the mellow bricks. 'They always used lime – marvellous for carnations if you find some of this mortar.' The old buildings are scheduled to be made into an old people's unit, with new buildings *inside* the old shell. At first the idea sounds grotesque, but if well done it could be more in keeping with this village which still lives, to use the place for people rather than exhibits.

As I left Mushroom Green that first time, I heard a bird singing so soaringly that I felt it must be a nightingale, at least a chaffinch. A man walking painfully uphill on two sticks smiled, 'I'nt it lovely, eh.'

'Yes,' I said. 'What is it?'

'A blackbird,' he said, with a mixture of pleasure and scorn, and plodded slowly on.

That is it, really. Why want a nightingale when a blackbird can sing like this? The Black Country is like it is. A man can stop to listen to a bird there; and he will plod doggedly on – and to hell with your fancy ways.

> Sutton for Mutton,
> Tamworth for Beef,
> Walsall for bandy legs,
> And Brum for a thief,
> Barton-under-Needwood,
> Dunstal in the Dale,
> Tattenhill for a pretty girl,
> And Barton for good ale,
> Walsall town for bandy legs,
> Bilston town for bulls,
> Hampton town for fancy girls,
> And Sedgley town for trulls!
>   (Traditional ballad.)

Not all Black Country industry is made up of small factories. Although ninety-five per cent of the population work within their own area, they may be working for large concerns such as Tube Investments, ICI or GKN. But the identity of each place has not been lost. Chains and anchor cables at Cradley and Cradley Heath; Oldbury with the Chance glass works down by the canal, and chemical industries; locks at Willenhall, where in the old days they were said to be humpbacked from bending over their work; leather at Walsall; glass at Stourbridge and Brierley Hill, more often the latter now. Black Country people are proud of their own district, are great collectors and visit their museums. The Black Country Society is 2,000 strong.

They have much to be proud of. Dudley on its hill, said to be 'an overcoat colder than Stourbridge', has its castle, now a zoo where the animals even look healthy, a thriving market-place round a curlicued fountain, much civic activity. Smaller centres such as Wednesbury, where there was a great battle between Saxons and Britons in 592, and Sedgley, with an overgrown churchyard and Victorian villas called 'Osborne' and 'Cremorne', have great charm. But much of the flavour of each place lies in the work, or craft, carried out there. Brierley Hill has a fine glass museum, showing English and foreign examples, ornate goblets and delicate scent bottles with orchid-shaped, spotted mouths. In the same building is the Brierley Hill Glass Training Centre, where apprentice glass workers go on day release. I watched some boys working there, so keen they were continuing through their tea break – as glassmakers traditionally do to make 'friggers'. They pranced round the furnace with red-hot bulrush blobs of glass on the end of their long blowing tubes, rolling them out on the smooth metal 'marver' (like most glass terms, derived from the French, from the Huguenot immigrant glassmakers) then blowing glowing bubbles, each movement dexterous – satyrs performing some phallic ritual to the god of glass.

'What's it going to be?'

'I haven't decided yet . . . a decanter . . . want to try?'

Surprisingly it doesn't take much breath. My bubble was ballooning out. The boy took it and blew the balloon until it burst, and gave me a piece of glass as thin as cellophane. Such is the skill of this craft that it may not be until he is forty that a man will be a 'glassmaker', the head of a 'chair' or team of four or five men who work together every day.

Glassmaking is taught at the Brierley Hill Glass Centre by Colin Gill, and I met his father Stanley Gill when I visited the Stuart Crystal glassworks near by. He showed me a leaflet of their trade union, the National

Union of Flint Glass Makers, which he said was the smallest union in the country. Had they ever had a strike? Not in this department, no.

We were in the glassmakers' workshop, with the teams working round the traditional long-armed chairs, while the great furnaces, which are fed on the floor below, gaped redly in the centre of the room. At the works there is still one of only about seven original glass kilns left in Europe, of beehive-shaped brick, but it is not used now, although the process can have changed very little through the centuries, or even since the Phoenicians first blew glass. The glass is heated in great clay pots which cost about £100 and last about twenty weeks at the terrific temperature, and it can be re-heated on the rods in 'glory holes'. The men work in jeans and vests, and look rather white faced. Tea bottles are much in evidence.

How satisfying is this craft? As a writer I know that it is the chiselling away at the craft of words, however inadequately, that is satisfying, rather than the self-indulgent emotional release some people imagine. But working shifts, day in, day out, with only one half-hour break for tea, in this heat . . . It only takes a glassmaker about five minutes to finish a beer mug or small decanter, rolling then blowing it out, smoothing it, cutting off the rim with scissors, putting on the handle which his 'servitor' brings him. And he is on piecework, so the same goblet will be made over and over again without a break. The satisfaction of the craft might seem a sentimental phrase. For the engraver maybe, working here on some decanters for the Duke of Edinburgh. And yet the bonus side must exist, possibly in the very restrictions, the team, the skill, and in the beauty of the material itself. There is something of magic in glass-making. And you can be proud of your position, your mastery. 'It is a craft you see, and I always try to make each individual piece better than the last . . . I am positive machines will never be able to produce lead crystal.'[8]

The same applies to leather. Walsall, the home of leather, is a patchy place today, with the planners just beginning to get their hands on it. It was the birthplace of Jerome K. Jerome. He wrote a moving letter to the people of Walsall on being made a Freeman of the Borough. 'I felt I was the guest of all of you: there were no class distinctions; your quiet, undemonstrative men, your placid, smiling women, your grave-faced little children, who clamoured to be lifted up . . . you gave me the freedom of your heart.' More recently another writer, John Petty, who was discharged from the army with TB, made his living there as a scrap-picker, scavenging waste metal. He describes his life competing with the 'tatters' for scrap at 3/- [15p] a hundredweight (you earned about 12/-

[6op] a day). The tatters were 'rough coarse men, they dislike competition, and especially from one not of their kind. I am of the working class, but I look something like a faded and haggard Shelley.'[9]

A pretty station with iron wreaths and an arcade topped with horse-shoes are swamped by large new shops. But little red-brick houses still cluster round the tall green mound on which St Matthew's Parish Church stands, with its thin tapering spires of soft yellow stone, unusual in this area of red sandstone churches. The 'bandy legs' of the ballad have been attributed to climbing up this hill to church, but a more likely cause would seem to be the number of horses that were kept in Walsall; even the football team is called the 'Saddlers'. In front of the church door, a slab commemorates Sir J. Cliff Tibbitts of the famous saddlery firm of Jabez Cliff, who died in 1974 aged ninety and who wanted his fellow citizens to walk past him as they went to church.

The saddler's craft has hardly changed over the centuries. In 1974 we visited the workshop of Harry Meads, 'Riding Saddle Maker', in Lime Street. The sun-filled workroom overlooks a green yard, and across to the church on its hill. The windows aren't often cleaned because sun spoils the leather. There is an iron stove, and three power Singer sewing machines, although much of the stitching is done by hand. Paper patterns hang on the walls, and there is a sweet smell of beeswax, as thread is rolled from a ball of hemp and waxed for use. Mrs Meads helps out with the stitching, and is a partner in the enterprise. Although her husband might remind her gently that it is time for his tea, her role seems far more liberated than that of more vociferous females. There are two women stitchers, one of whom, Betty Easthope, worked for Harry Meads when he started his business in 1955.

'Will there ever be women saddlers?'

'They are taught it in London,' Mr Meads smiled. 'But I don't think anyone would take them on.' (The stuffing, particularly, is hefty work – a stuffing mixture, but 'real wool for Scotland Yard'.)

Very dignified, almost military in appearance (during the last war he served in the army), he wears a grey overall, looks you straight in the eye, then suddenly peers above his spectacles if you are taking him too seriously. His blue eyes cloud slightly with embarrassment when he expresses one of the kindly sentiments which are obviously a part of his nature. He has a craftsman's shrewdness, and the wisdom of experience.

'What do you think of modern commercialism?'

'Plastic seats and so on [saddle trees are made of beech and steel] take the craftsmanship away. *If I was younger*, I would be unhappy about commercial trends . . . Nothing here is mass produced . . . Plastic is a colossal failure, although they get away with it in Germany . . . No one in America could make a saddle all the way through, but they do hundreds of 'cowboy saddles' – they'll have 200 flat out on automatic production of cowboy saddles. They appreciate quality though, and send English saddles to be recovered after many years' wear. They always say, don't bother about the cost . . . I won't touch cheap saddles; people who buy one always regret it. There's a line from Pakistan . . .'

His father was a bridle-cutter. (Mrs Meads's mother, who lived to ninety, was a stitcher.) He showed us his 'unfinished symphony', a racing saddle quilted underneath with yellow silk by Mrs Meads and weighing 14 oz. And an old catalogue of *c.* 1872, of Thomas Newton of Walsall 'Leather seller, saddler and coach ironmonger' – with illustrations of the 'Officer's Hussar Saddle with Wallets', the 'Light Dragoon', the 'Servant's Saddle with Portmanteau pad', and beautifully quilted saddles of flowered doeskin (110 shillings [£5.50p]) . . . 'Foreign and Colonial Harness and Saddlery Ship'd to order.' (In another catalogue I saw saddles for Mexico, Japan and Russia; military saddles and appointments for 'Princes, Field Marshals . . . Knights of the Star of India, Rajahs, Nabobs'.)

Five saddlers work here, on piecework, with one cutter. The pace in the workshop is tough and fast, but the atmosphere seemed calm and full of a durable content. The leather gleams. We are shown a minute scratch on the underside of a flap: 'I won't sell that – that's scrap now.' The floor is littered with parings and scrap.

'There must be a use for that?' John suggested. But Harry Meads waved his hands with a Renaissance-like grandeur. 'If I can't make a good honest living out of making quality saddles, I might as well pack up, mightn't I?'

When I visited him next, in 1975, the economic slump had hit Walsall badly. Even the export market had declined, and saddles were piling up unsold. 'There's no trade at all in Walsall,' Mrs Meads told me. 'We'll have to go on short time.' The sun still streamed in, but the workroom seemed half empty, although I was still greeted with smiles. Mr Meads seemed cheerful and philosophical, although it was clearly a tragic time for him.

I left them, and ate some sandwiches in the market square. Posters told me cancer could be cured and to 'fly on a cruise'. Litter blew round the street corners. It seems more than hard that the saddlers should be crushed by the shaky economic system, our overreaching times. As Harry Meads wrote to me recently, 'I have never known any "strike" action in the saddle trade in my lifetime.' And there have been bits and spurs and saddles made in Walsall since the sixteenth century, with a great flowering of saddlery after 1760 when improvements to the roads set Walsall on the map as a staging post. 'Walsall for bandy legs' – and leather.

*

But Black Country people are resilient, adaptable. They are able to suffer more and put up with more than other people. The 'little big men' with their thick shoulders, can bend things to their own way. They have literally wrung their living from the available materials, and even their traditional recipes are miracles of economy – tripe and onions, cow-heels, faggots, pork with everything, even with the Christmas turkey or fowl, from the pig kept at the bottom of the garden – or two pigs, one to sell and one for Christmas. Industry has been able to diversify – from iron manufacturing there has been a switch over to the present-day metal fabrication and light engineering. The area has absorbed outsiders – Welsh in the 1920s and 1930s, the Irish navigators of 1769 who started to dig the canals and who may, Winston Homer, Anglo-Saxon lecturer in Modern English at Dudley Technical College has suggested, have been partly responsible for the traditional Aynuk and Eli stories which portray a wry acceptance of everything that happens. They have absorbed outsiders but stay there themselves. The dialect is inimitably their own, but the pronunciation differs in each place. 'We still speak Anglo-Saxon,' Winston Homer said proudly on a recent radio broadcast. There is a great predilection for the letter 'n', with 'n', 'an' or 'en' endings, from the Anglo-Saxon (flannen for flannel, groun for ground).[10] 'Her' is used instead of she; 'hisn' and 'hern', 'yourn' and 'ourn'. You can say 'howbin you?' (or yo) although the usual greeting in Wolverhampton is 'All right?' John spent many months trying to find out the correct answer to this, and eventually decided you come back with the same words in an even more aggressive and crisp way.

'All right?'

'All right?' on a rising note.

The verb 'to be' is the most confusing. 'I bay' is a negative, 'I bin' the positive. Which can result in a sentence like 'Them bay bay winders bin they?'[11] Some negatives have no 'n'. 'Cor' means 'can't' (You cor do that); 'ay' means 'ain't'. Not to mention a whole vocabulary of special words such as 'sneap' for 'snub', 'moach' for 'to dawdle', 'forby' for 'near'.

*

The Black Country is a planners' paradise – they long to get their hands on it. It can't be denied that some parts are devoid of any attraction or hopefulness. If you travel on the top of a bus from Walsall to Wolverhampton for instance, you will see derelict houses, bleak factories away to the south, and between-the-wars villas that a Cyclops with vertigo must have designed. The faces in the bus are quizzical or hopeless, not happy. What percentage of the human race leads dreary lives? Any mother who proclaims that all children have equal chances now, that they can get on at any school, therefore let us keep the best schools for the brightest kids, should be forced to travel on top of this bus. Stunted small boys light up their cigarettes as soon as they are up the stairs, not with bravado, but with a weary addiction, pulling on them desperately. Looking out of the windows you can't blame them.

As I write, planners are getting out their plan to 'improve environmental standards'. The West Midlands County Council has put forward a twenty-year programme, which seeks to obviate pollution near houses, make more amenities, reclaim land, without spoiling the character of the area. But in phrases such as 'we shall have green wedges of park land where old tips are' one sees danger for the marvellous spontaneity of the Black Country environment. The derelict areas are half its secret. And planners, one always suspects, are like those people who root out overgrown, softly tangled and twining English country gardens, to make trim lawns and stiff rows of red and yellow flowers. 'We . . . hope it will be able to change its name to the Green Country,' a councillor is quoted as saying. No, Councillor Chapman, no.

But I have an inkling that the Black Country will defeat the planners yet. That the meadowsweet will rampage over linear parks, scrap lorries dirty up the concrete walkways, cocks crow from the landscaped lawns, whippets race over golf-courses, dominoes and a quiet game of cards go on being played in redecorated pubs, and birds find somewhere to nest. I hope so.

We heard a BBC Third Programme talk, 'Village Prospects part IV, The Last of Gornal Wood'. 'There'll always be Gornal,' a sturdy voice told us. 'Gornal'll never die . . .' But wasn't the postal address now Lower Gornal? the interviewer asked. This was clearly irrelevant. 'It's an arrogance that we're different . . . it's nice to have roots . . . I always have faggots and peas . . . most Fridays . . . It's still roots to put down . . . it's still, you know, an identity . . . all outsiders are regarded as friendly people . . . but they could never become part of the community.' They spoke of the local dialect, from the days when Gornal had 'lily white sond' to sell.

An ex-miner spoke of the 'big happy family' in the mines and the 'total lack of comradeship' in factories. It had been one of the 'greatest dramatic experiences' in his life when the local pit closed in 1968. Some admitted Gornal could die. 'The schoolchildren speak differently . . . Would you sit around Gornal if you'd a car?' The puzzled interviewer was told the story of Johnny Long Stomach who put a pig on the wall to watch the band go by. Why was it funny? the interviewer asked again and again. The teller of the story couldn't explain. It was so obvious. A pig on a wall. And Johnny Long Stomach.

There'll always be Gornal.

> With coal and steel and shovel and pick,
> Two hundred years the building took;
> From running brooks to singing streets,
> From wheat to mine and coal slag heaps.
> O black the name and black the age and black the sweat that runs,
> And black the day the name should change the birthright of our sons.[12]

5 Birmingham

A future archaeologist, meditating on the excavated remnants of
Victorian and twentieth-century daily life, would be compelled to
note, as one of his most important clues, the label 'Made in
Birmingham'.

Asa Briggs, *History of Birmingham.*[1]

The city of twelve hundred trades – the small man's city – Brummagem –
Brum. To those who don't know the city, and some who do, it retains an
aura of dingy red-brick streets and stifling Victoriana, crude commerce
and Brummy jokes. The reality can come as a surprise.

Birmingham is visually exciting, surprising – often beautiful. Its centre
is much more hilly than that of London for instance, and it is not in a
basin, so that it is a city of unexpected views and vistas. You can look down
and up a switchback street and see a perfect turreted Victorian building at
the end, pockets of the old tucked away behind the new and given more
room to breathe by recent demolitions. From the overpass over Small-
brook Ringway there is an exhilarating townscape of tall blocks and thin
spires, cosy warehouses and swirling ringways, pinpointed by lights in the
evening as the wind scuds from a turning, crimsoning Midland sky. There
is flashing neon, but it has retained a human scale.

An area which at once gives the flavour of modern Birmingham is that
by the new library. This is a long-lined, uncompromising building by
the John Madin Design Group, surrounded by concrete steps and uncluttered, water-divided walkways. Below the steps is the pretty, pinnacled,
small lacy stonework memorial to Joseph Chamberlain, which in spite of
recent cleaning still manages to have ragwort or something very like it
sprouting from its crevices, and which the corporation have surrounded
with a bed of posy-like Victorian flowers. The two make up not so much
a contrast as a synthesis, a whole. Those who loved this part of the town
in the thirties will tell you it has been spoilt, but as evening draws on and
the clock (Big Brum) booms from the City Museum and Art Gallery
next door, its pillars and friezes and tiled clock tower warmly floodlit; as

darkness settles round the Roman columns of the Town Hall, and the scent of stocks floats from the window boxes of the intricately domed Council House; as starlings chatter and resettle, the scene is both reassuring and luminous.

> Full twenty years and more, are past,
> Since I left Brummagem;
> But I set out for home at last
> To good old Brummagem.
> But every place is altered so,
> There's hardly a single place I know;
> And it fills my heart with grief and woe,
> For I can't find Brummagem.
>
> But what's more melancholy still
> For poor old Brummagem,
> They've taken away all Newhall-hill
> Poor old Brummagem!
> At Easter time, girls fair and brown,
> Used to come rolly-polly down,
> And show'd their legs to half the town;
> Oh! the good old sights in Brummagem.[2]

So sang one Dobbs on the nineteenth-century stage, and many citizens echo the thought today, with the stampeding motorways and ringways, trembling 'temporary' overpasses and sinister underpasses. Spaghetti Junction is no joke, and you pay for being at the centre of the country's road communications. 'You take your life in your hands, don't you,' said a woman clutching my arm in Digbeth; and walking along a road in Edgbaston, another who had in typically friendly manner given up her own bus to show the way (there were soon three of us as another stranger hailed us), told me how she had had her bag snatched in an underpass, at night. This is apparently a frequent occurrence – 'It's usually immigrants, and the police don't dare take any action' – a statement which may or may not be accurate, but which if it is seems to call out for more equality for all, both to prevent the need for the snatching and to eradicate it. One has to sympathize at least with an old citizen such as she, who has to walk a long way from a modern council high-rise flat she dislikes to shops at Five Ways, who has no feeling about colour or race but who sees attractive 'maisonettes' logically given to the families with the most children, who may smash them up. At fourteen she worked at Fort Dunlop and had to be there at six thirty and make seventeen tyres on her machine for one shilling [5p] and now she sees a younger generation unwilling to work 'because their parents give them money to get them out of the house'. One who in a crowded city in fact is the loser.

Some have managed to hold on to what they liked about the past, just as some districts in Birmingham are cannily full of their own particular character. The jewellery quarter for instance, which stretches beyond the eighteenth-century square of St Paul's church, the only true square in the city – quiet and green under the shadow of the huge GPO tower, with a turreted Barclays Bank of later date than the silversmiths and electro-plating works and gilding works in shabby, elegantly porched buildings, which surround the church. A church which has its pews firmly enclosed for rich jewellers' families and labelled with enamelled, numbered plaques, delicately bordered.

Narrow streets strike out from it, leading to the hub of the quarter with Frederick Street and Vittoria Street running up to a green clock tower erected in 1903 to commemorate a visit by Joseph Chamberlain to South Africa. ('We have shown that we can be strong and resolute in war: it is equally important to show that we can be resolute in peace.') There is curly pale-blue ironwork on an ex-butcher's shop; there are towered warehouses in patterned brickwork like Venetian palaces; a maze of little courts and courtyards and workshops down alleyways and up stairs, which have escaped the bulldozers (this is a conservation area, one of thirteen in the city). Not only silversmiths and jewellers, but bicycle-bell factories, works for 'tea and coffee pot hinges and condiment hinges', and other such unlikely wares, and the Polytechnic School of Jewellery and Silversmithing. On the pediment of a warehouse wall a plaque of Queen Victoria looks steadfastly away from the Ramgarhia Sikh Temple which is a blaze of colours and has had bricks slung through its windows. Down the street singing rings out from the Elim Pentecostal Church.

Not a residential area though. The corporation have built the Hockley Centre, with smart new flats for craftsmen. But the flats in this new factory complex could cripple the thriving jewellery trade, some think, as master jewellers might have to treble their trade to meet the rents. This means that some manufacturers cling to broken-down, lightbulbless, stairless quarters, while many are luckier with their little workshops. Mr Corbett, who studied at the jewellery school and worked for a big firm before owning his own business, let me see his workroom. The majority of the tools were the same as those used a hundred years ago, and the drill-stock was obviously, as he said, based on caveman principles. A beautiful blue water-globe of 1896 gave a much cooler ray to work under than viciously magnified light, he explained. (Elsewhere I was told a setter usually has to have glasses after two years at the work.) Much of his own work was repairs or in semi-precious stones, but clearly demanding the same high skill as more highly-priced jewellery.

At the front of this court is Mr Hollins's shop. Mr Hollins is eighty-four and has been seventy years in the area. 'It isn't a jewellery district as we knew it . . . when I was a lad, at one o'clock the crowd was like going to a football match. Before the first war it was the wealthiest district in the land. The jewellers had *millions*. My mother used to be taken by her father when she was a little girl to see the jewellers and their wives come out of St Paul's Church all decked out in their jewellery. I was married in St Paul's Church sixty-one years ago. Now we're the only people who live in this street . . . I've lived here all my life except for a free holiday in the First World War. I wouldn't move . . . you can't pluck up your roots. Birmingham suffered a lot in the last war . . . if it wasn't for the cathedral you wouldn't have heard more about Coventry than Birmingham. But give me the bad old days. I was one of six children and I only had 1d [½p] a week pocket money although my parents were fairly comfortably off. They were happier days altogether than today. Vandalism . . . the young are shirkers not workers. I'm an old man but I don't feel it.'

He doesn't look it. He looks about sixty. I have never seen a tidier shop, with sweets and tins and matches and Fisherman's Friend cough pastilles. His wife has arthritis, so he does all the cleaning, drives to the Cash and Carry, is open ten hours a day – 'Not so bad for an old crock.'

The genuine article. There is enterprise as well as the genuine in the jewellery quarter, however. The precious metals go cheek by jowl with trinkets, in typical Birmingham manner. In the old days old men or boys would carry jewels to the Assay Office casually in leather bags. Equally there was a saying 'Give a Birmingham maker a guinea and a copper kettle and he will make you a hundred pounds' worth of jewellery', and one ingenious individual cut and polished some cinders from the calx of Aston furnace, set them in rings and brooches and sold them as fragments of Pompey's pillar.

Brummies are on the whole extrovert, unselfconscious and self-assured. They are quick and quirky. Coming from the Black Country their faces look very alert, although some of the faces are knobbled in a Dickensian manner, bespectacled and Dolittle-nosed and bald pated like something out of an old *Punch*, flushed and intelligently Jewish and surrounded by white hair – small men with lined Hogarthian faces, large tramp-like men, keen executives, calm students. A live variety. Canny and laughing and talking and absorbed in their conversations – prepared to laugh at themselves. In a pub they will include the whole room – 'Every chance in the big race. Fler d'amer – flower of love. Right or wrong? A foreigner? Do I look like one? I was born in Brum . . .'

*

The city centre as such is very small, with shopping precincts – the Bull Ring centre which teems uncomfortably or that into which you step direct from New Street station, which has a cool terrace café selling Italian ices, opposite Habitat – which together with New Street make shopping in Birmingham far less of an ordeal than shopping in Oxford Street in London. Beyond the central streets you are immediately in shabbier, more idiosyncratic territory.

Digbeth, for example. Dusty streets open suddenly on to a deserted churchyard on a hill. Ugly buildings, old warehouses, derelict gaps, squalor and promising-looking corners. At the corner of New Canal Street and Fazely Street a green ironwork, frilled urinal, very much in use but looking like something out of a classic French film, only Victorian, prettier. There are others here, and farther up New Canal Street is the monolithic, Ionic-columned old British Rail parcels depot, once Curzon Street station and the terminus of the London–Birmingham line, the twin to the old Euston Arch. It seems almost awesomely, elephantinely vast now, rising grey from the little streets where once it was an entrance-way to the empire's capital, new realms. Will Concorde's hangar one day look like this?

More attractive is the Birmingham Gun Barrel Proof House, in Banbury Street. In mellow brick with curved gables and a plaster coat of arms, it was built in 1813 when Birmingham won the right to its own proving authority by special Act of Parliament. Rightly so, as the gun trade was one of the most flourishing traditional trades in Birmingham, with its own district, and there are still many gunmakers here. Although tucked away in this peaceful road-end (peaceful that is when barrels are not being tested), the proof house is very active, with barrels being brought for provisional proof and then definitive proof and stamping. Under the Gun Barrel Proof Acts no gun may be sold or exported unless it is duly marked.

Swords, and more recently Hurricanes and Spitfires, were also made at Birmingham. It is said that the swords used at the charge of the Light Brigade were ground at Hazel Mills, Strickley. In the Middle Ages and Tudor times the town was famous for its smiths, tanners and gunsmiths, then lorimers and naylors. There were mills on the banks of the Rea, water-wheels for power, and good drinking water for the workmen of Digbeth and Deritend. In the seventeenth and early eighteenth century there were no trade guilds or companies and men were free to come and go – Birmingham became the town of 'free trade', with few municipal restrictions. Then came the great era of the eighteenth century, with Matthew Boulton, as Sir Arthur Bryant has said, looming through the century like a Titan in the mist. This was the age of the Lunar Society and Dr Priestley (who discovered oxygen, nitrogen, and sulphuric acid among other things), of the printer John Baskerville, of men taking out patents for everything from papier-mâché to steel pens, and the invention (before the Spinning Jenny) of an engine to spin cotton yarn.

There is a portrait of Matthew Boulton in the Assay Office, a fine building with pillars outside and tiles and old flowered iron radiators inside, which is unfortunately being partly rebuilt. He founded it in 1773. Before then gold and silver had to be taken to London or Chester to be hallmarked, so hallmarking in Birmingham naturally increased the trade: one of Boulton's chief characteristics was an insistence on high standards and non-counterfeit wares. Boulton's greatest achievement was at the famous Soho works, however, where he told the visiting Boswell: 'I sell here, sir, what all the world desires to have – power.' The factory produced buttons, buckles, swords, gun furniture, by water power; then after Boulton met James Watt – who later became his partner – and enabled him to commercialize the steam engine he had improved from Newcomen's model, the factory led the way into the industrial revolution. William Murdock was another who worked at Soho, who first used coal gas for lighting a house.

Nothing remains of the Soho factory now (the works later became Averys), but in Soho Avenue, Handsworth, overlooking its site, is Soho House, Matthew Boulton's home. Handsworth has crumbling villas, housing chiropodists or selling hot curry patties, in windblown streets. But from the hill there is a marvellous urban skyline. Among run-down gothic villas, Boulton's house is oddly disappointing, although partly designed by Wyatt. A man wandered towards me in a dressing gown. A rest-home for business-crazed tycoons? (It is in fact residential police quarters, I was told with some degree of secrecy by a policeman.)

Opposite the Assay Office is the Museum of Science and Industry, and nearby under the giant GPO tower a dark strip of canal emerges briefly from a tunnel, with a rotting hulk of a narrow boat sinking in the treacly water. But the Birmingham canals aren't dead – you see a few strange boat-loads chugging along them guided by independent, rough-hewn individuals who look rather like contemporary poets on a day off. Most of the traffic is now pleasure cruising, however. Birmingham reputedly has more canals than Venice. Gas Street Basin, where boats can be hired, has the Opposite Lock bar and restaurant in the old stables where horses for the narrow boats were housed, and the Rum Runner Club's lighted restaurant opens on to the water. It is an amazingly foreign-looking scene, with its old roofs and painted boats. Narrow boats can be hired from Brummagem Boats. The boat owners may spend the out-of-holiday season carrying coals down to Worcester, selling to farmers or house-holders on the way. Not a very lucrative operation I was told by one man who does it, but one could envy him the life. Bearing in mind, however, that there are thirteen locks in Birmingham alone, for a start. The genuine narrow boat people are almost of the past. Caggy Stevens still works the last horse-drawn boat. Here in Gas Street the oldest resident was lumping a heavy board belligerently on to her boat when I passed, her white hair firmly knotted in a scarf. 'I've finished with boats,' she said. But she was clearly going to stay there till she dropped.

Attractive as it is, the basin has the air of waiting for the next television crew. 'We've had too many of those sort of people,' my old resident said.

Boat owners sit and drink mugs of coffee and read the Sunday papers. In a boat neatly (and permanently?) moored to a tidily painted bit of wharf, decked out with neat tubs like a garden, there is a sticker in a window of the cabin proclaiming 'Freedom is a boat . . .'

*

It was in November 1769 that the first boat-load of coal was brought to Birmingham by canal, and thereafter the town was linked to Bristol, Hull, Liverpool, London. The impact on trade was tremendous. Two years later transport per ton from Liverpool to Brum was more than three times cheaper by water than by land. Macadam's road surfaces and lighter coaches followed and in 1837 the railway to Liverpool and Manchester, a year later to London. During the railway age Birmingham was the 'workshop of the world'; this was the great iron age, and also the age of the electro-plating industry, with vases, shields, gold and silver services, spoons and forks, and pins and souvenirs going all over the empire. The phrase 'the best governed city in the world' was also coined. The boom in the 1870s provided a climate in which Joseph Chamberlain, preceded by others, could undertake his great municipal reforms. He retired from

Nettlefolds at thirty-eight with a fortune, and devoted himself to civic life. 'The town shall not, with God's help, know itself,' he declared on becoming mayor, and he proceeded among other things to clear a large slum area and build Corporation Street in its place – reducing the death rate of the district to a half or even a third of its previous level in five years. Courtyards and muck heaps, and with them the 'Brummagem rough' were cleared away. The corporation took control of gas and water undertakings, and the National Education League was founded. In the 1860s and '70s Birmingham led the way in social reform.

Birmingham was also the home of the protection movement. The Black Country and Birmingham had always been open to the threat of foreign competition, and although Chamberlain was not originally in favour of protection, he became convinced, and in the House of Commons in May 1903 pronounced: 'We are the one open market of the world. We are the one dumping ground of the world.'

The great iron age had moved into the age of steel. But Birmingham is not all metals and nostalgia. It has a present, and a recent past. In the thirties there was a strange powerful flowering of poetry and music, a golden age as if tiger-lilies had replaced ragwort on the slag heaps.

> Sun shines easy, sun shines gay
>   On bug-house, warehouse, brewery, market,
> On the chocolate factory and the B.S.A.,
>   On the Greek town hall and Josiah Mason,
> On the Mitchells and Butlers Tudor pubs
>
> Eight years back about this time
>   I came to live in this hazy city
> To work in a building caked with grime
>   Teaching the classics to Midland students;
>
> And to hear the prison-like lecture room resound
>   To Homer in a Dudley accent.[3]

Louis MacNeice was a lecturer at Birmingham University, as were Henry Reed and Helen Gardner. Auden's father was children's medical officer for the city – so Auden was another of those who gathered there. Professor R. F. Willetts who is currently Professor of Greek at Birmingham University and who was one of these associates with common interests, told me that they often met in the Hope and Anchor pub (no longer standing) in Edmonds Street. He remembers Auden chainsmoking Woodbines as a young man, and how politically aware they all were – 'One lived more intensely.' They were of course on the Left, joined demonstrations, went to London for 'Arms to Spain'. Some got caught up in the war; one poet giving it all up for an ironmonger's shop when he returned.

Others there were Walter Allen, Henry Treece, the poet and novelist, who was already a graduate, and boxing champion, something of a legendary figure; R. D. Smith, who with Professor Willetts edited the university magazine *The Mermaid*. The composer Benjamin Britten, and Peter Pears, would come over from wherever they then were. (Another Birmingham student who came from Smethwick, and who studied French, was Madeleine Carroll. Professor Tolkien had also spent formative years in Birmingham.) What sparked it off? Could it happen again?

In the fifties there was a group here with poets such as D. J. Enright. Today there are young poets, and playwrights – Gareth Owen for instance, who has worked with Walsall's successful Tangent Theatre Company; also Dr Edward Lowbury, who has an international reputation. *Muse*, a magazine edited by Geoff Charlton, is full of Midlands talent, and *The Little Word Machine* was hailed by the *Sunday Times* as 'one of the liveliest magazines'.

I went to the Arts Lab., which is one of the places where poetry readings have staying power. To get there I walked past the derelict Snow Hill station with its curved arcades, through St Chad's circus below Pugin's red-brick church, round a colourful 1969 Great Western Railway mural and a red-faced mosaic of John F. Kennedy with a martial slogan; through a subway incongruously named 'Pugin subway' and on to a drab part of the city called 'New Town'. The Arts Lab., which is mainly run on grants, is housed unspectacularly. Inside there were good screen prints on display and posters advertising local theatre companies. Faces looked lugubriously at us from the latest film posters. Four of us sat waiting on striped wooden boxes by a bar which sold coke and coffee, and which had bottles of milk and orange colanders and posters of *Occasional Work of a Female Slave* – 'A Witty Sôcial Satire'. Oh where were Auden and his Woodbines, the fire, the Mitchells and Butlers brew?

The poet of the day did not turn up ('Poets are sensitive, temperamental,' it was explained). So we moved our boxes, and young poets read what they had with them. The standard was promising: light lyrics were read by a poet from Walsall, who sported a Saddler's tie (where else but in the Black Country would you find a girl poet wearing football colours?); a guitar was strummed; John Keetley the publicity officer and in charge of poetry readings deftly included everyone. The poetry was somewhat introverted, despite its coin-in-slot modernity; the voices a little defensive.

Where was the outside world? Spain? The tiger-lilies? Perhaps they will flower later.

But there are poets with roots in the Black Country or Birmingham, who are writing here, or elsewhere – Bryan Walters, Roy Fisher, Edward Lowbury who is reviewing the work of five of them in a book which will also consider poets such as Shenstone, whose garden and *ferme ornée* at the Leasowes were possibly better than his poetry.

Dr Lowbury finds no conflict between his research work and his poetry. He keeps a notebook in his pocket marked P and M (poetry and medicine) at opposite ends. He is a well-known bacteriologist, heading research at the burns unit at Birmingham Accident Hospital. Before that he researched into the common cold at Salisbury, and it was on coming to Birmingham, he says, that he first felt he was in a community. In his poetry collection *Time for Sale*[4] there is a poem 'Night Train', in which he describes faces on a journey on the Euston–Birmingham line with a golden sun on one side, the moon on the other. It was then that he first became aware of faces, he says, and from then on he became more aware of people, more extrovert. It is easy to understand why – you couldn't be in Birmingham and ignore people; it is a town made by its people. Although Dr Lowbury and his wife Alison, the daughter of Andrew Young the poet, live in a quiet, tree-filled area, his writing is concerned with outside scenes, faces, old age. Every six months or so he succumbs to what he calls 'relapsing fever' and writes furiously, and one has the impression that it is because he is so busy in his dual role that he achieves so much, rather than vice versa. He has a sparkling, gentle wit, and talks without pomposity of the similarity between poetry and research – the following of the unexpected hunch.

His modesty ('You were the first medical student to win the Newdigate Prize at Oxford?' 'I'm told I was.') reminds me of another Birmingham citizen who wrote, 'I did not know I was an antiquary till the world informed me . . . but when told, I could see it myself.' He was William Hutton, who on first seeing Birmingham, was, he says, 'much surprised at the place, but more at the people. They were a species I had never seen; they possessed a vivacity I had never beheld: I had been among dreamers but now I saw men awake: their very step along the street showed alacrity . . . Hospitality seemed to claim this happy people for her own.' He set up a stationers and bookshop in Brum, shortly after having run away from being an apprentice in Nottingham. His *History of Birmingham* was published in 1782; his autobiography in 1816. He is an immensely charming character, writing neat maxims and speaking delightfully of his courtship and marriage. A great walker, the last sentence in his life story reads: '1812. This day October 11th, is my birthday. I enter upon my ninetieth year, and have walked ten miles.'

Now, many of Birmingham's second-hand bookshops have had to close or move to more leisured towns. But there is still the busy Hudsons for new books, and the new library. This is a streamlined and comfortable place to work, with black armchairs and most of the books on open shelves (I write as one who has waited all day for a book in the British Museum Reading Room, only to be told that it had been bombed in the blitz and had not been taken out of the catalogue). The library also houses a famous Shakespeare Library, the Stone collection of photographs, and books printed by John Baskerville, including his 1763 Cambridge edition of the Bible, possibly the finest example of typography ever produced. The title page, the headings to the side margins and the wide spacing of the chapter titles are a typographer's dream. His books, Macaulay says, 'went forth to astonish all the librarians of Europe'. Sadly, there was no purchaser for his printing equipment at his death, and after four years it was shipped to France.

*

A town of variety, possibilities – for the ludicrous, the sublime. The old hub of Birmingham was the Bull Ring. A Saxon foundation, at the time of Domesday Birmingham had fewer families than Coventry, but in 1166 the town was granted a charter for a market, and there has been a flourishing one ever since. Today there is still an open-air market at the Bull Ring. Among the plastic and floss and sequins and leather carriers and buy-now-pay-later are flower and plant stalls. Birmingham people love flowers, gardening. The market stalls thrive, there are flowersellers at street corners, and the corporation's flowers are the best I know, with tubs of stocks and simple daisies and trailing greenery. The city's 20,000 allotments produced £250,000 worth of food annually during the last war. Predecessors of the allotments were the 'guinea gardens' which surrounded the town. And there were tea gardens, bowling greens, skittle alleys, music and dancing at Vauxhall Gardens – leading up to today's Botanical Gardens.

The Bull Ring is also the site of the Parish Church of St Martin. Here lie the de Berminghams, once the lords of the manor. The church's delicate black spire, tree encircled, is almost, but not quite, crushed by the mammoth circular edifice of the Rotunda.

The cathedral is luckier, surrounded by green, and some of the best modern architecture in Birmingham – the Bristol and West Building

Society building, the tall Bank House which is solidly and restfully modern, with brown tinted glass. And the old Grand Hotel, in French town-hall style, which boasts its own natural water supply. This is the luxury part of the town, with shops selling glass and silver, flowers, and expensive clothes. It continues up to Colmore Circus where there is more Louvre-type architecture in the Wesleyan and General Insurance building; then the tall new block of the *Birmingham Post*, and on to Steelhouse Lane where the General Hospital raises its dark-green gothic turrets and red brick, emulating the Victoria Law Courts in Corporation Street.

The cathedral itself is elegant English Baroque. It contains one of Birmingham's most fiery ornaments – stained glass designed by Burne-Jones (who was born in Birmingham) and made by William Morris. Behind the altar is a red and blue 'Ascension', and the west window is a 'Last Judgement' which glows with pointed, flame-like movement. Somehow Burne-Jones has achieved a mixture of his water-lily coolness, and red fire. The design, cleverly echoed in an embroidered hanging by Carole Raymond, dedicated in 1975, is much freer than the style one associates with the Pre-Raphaelites, of whose paintings there is a major collection in the art gallery. This also houses paintings by David Cox. Son of a Birmingham blacksmith and steel-smith, his golden, sunlit and to us nostalgic paintings of the seaside and countryside, are so eminently in the English tradition, so full of shifting light, and charm.

There are many smaller galleries in Birmingham – the Ikon Gallery, the Compendium Galleries, the Royal Birmingham Society of Artists. The work of poets and artists is on show in the decorative West Midlands Arts Shop, and there is an arts centre in Cannon Hill Park, which has a club membership, with family films and classes. The council-run 'Birmingham Volunteer' students also enlist children from school for sessions there at 1p a time. Even if teenagers only patronize the crowded coffee-bar, as some say, it is at least an enlivening place in which to drink your coffee. There is this Puritan streak in Birmingham people still, which hasn't vanished from the days when Quakers and Dissenters flocked there from more contentious areas. 'They had a talent for getting rich . . . it was a sort of puritan stronghold . . . a little of this lingers,' I was told by Barbara Foxall, who lives in Edgbaston, where the successful manufacturers built their houses. The wife of a present-day successful business-man, she is Barbara Morgan the actress, who acted in the first season of the Crescent Theatre when it moved into its own premises – a barrel-like, vaulted ex-factory, ex-meeting house, with old tramcar seats – in 1932, and she both acted in and translated the opening play when the Crescent moved into its modern theatre. The Crescent pays none of its actors (the stage-manager and canteen lady get paid), was putting on plays such as Sartre's *Nekrassov* and Lorca's *Blood Wedding*, and plays by Ionesco, before George Levine and the Royal Court brought this type of play to London, and was a leader in the Little Theatre movement in the '50s and earlier. The theatre has always made a profit, has no subsidy, is ungimmicky. 'One of the great joys is to be near to important plays and the great old plays,' Barbara Foxall says.

Birmingham theatre is active. See a pantomime at the Alexandra and you have seen the genre at its best, with actors and audience in roistering form. There are experimental companies, and the New Repertory Theatre opened in 1972 as the successor to Barry Jackson's original Repertory Theatre, which first brought quality plays to Brum. The Rep. can collect audiences for plays such as *Equus* or *Jumpers*, and with its circular promenade like a modern version of the Covent Garden Opera House, where horseshoe-shaped windows overlook the city, and with a competent system for booking interval drinks, it gives theatre-going an edge on the cinema once more.

It is of music that most people rightly think in connection with Birmingham, however. At present conducted by Louis Frémaux, the City of Birmingham Symphony Orchestra, which was founded in 1920 after the famous Triennial Festivals had been going for a long time, lives up to its great tradition. Its home is the Town Hall, which was opened in 1834. Here in 1837 Mendelssohn conducted after his honeymoon, and in 1846, conducted *Elijah* which he had written especially for one of the Triennial Festivals. 'No work of mine ever went so admirably at its first performance.' The windows were open, and the chorus could be heard at the Grand Hotel. He was however critical of the organ, a magnificent gilded structure topped by a cameo, and later Sir Thomas Beecham was to say, 'What is that monstrosity before us, Mr Beard? Do you think we can possibly have it removed before this evening?' But Paul Beard explained they were very fond of their organ.

Dvořák also composed for the festival, and Elgar's *Dream of Gerontius* was commissioned for it, but was a failure at the time. In 1912 Sibelius conducted his *Fourth Symphony* here, a year after its first performance in Helsinki.

During the 1973 Triennial Festival we heard Yehudi and Hephzibah Menuhin play in the Town Hall, which in spite of its size can seem curiously intimate, with its stuccoed ceiling. It was not only their effortless virtuosity that made the applause so thunderous after the Beethoven sonatas. The legendary pair radiated a brand of simplicity and sheer goodness that the setting did nothing to destroy, and which was very moving.

*

I had written to Keith Brace, Literary Editor of the *Birmingham Post*, for some tips on literary Birmingham. We met for lunch at the Midland Hotel, which is solidly and splendidly anachronistic and where you can sit downstairs for half a day drinking coffee. With a generosity I feel must be unrivalled in an editor, let alone a fellow author (Keith Brace has written a very evocative book on Bristol), he had brought me a typed sheet of information, ending up characteristically – 'and there's me, of course'.

His columns in the *Post* are models of quiet humour – ('I try to be a moderate voice') in a world gone mad. The *Birmingham Post* literary lunches and dinners are admirable, but also pose problems. The literary lunch doesn't attract aristocracy as does the Yorkshire one, he says, where people go to talk to Feversham or others, and then to meet the authors. 'There are no aristocrats in Brum . . .' The Midlands are far less feudal than Yorkshire, he pointed out, and both Shakespeare and George Eliot were typically Midlands and middle class in this respect. 'Most writers have been from the middle classes.' A great Shakespeare devotee, Keith Brace's heart obviously lies in Stratford where he lives, and although so much part of the Birmingham scene, I got the impression that this is the town where he comes to work, as with many people perhaps.

I don't think it over-euphemistic to call the *Birmingham Post* an outstanding paper. With columns or reviews by Leslie Duckworth on the local environment, Vivian Bird (of the *Sunday Mercury*) a leading Midlands topographical author to whose books I for one have been greatly indebted, Anthony Everitt, Features Editor, on theatre, and others on specialized interests, and a coverage of local and general news that strikes a sound and un-solemn balance, it is above all a satisfying, un-irritating paper to read. Of how many newspapers can one say that?

One man who came to live, in the most literal sense, in Birmingham is Andre Drucker. A Czech-born Viennese writer and artist, he had to leave Vienna in 1936 after the Nazis took power, for Prague, where he worked, and starved. 'My most creative time was when I was hungry. Under pressure you grow and your imagination grows.' Then in 1939 he was 'publicly displayed on the Nazi blacklist', and came to England, where he has worked as commercial artist, broadcaster, and critic; has written *Ach to Be in England*, and recently a novel, *Little Men in a Blind Alley*, which is very Brummy, spills out words like firecrackers – 'a Venetian bridge of sighs arching a cat's back on to scrap yards; a painted barge blowing bubbles on a silent water maze . . . swans picking the windows out of the reflection of giant council flats, light crumbs . . .'[5]

When he first came to England he found honesty, generosity and kindness. A policeman lent him a bicycle, and he could leave it against a wall without a lock, quite safely. He loved the stiff upper lips and pipes; 'they didn't talk so much but they did it'. The honesty he feels has gone. But he can't remember more than four or five occasions in Birmingham when people have called him a bloody foreigner, although in one of the coffee bars he runs he has had someone try to cut his throat with a knife. 'The measure of freedom makes things bad – there's no fear any more – religion too is fear of a kind . . .' His coffee bars have true Viennese-style cakes, and the first one, La Bohème, sadly a prey to redevelopment, had classical music only, magazines and newspapers, and was open seven days a week until twelve. 'Who could you get now who would work those hours?'

With typical friendliness he drove me to his home for coffee, showed me his garden and a mosaic of marble chips, in a road near Augustus Road, which used, he told me, to be called Millionaire's Road. This is the Harborne, Edgbaston area. There are villas which are flaking a bit now, but which one can imagine in their original prime, with their ironwork verandahs and gothic gables. Edgbaston is widely acknowledged to be the finest nineteenth-century suburb in the country, but there are no conservation areas in it. It is a leafy area, and here are the Botanical Gardens, which we thought disappointing – on a hot day unbearably crowded and no longer a fit place for small, rich manufacturers to walk with large wives on their arm, beside the rot-threatened conservatories.

But Birmingham has plenty of lungs, green spaces. Traditionally a town of junketing and fireworks, wakes and pole climbing for legs of mutton, bowling-greens (these are now a bit expensive for some pensioners, I was told), it now has parks such as Cannon Hill Park for tulip festivals and angling, Sutton Park, the wilder Highbury Park, its own stately house in Aston Hall near Aston University, and a recently-opened nature centre, where animals such as foxes and squirrels, and also flora and birds, are given a natural habitat in which they can be observed – 'None of the animals will be sitting on perches with a label round its neck saying "Owl" or "Squirrel",' says the deputy keeper.

The Edgbaston Priory tennis club is renowned. It was once two clubs, the Edgbaston one being very exclusive and a stronghold of male chauvinism. There is also Test cricket at Edgbaston.

Birmingham University, in this same area, is another green enclave. It is dominated by its landmark, the Chamberlain clocktower, called Joe by students, and modelled on a tower at Siena. This rises beside an ornate extravaganza of a hall, which is uncannily matched by the modern staff house of Sir Hugh Casson with dazzling broad window frames which demonstrate that recent architecture need not grovel in order to match the old. The halls of residence have an enviable setting with lakes and green slopes reminiscent of the backs at Cambridge.

A place equally living up to expectations is the Oratory Church in Hagley Road. Mainly built as a memorial to Cardinal Newman, it has a Roman interior, with tall pillars of mottled marble, which were shipped in one piece, marble altars and inlaid walls in the side chapels, hung with chased silver lights. Long yellow candles are replenished from rush baskets. The atmosphere is Italianate, silently bustling; it is also holy. Newman, who lived here and preached in the earlier church, might well be horrified at the skyscrapers near by, some of Birmingham's most soulless. But he would have liked the school playground. Less world-shy than he seemed to some, Meriol Trevor tells a delightful story in her biography *Light in Winter* of the small boy who bought a guinea pig and who took refuge from rough street boys beside the striding figure of Newman. He felt that he was looking rather obtrusively at Newman's protruding chin, for 'after we had walked some way the chin dropped and I saw a smile steal over the fixed mouth'. The boy told him about his pet, and they talked about guinea pigs – 'I observed with some wonder that he [Newman] did not know much about them.'[6]

But he knew about the world, spoke then as if he were speaking now:

What we call human society now. . . . in its width and breadth it is so much better educated and informed than it ever was before, and, because of its extent, so multiform and almost ubiquitous . . . It has triumphed over time and space . . . But can religion hope to be successful? It is thought to be giving way before the presence of what the world considers a new era in the history of man.[7]

Other suburbs of Birmingham have their own distinct character; one can still discern small village centres, with their particular type of architecture. There are also areas lacking in any kind of charm, such as that along the Coventry Road, at South Yardley, or at Bordesley Green. Bournville too, estimable as it no doubt was and is as a garden suburb, originally a model village, is disappointing as the home of chocolate. The Bournville

Baths are an exotic eyecatcher of 1902-4, but apart from that one could apply William Morris's term 'man hutches' to most of the villas, although they are elaborate hutches, with gardens obviously pleasanter than the traditional slum surroundings of many industrial workers. Nicolaus Pevsner writes that the style here 'established the vernacular for suburban living for the first half of this century'.[8] What a pity, one is tempted to add.

Present-day planning is decried by many, but to one like myself who never saw the pre-war Birmingham, the new face of the city has an integrated, exciting aspect. It is a city where there are many striking modern buildings, which cannot be said of all towns – there is a positive as well as a negative side.

Talk of a 'living museum' in the city centre, with old gas lamps and a village atmosphere, has not to date taken concrete shape. But old buildings, such as the Town Hall and Art Gallery, can be clearly seen at the end of opened-up vistas.

Birmingham owes much of its present skyscape to the architects James Roberts, who built among other things the Rotunda, and John Madin, the son of a master builder, who designed his first house with only his army gratuity behind him. The John Madin Design Group have acted as consultants for the Calthorpe Estate in Edgbaston, which has not lost its character, although some residents say wistfully, 'it used to be like a village here'. In this area the different density capacities, or in layman's language, heights, of buildings, follow the example of the earlier city architect A. G. Sheppard Fidler, who aimed for variety, and to whom can be attributed much of the quality of surprise and contrasting intimacy in Birmingham's views. Unlike the great father of post-war reconstruction and road planning in Brum, Sir Herbert Manzoni the city engineer, who wrote with a sense of humour of his low-density houses: 'Tens of thousands of acres were developed to this standard between the wars to form the dreariest and most depressing monuments erected to my generation – I plead guilty to over thirty thousand of them.'[9]

*

Civic life at present enjoys the tumultuous almost daily drama of rivalry between the newly-formed West Midlands County Council and Birmingham City Council. Councillor Sir Stan Yapp, a former toolmaker, now leads the former, and Councillor Clive Wilkinson, who was a self-employed carpenter and only thirty-four when he took on the job, is Labour Leader in the city council. Both are hard-headed and confident, shrewd and capable; their clashes make lively reading. A typical quote from Clive Wilkinson – 'There is a touch of arrogance about me. I am arrogant enough to believe that when I make a decision it is the right one.' Birmingham clearly resents the creation of the new authority; ratepayers may equally resent the feuding, although Conservatives seize their chances when the two Labour giants differ. Two of the many problems both have to tackle are derelict land, and education, which is a much vexed field in the city.

Birmingham is to receive one of the biggest grants yet made by the EEC, towards its wholesale markets complex – the first grant to be made in this country, which was applied for on the day Britain signed the Treaty of Accession. The complex is being built on a 22-acre site close to New Street Station and the Bull Ring. The meat and fish markets are open.

In industry, Birmingham is poised in a position of vulnerability which the rest of the country can only ignore at its peril. During the nineteenth century, Birmingham was not only the hub of the mining and manufacturing district of South Staffs, but also grew in importance as a provider of services and trading facilities. South Staffs felt the effects of the waning of the Iron Age, but Birmingham suffered less than the Black Country because of a large availability of skilled labour and a wide variety of products. As steel took the place of iron and brass, Birmingham tended to make the finished products while the Black Country made components and parts. After 1931, the city was able to lead the national revival in employment after the depression, because of the variety of its trades and the adaptability of the businessmen; it was able to be resilient and to tackle new industries, also to lead the way, with the rest of the Midlands, in the use of automated machinery. By the 1960s exports of metal and engineering products accounted for about sixty per cent of the total United Kingdom figure compared with thirty-three per cent between the wars. By 1949, 84,000 Austin cars, for instance, had been exported since the war and the introduction of the Mini in 1960 gave a further impetus. Smaller firms were helped to export by the Chamber of Commerce, which in the 1950s began to support Britain's entry into the Common Market – typical of Brum's outward-looking attitude.

Today there is an even greater swing to the service industries and professions. About sixty per cent only of industry is in the manufacturing sector. The National Exhibition Centre, backed by Birmingham, is a prime example of the lead in promotional as opposed to production activity. But still one-third of the country's exports begin their life in

Birmingham and fifty per cent of the region's industry is tied up with the motor car in one way or another.

Four thousand firms belong to the influential Birmingham Chamber of Industry and Commerce and of these over half employ less than fifty people, and about one thousand less than ten. It is still the city of small trades; its industry is still resilient and adaptable. But those involved in the short-term outlook are aware of the present precariousness of the situation. The Birmingham Chamber is active, for instance, in promoting industrial development certificates which aim to help keep industry in existing premises, on the old backyard principle, as opposed to the government offer of cash grants for moving to new areas where industry is needed. If too many industries leave, Birmingham will be the loser.

6 Bridgnorth, Ironbridge, Telford New Town, Wellington; The Roman City of Viroconium at Wroxeter; Newport, Tong

All friends round the Wrekin.
Traditional toast

Until the coming of the railways, the River Severn was the great trade artery of the Midlands. In the seventeenth century it was navigable up to Welshpool, and craft could carry cargo down to Gloucester and so round the coast to London, or across to the Continent. Perched on a red sandstone rock 200 feet above the river, as well as below on its banks, was the small town of Bridgnorth, an important port and barge-building centre. The scene here was later painted by Cotman and Turner, and it is easy to see what attracted them in this combination of swirling river and legendlike cliff-top town. In many ways the setting has changed little, and it does seem remarkably like a stage setting – theatrical and improbable, and attractive in its way. But it *is* attractive, in the right mood, when the sky is scudding with dark clouds, or aquamarine, with shining pink and white cloud-skeins, rain hanging softly in the air, the dark outline of the Wrekin and of trees silhouetted on the skyline. And with a rainbow. Each time I visit Bridgnorth a rainbow seems to appear, brilliantly arcing down to the green fields on the opposite bank and well matched by the spires and tower of the town, the black-and-white houses, cable-railway and happily chuffing steam of the Severn Gorge Railway.

What will happen to Bridgnorth? Its narrow streets are not yet riddled with tourists and nick-nackery; it has industries but would hardly be termed industrial now; it has not been bought up and strip-lighted by the leisure kings. Perhaps the first alternative would be the least harmful, or so those that live near by seem to feel. It is certainly a commuter town for Wolverhampton, but it also retains a certain leisureliness. Many young married couples live there, and there are the old residents who say 'it's all foreigners now'; there are shops laden with Shropshire fruit, mushrooms, pigeon, game; on Saturdays there is a market under the arches of the black-and-white town hall, with produce from local smallholdings on the centre stalls; in the newsagent's the *Farmer's Weekly* is in keen demand, and waitresses in cafés talk about the crops. The seventeenth-century Castle Inn and Swan Hotel are unchanged, and there is a small museum, run by the Bridgnorth Historical Society, in the arch of the North Gate, which is the only relic of the old town fortifications. (In the twelfth century Bridgnorth was laid out as a 'new town'.)

Down by the river, in certain moods, is another stretch of calm. The Severn is one of the best angling rivers in the country, and lower down near Quatford, the stretch of wide river between hills, with its anglers and green fishing umbrellas, the occasional boat, is like something seen in an old French film. In Bridgnorth itself, the town water is free fishing; anyone can get a Severn licence and those under fourteen don't need that. Consequently, by bus and on foot, accoutred with the utmost seriousness, swarms of boys hurry down to the banks for a day-long stint catching barbel and chub. They wear sober green or brown water-proof jackets, and caps, or fishing hats, and carry smart canvas stools and fishing baskets which have probably been made by Archie Deans, the basketmaker in the town, one of the masters of this craft now becoming rare.

I asked one of them if he fished often – it was the last week of the holidays and the banks seemed feverish with activity. 'Yer –' was all he said, but his smile under his neat hat was explicit.

*

By the river too, is a timbered house of 1580, in which Bishop Percy was born, who was inspired by an ancient manuscript found at Shifnal to build up the collection of *Reliques of Ancient English Poetry*. The house should be seen by those who are not *aficionados* of black-and-white architecture, because it is tall and well-proportioned, with unusually delicate black feathering curling from the larger beams to give an effect of lightness and space.

This is in the Low Town. The High Town is quite distinct, above on the cliff, and the two are joined by the cable-railway and a mossy set of steps, beside which is a small theatre, the Theatre on the Steps, which sadly seems to lack funds. Until the 1930s in fact, an elderly resident assures me, the two parts of the town kept themselves to themselves, the Low Towners being clannish; and earlier still the High Towners looked down on their brethren in more than one sense, because it was down by the river that the rowdy bargees lived.

The earliest craft on this stretch of river were possibly coracles, and until very recently coracles were used at Bridgnorth. But the cargo of the seventeenth and eighteenth centuries was carried in barges or 'trows', flat-bottomed craft with a single mast and sail, or two or three masts. They were navigated downstream, but upstream, until about 1800, were pulled by men – two or four to a barge, five or six to a trow, hauling from 20 to 80 tons. The heavy work naturally called for beer, and this was conveniently housed by the vintner in some of the caves overlooking the river which were also rented out as homes in the cliff. 'Shropshire born and Shropshire bred, strong in the arm and weak in the head' – could have been an apt saying for the watermen. In 1835, there were twenty-one maltsters, and cargo carried during the earlier centuries included hops, spices, sugar, wines and brandy. Given caves, the possibilities for smuggling seem endless, and the last barge to go down the river, in 1895, which sank with a load of firebricks, can hardly have been the first casualty. But the river traffic prospered. Coal from the pits in and around Broseley was carried down river, and also farm produce and 'Cheshire' cheese, North Welsh cloth, and later the products of industrial Coalbrookdale near by. In 1756 the stretch of the river between Buildwas and Broseley was the busiest stretch of the Severn; in 1766 the canal joining the Severn at Stourport gave access to Liverpool; passenger traffic thronged downstream to take the waters at Bath. But with the opening of the Severn Valley Railway in 1862, the trading boats diminished.

Besides all this activity, Bridgnorth had tanneries, and was known for gun-making, stockings and black silk lace. Sulphuric acid was manufactured in or near the town, and there was a pioneer engineering works which supplied Robert Trevithick's Catch-me-who-can, the first steam locomotive to draw fare-paying passengers. Weavers worked here, and in the early nineteenth century a hand-loom carpet factory was opened at The Friars, an old monastery site by the Severn. The building still exists, with the round-headed windows of the era and wooden balconies running round the top storey; the works was closed in 1940, but is now run by the Carpet Manufacturing Company of Kidderminster. Another industry which seems particularly suitable for Bridgnorth was Phillips's ginger-beer factory. The bottles for this were sealed with a marble in the neck. Mr Walker, the treasurer of the Bridgnorth Historical Society, remembers that at school they used to put carbide and water in the bottles to make them explode, and disgorge their marbles. But such fruitful industries have given way to electronic equipment and aluminium works. A relic, seemingly, is Archie Deans's little whitewashed basket workshop. In an old print of 1570 I see 'cane croftes' on the far bank of the Severn, but can trace no details of them. Willow now comes from Somerset, but there were two brothers working in Archie's place before him who grew their own supply. Archie, who is blind, has 'seen the good times and the bad times'. 'I could have used this fame then,' he says (a keen American with a notebook was scenting round his room as we talked), remembering when he walked twenty miles a day in the '30s to get 3/- [15p] for a washing basket. The supple willows stacked round the walls have to be soaked in a rainwater tank in the garden. 'It's a lousy job in winter when the ice is on the water.' But he likes meeting the people who come to order their baskets, and everyone in the town knows him; the grocer where he shops keeps sugar, or other scarce items, by for him. In fact Bridgnorth still seems small enough to have a sense of community, of belonging, for some of its residents at least; although elderly brows furrowed at the thought of the coming of the RAF station at Stanmore in 1939, and more recently the spread of the housing estate on the borders of the town.

Determinedly anachronistic is the Severn Valley Railway, reopened on the GWR track down to Bewdley. It is not so very long since one went in steam trains, after all, but the sight of the cream-and-brown carriages, with their gilt lettering saying 'Guard' and 'Luggage', of the old views of resorts in the compartments, fills me with nostalgia. I can feel the sand in my plimsolls as my feet dangle on the floor amidst buckets and spades; experience the excitement as a holiday station slides into view, with its wooden slats and hedge of salt-sprayed flowers.

The Severn Valley Railway station buildings are suitably frilly, decked with hanging baskets. The company buys engines or gets them on loan, and repairs them. The price of an engine from the scrapyard has now gone up to £6,000; but they had broken even, to date, for the year when I visited them. Besides pleasure trips, the line provides a real link to the market and runs a Saturday 'shopper's special'. It also carried coal during the fuel crisis of 1973. We *do* need local trains.

Volunteer workers carry out repairs, drive trains, besides doing their other jobs, of any kind. David Reynolds, who is nineteen and works for British Railways at Crewe, showed me round and pointed out the features of the Great Marquis, the Duke of Gloucester, and the Warwickshire – 'an admirable shunter'. We sat snugly in the driver's compartment of engine 461, he on the fireman's seat, I on the driver's. I looked out of the front window down the line, and felt what generations of small boys must have felt in their bones – the desire to set off down the track. David's expression was earnest with intense enthusiasm under his red hair. It can take eighteen months to paint an engine – by hand of course, not sprayed on like the BR – with six coats of primer, six of undercoat and nine top coats. The finer points of axle boxes and the white-metalling of bearings escaped me; but it was an unusual pleasure to see someone so passionately keen on his work. He showed me the piece of mammoth machine he was working on, happily alone in his shed; but at weekends volunteers can sleep in an old sleeper in the siding, and there is a bar on the platform. They have a great time.

Diesels, it appears, are more expensive to maintain than steam trains, but have the advantage of being able to return immediately after a trip without having to drop the fire. But this steam line is proving its worth. From above, on the Castle Walk, which Charles I called 'the finest in his dominion', one can see the white puffs of smoke floating like cottonwool. The Walk encircles a church by Telford, graceful outside, but inside illustrative of the fact that he was better at viaducts than churches. There is also a fragment of castle wall, leaning at a precipitous angle, which is a remnant left from Cromwell's demolitions. (He had previously aimed to tunnel into the castle and blow up the Royalist garrison, but the latter wisely surrendered.) From here one gazes out over the countryside, the wide Severn, the modern estates, the stream of commuter traffic. In his book with Edwin Smith, *England*, Angus Wilson has written:

Each area has its traditional forms and prejudices, preserving visual individuality for the visitor often at the cost of an inertia, a self-satisfaction that stifle the young or the lively who live there. Each area, equally, is fighting to preserve that prejudiced individuality against a more lively, though more uniform modern general culture that threatens scenic variety while it offers release to those to whom the old ways are an imprisonment. The paradox is not, of course, peculiar to England, but in so small a country, where there is so little room for compromise or evasion, its pressures and tensions are fierce.[1]

Scenic variety, at least, seems assured in Bridgnorth. When I was a child we used to go each year to *Where the Rainbow Ends*, had a friend who took the lead boy part. On the Castle Walk one day, buffeted by wind from a grey sky strewn with solitary gulls, John and I suddenly saw another rainbow here – startlingly purple, pink, yellow. About a mile separated its two bases, and we could see where the rainbow ended, in a green field. Then suddenly, the wide arc was encircled by another arc, another rainbow, glistening in the rain – its shadow. A woman hurried past us beneath her umbrella. 'I've only seen that once in my life,' she said.

> Meanwhile, at social industry's command
> How quick, how vast an increase! From the germ
> Of some poor hamlet, rapidly produced
> Here a huge town, continuous and compact,

Hiding the face of earth for leagues, and there
Where not a habitation stood before,
Abodes of men irregularly massed,
Like trees in forests – spread through spacious tracts,
O'er which the smoke of unremitting fires
Hangs permanent, and plentiful as wreaths
Of vapour glittering in the morning sun.
And, wheresoe'er the traveller turns his steps,
He sees the barren wilderness erased.

(Wordsworth's *Excursion*, 1814, at the
dawn of the steam age. On the northern
industrial region and the Black Country.)

Nowhere did fires burn more unremittingly than at Coalbrookdale, which lies to the north of Bridgnorth, nestling below the Wrekin. This is the spot which has been accurately called 'the cradle of the Industrial Revolution'. This small valley holding the River Severn saw the emergence of England's greatness as an iron and steam power. Here Abraham Darby I was successful in smelting iron ore with coke, in 1709, the process which Dud Dudley had discovered earlier, but which did not become general until much later; even in 1747, one iron furnace producing a few tons of iron a week (by burning charcoal) might consume up to one acre of woodland every day. Here at the Coalbrookdale Company (now part of Glynwed Foundries and also a museum) the power of steam was harnessed to iron-making in 1742, and in 1851 the foundry was the largest in the world. In that year the Hyde Park Gates were made here, which were exhibited at the Great Exhibition and now stand in the park. From here came the world's first iron rails, components for iron bridges for South Africa and South America, a curlicued plethora of pretty Victorian wrought-iron furniture, Rayburn cookers . . . the list is endless. The most striking example is the world's first iron bridge, which crosses the river at Ironbridge a little farther on. It has been reproduced on countless mugs and prints, but the original is just as finely worked – a delicate tracery of circling ironwork which crosses the river from the small warm-bricked houses of Ironbridge to a hillside tufted with trees. Round the corner belch the red cooling towers of Buildwas power station, symbolically juxtaposed to the ancient Buildwas Abbey with its Norman arches.

It is this symbolism, this contrast, that makes Coalbrookdale such a powerfully evocative place. Here open-air furnaces once sent up their cones of flame day and night. Were these hell fires preferable to assembly lines? But 'Bedlam Furnaces' now lie empty and crumbling, overgrown with soft old-man's beard. Willowherb and willows grow over the scarred earth of Blists Hill (an open-air museum with relics of the steam age). Grass and lichen have encroached on old kilns, canal cuts, sawmill wheels and pithead gear. Men have taken coal, and wood, and clay, and their ghost engines stand here as witnesses to their rapacity – and also to their loving skill and craftsmanship. But nature has proved an equal in the battle, and has won back her territory. She can stand up for herself, in spite of all our fears.

*

The old Coalport China works in the valley is now closed, but will be opened again as a museum showing the old processes. (Coalport is now in the Wedgwood Group.) The whole Ironbridge Gorge Museum complex in the area is designed with care and lack of vulgarity. From April to October 1974, 130,000 visitors, many from Europe, visited it. In 1975 the figures were about 150,000. Blists Hill, part of the complex, never seems over-peopled, however, and in the evening when the gates are shut it is broodingly lonely.

Roy Evans has a pottery studio here. He is a native of Pontesbury in Shropshire; short and with a dark craggy face and deep-set blue eyes, reminding one of those small dark people who lived in the West Midlands long before the Romans came. He is a consummate craftsman, an extrovert.

On our first visit to him the site is deserted, except for a Conservation Corps team working on an old iron furnace. His two blond sons who often dart about among the pots are not there (he is, as he puts it, 'married with a wife and a mortgage'). We open cans of beer, and he sits at his wheel like a centaur, an organic whole made up of one part man with hands beautifully shaping the clay at lightning speed, the other part bench and circling wheel. The pot flowers up from this union. The clay tapers to incredible fineness.

'I decided I'd *be* a bloody potter,' he says, beginning his life story.

He left Pontesbury at eleven to go to Birmingham. He studied at the Moseley School of Arts and Crafts, but later became an engineering draughtsman. 'I hated engineering, bloody hated it, because I'm a bloody hopeless mathematician. I thought I just don't fit . . . draughtsmen always get the blame if anything goes wrong, because you've put the dimensions on and you're the last in the line . . . In the firm I thought, my God if this is what I've got to face for the rest of my life I might as well shoot myself.' His wife was going to pottery classes and one evening he joined her. 'As soon as I touched the clay, then it sort of happened. I thought, this is what I want.' Looking at him it seems so obvious.

'I had a disrupted childhood but I remember always feeling happy. I liked solitude . . . I liked sounds and smells. I remember picking up a dry piece of grass and thinking it was beautiful . . .' He uses a grass as a sign on some of his simply designed dark-glazed stoneware pots.

He took the plunge which many have taken. Some, like him, to succeed. His work is hand-thrown, but he also makes a range of cast mugs and tiles about which he is a little apologetic, although they show very attractive local scenes from old engravings silk-screened on to transfers. He sells to people who visit the pottery, or takes special orders from them. (The 20s age-group and children are the keenest buyers.) He also lectures part-time at Wolverhampton Polytechnic.

It is appropriate that he should be here, where pottery was once an industry. His workshop is an old roof-tile kiln. Broken red tiles lie outside. His clay comes from a mine at Broseley. He built his own kiln, works on an electric cone wheel. Kick wheels are too slow; in the old days a woman sat opposite or beside the man to kick the wheel, and there are still women alive who did this at the Coalport works.

I ask him if the crowds of visitors who come to watch him work worry him.

'I didn't want to hide in a little workshop somewhere . . . this is my contribution to the craft. Here I can show the other side of it and dispel the popular image that the potter's life is idyllic.'

'Do you ever worry?'

He seems puzzled. I have never before seen anyone thinking out the meaning of the word; most of us know the symptoms.

'I'm too busy making pots. I worry about the world. Today "civilization" is at a very low ebb. Spiritual things have gone wrong. Through our industrial society we have lost our love of each other. It's all keep up with the Joneses – we've forgotten how to be kind. I'm an atheist, I don't believe in God, but I believe in another force inherent in all of us . . . Everything goes in circles . . . I feel some great change about to take place . . . a change I think and hope for the better . . . but the world needs a shock to make us all take stock of ourselves.'

He empties his beer can exuberantly. The pots and bowls stand in gleaming rows.

*

Everything goes in circles. The small workers' cottages at Ironbridge, and at Madeley, where the old bricks have a distinctive smoky-orange colour mottled with black, often set-off with white-painted ironwork, look cosy and decorative now. They give no hint of hard labour conditions. Autumn trees burn their colours on to the hillsides where once the furnaces stood. But encroaching on this old heartland of the Industrial Revolution, is the new industrial complex of Telford, with its cottages, not so decorative, its more inhuman industries. Will these in their turn run the full circle? Will new trees, hopeful new people cover the scars?

*

'THIS IS TELFORD – YOUR OPPORTUNITY', the roadside notice proclaims. Telford New Town got off to a slow start, but now in the early '70s has opened its 222nd factory, whereas from its inception as Dawley New Town in 1963 (it was renamed Telford in 1968) until 1972 only about eighty factories were let. It is planned to have an ultimate population of 220,000 plus, by the 1990s. (The target is 145,000 to 155,000 by 1986.) For whom does opportunity knock?

We lived in the area for nearly a year before discovering where in fact Telford was. It is always in the press, but vague on maps, for the simple reason that it is welded together from three towns in the shadow of the Wrekin – Wellington, Oakengates and Dawley – not to mention smaller villages which it has devoured. But it has an attractive reception centre at Priorslee Hall, and talking to Mr Riley, the public relations officer, who used to be deputy editor of the *Shropshire Star*, and who produces *Telford News*, I was convinced not only of his sincerity, and faith in Telford, but of the altruism of the planners. After all, one must have progress; but as always, planners seem too altruistic, too idealistic. Human nature isn't like that; in our cold climate there is a longing for plush and garrulousness, if not for streams and fields.

The slow start to the construction work was part of the plan. A quarter of the land was derelict and had to be reclaimed; about 3,000 mine shafts had to be filled in; £10 million was spent on sewering the southern area alone. For an area that was 'dying on its feet economically' this seems sound sense. The Telford Development Corporation has no government grants and rents its own houses out. Mr Riley gave me a very sane estimate of the social problems (the Samaritans and social workers get many calls from unhappy housewives, and there are suicide bids): 'There are always some who can't fit in – the more resilient younger generation may be able to cope better.' He also said, wisely, that far too much was written in the press on vandalism, that it was imitative and the less said the better. The local people, who have not quite lost their belief that Telford isn't here to stay, are kind, as Shropshire people are, but naturally don't like bulldozers outside their gates. The three old towns also had a tradition, because of poor communications, of being independent and of not mixing. Surely the aim of linking all these people, of creating a new community is a shining ideal, a planner's grail? A new town must have its problems, but are they not the problems of modern life intensified for all to see?

Armed with this belief, and all that followed has not entirely shattered it, we set out to look at Phase One of the planned 'City Centre'. (Phase Three, which was not then begun, would cope with concerts and 'participation sports' – 'culture'). Given that a 'city' centre below the green slope of the Wrekin and amidst fields is odd, if pleasantly airy, there seemed to us other drawbacks. In spite of all the money spent on drainage, there was in this vast shopping centre, which is what it was, one portaloo. On tarmac on one side of the buildings pensioners patiently waited for buses; on the other side, which couldn't be reached without braving main roads or supermarkets, was an even vaster expanse of tarmac, with serried ranks of cars. Into the boots of these cars women were heaving vast plastic sacks of groceries, unloaded from shopping trolleys. 'Like sheep surrounded by their movable pens,' said John. And when we had seen the interior – a marvellous Sainsbury's, a Carrefour – he reiterated, 'I'd no idea it would be so inhuman.'

There was none of the bustle and warmth of a town, and yet the people shopping looked like town people, in the country. Telford Corporation employees wore crisp scout-leader badges; the café waitresses were strained and argumentative. In the heart of the complex was a well-designed space which was currently showing an exhibition of wooden sculpture beside the plastic fountain, on the edge of which a grandmother from Bridgnorth was sitting to rest her feet. 'I think it's called modern art . . .' she said, and then, '. . . I don't think I like it.' But she added, 'It's progress isn't it, and we've got to have progress.' She liked the old market at Wolverhampton – now pulled down.

We decided to see the homes where all these groceries would be refrigerated, and, presumably, eaten.

The matchboxes were multicoloured shades of brown and red, crammed on top of each other. They were set in 'Woodside' which lies beyond the old village houses in Dawley, where there is now the pathetic label 'To Local Shops'. But the notice that met our eyes on the outskirts of Woodside was even more expressive: 'PROPOSED SITE FOR PUBLIC HOUSE'. *Proposed site*. Glum, we plunged into a maze of roads, called 'Warrensway', and I still do not know if this was the irony of suicidal despair on the part of the architect, or a genuine expression of his belief that people like living in rabbit ghettoes. They didn't seem to like living here. It wasn't very surprising; the roads were bare of passers-by; some houses seemed to have very small, high windows. 'Have you noticed,' John said, 'no *child* could see out.'

We talked to people of all ages. A widower from Birmingham visiting his daughter, claimed she didn't like it. 'Once they get in they can't get out.' He said there was no life in the place. Cars raced at forty miles an hour down roads where children played; housewives didn't get up till one or two, and then couldn't rest in their houses, had to rush, hounded, to their neighbours. A young girl pushing a pram, when asked if she liked it, said 'No'. Were people friendly? – 'No'. She, too, was used to a lot of talkative people in Birmingham. No one spoke to her at the clinic; she claimed the nearest library was in Madeley. In some ways perhaps life is made too easy here. When one thinks about it, freezers and shopping centres eliminate all the communication necessary for getting to know a good shoemender, borrowing a tin of paint, the therapeutic gossip at the village shop.

Talking to an extremely kind middle-aged couple who asked us into their house, we came to the conclusion that to some extent people weren't helping themselves. For there was a community centre, we later discovered, with a hall for Sunday School, a children's film club, concert bills and notices of planned poetry readings. But we saw this couple's point of view. They felt isolated. Like many others they feared to become involved with their neighbours, in case they should become over involved, people take advantage of them. The vicar didn't call (although Telford Development Corporation does work closely with local vicars). There was no club, they said (there is one, but possibly too much in the Knees-Up-Mother-Brown style for such an articulate, educated couple). Not everyone, after all, is cut out to be the game, team-spirited girl of the class who leads all the societies, joins in; others may long to slink in peaceful anonymity into the noise of a bar, where they can brood in peace, or for the convivial pretentiousness of a 'county' hotel; for sedate middle-class pleasures. Why in heaven's name hadn't they built that pub *first*?

But Telford does try. At Christmas Miss Telford Centre threw the switch of a laser beam sky sculpture. The crowds peered into the sky. They could see nothing. Officials told them that the beams were working, but they could not be seen because it was not dark and raining. The crowd waited. The brass band played on. Two helicopters with photographers had to be grounded. A public relations officer said, 'We may well go back to the traditional lights next year.'

*

Beyond the houses we visited, but not from them, or from the perfectly-shaped, litter-strewn corporation flowerbeds, there is a view of the Wrekin. To live near this one would put up with a great deal.

In his *Journal of a Tour through North Wales and Part of Shropshire*, published in 1797, Arthur Aikin writes, 'The Wrekin itself . . . is craggy at the top, and so much higher than the surrounding hills, as apparently to rise alone from the middle of the plain . . . its figure very exactly resembling that of a *whale* asleep on the surface of the sea.' The description is apt. True also, is what a modern writer, H. W. Timperley, has written: 'Once the Wrekin has been seen and climbed it seems to have the power to stir our feelings in such a way that it cannot be forgotten. I do not mean simply by its shape, or by the view from the top, but by something that impresses the mind more deeply and less describably – the feeling of having been close to the hill as a presence.'[2]

We walked up it in the evening. It is an extinct volcano – some say the oldest mountain in the country. Perhaps its secret is that it is a very feminine mountain or hill – fairylike. It has uncrowded beech trees and graceful silver birches which rustle in the wind. Pink willowherb, and ferns. Farther up its slopes the beech trees interlace curiously in a tangle of twisted arms which seem bound by a spell. There are pools in moss which children call fairy pools . . . It is full of lightness and dappled shadows. The army once used the slopes as a firing range, but have now given the rights back to the public. A television mast has been built near the summit, which seems more than sad, but when we first saw the Wrekin the summit was bare and open, with a fleece of very dark, richly-coloured heather. To reach the top you pass through the Gates of Heaven and Hell, narrow passes between twin mounds, through the first of which you look up to see nothing but sky, from the latter down to the bottom of the hill.

Seen from here, the pale outcrops of Telford seem insignificant. They have perhaps not marred so very much of the countryside. To the north are the Weald Moors, with flat cornfields and canal cuts. There are lines of poplars and black-and-white cows. What would England be without black-and-white cows? To the south the curved cylinders of Buildwas power station catch the last rays of sun on their red sides. To the west –

To the west the light falls on the grey Welsh mountains. Thick rays like prophet's fingers break through the dark clouds and stream down-wards, illuminating the silvery distance, the shimmering hills – ridge after ridge of them. One is filled with a longing, to travel, to go westwards, to the west where the sun sets, on and on westwards to the gleaming distance. We are all explorers; at moments like these almost unbearably so.

*

As we came down the hill, occasional pairs of lovers were still walking up it in the twilight, up to the Gates of Heaven and Hell.

At the foot, there is an entirely suitable 'pavilion' – the Forest Glen. It is a long building with ivy and ironwork outside, and inside are mirrors, long white-clothed tables, cakes on lace doilies, bentwood chairs, hanging gas fixtures, and up by the raftered roof, magnificent oil paintings in gold frames. It seems set as if for a French Sunday meal, or for a visit by Queen Victoria. It was built by the owner Percy Pointon's grandfather in 1889, in the days of the wagonettes which would bring sightseers to the Wrekin from the railway. One painting shows iron being smelted at Wednesbury, with belching furnaces flaming in the dark. In a glass-fronted cupboard is a beautiful collection of Coalport china, and Mr Pointon has already given a major bequest of china to a museum. Turkeys, and I am sure, trifles, were laid out for a society dinner of Oddfellows – or maybe Buffaloes? In the kitchen were rows of plain white china jugs, no frippery.

Mr Pointon led us into his own house, which is joined to the main building. The sitting room was even more richly Victorian, with portraits each side of the fire, china, a glow of dark red and gold. On the wall were Dresden china wall plaques of the Four Seasons.

'I've never seen anything like those,' John said.

'No,' said Mr Pointon, gently proud, 'I don't suppose you have.'

I am sure the Buffaloes, or maybe Oddfellows, drank a hearty toast later, with the old toast – 'All Friends Round the Wrekin'.

*

Some way to the east of Oakengates and Wellington is Weston Park, which is one of the most pleasant historic houses to visit. It is a graceful seventeenth-century house and the interior has been arranged so that it is close to the spirit of the original, a good backdrop for the magnificent art treasures. The bedrooms are particularly well done, and there is a double, partitioned bathroom with old-fashioned baths, where you could lie in friendly privacy with your glass of sherry. The grounds are equally attractive, with fine trees. The Earl of Bradford is noted, amongst his many activities, for his strong interest in forestry.

Wellington itself lies below the Wrekin, and in spite of being swallowed by Telford, has hung on to some attractive Victorian streets, and its old station. Beyond, the land flattens out to Preston upon the Weald Moors and Kynnersley; an area, threaded by narrow canal cuts and a disused section of the Shropshire Union Canal, which John Hillaby has hauntingly described:

Here are the Weald Moors of Shropshire, a relic of a long time ago when ice-sheets changed the course of the Trent, and the Severn and the Midlands were deep under lake water ... Against the silvery-grey mist the wire-thin stalks stood out like the brush-strokes of a Japanese print. And at dawn when the sun caught the top of the giant grasses the plumes glowed with cold, incandescent fire. Out of this wilderness of vertical lines came the yelp of moorhen and the almost ceaseless jig-jag, jangly notes of reed- and sedge-warblers.[3]

Here Hillaby met poachers, but we only saw the opposition's work, in the shape of a line of dead rats and crows by some pheasant pens. There was no morning mist, but pale fields, pheasants, wheeling swallows and crows. It is a sedgey, desolate area, cut through by the straight channels of water. By one of these lay an unattended canoe. Suddenly round the corner of a cart-track came a ten-year-old Ford Anglia van in second gear and going like a rocket. Through the wheel peered a ten-year-old Stirling Moss, with his sister of eight beside him. They cornered again rapidly and roared off into the corn over a hump-backed bridge.

A big articulated lorry lumbered up, looking lost, and after much backing disappeared down the long cemented farm track into the distance. It was all very silent again; we could have been in the farmland scene in *North by North-West*. It seemed incredible that we were only a few miles from the 'city of the 21st century'.

*

To the west of the Wrekin, the Severn curves round from the south and up to Shrewsbury. Close to the spot where the river is met by Watling Street, lies the site of the Roman city of Viroconium, at Wroxeter. It is the largest Roman site in Britain not built over and was the headquarters of the XIV Legion. The remains of a great brick arch tower up from the plain; the bricks are picked out with a line of light-red bricks which looks almost new. The efficiency of Roman civilization is also brought home to one by the construction of their baths, which can clearly be seen here. Coal and charcoal used to heat them was even found in a storehouse.

The Romans built a bridge over the Severn, and besides being a military headquarters, Viroconium was a market town. There are columns from the forum, and some of the houses had shops in the front. Many of the buildings were timber. A field near the forum has been excavated, and pottery, mosaics and coins were found.

Some of the area is ploughland once more. The evening sun was shining on this field when we were there, and suddenly I saw something glinting on the earth. I started scrabbling over the spot, and found a piece of glass, which is probably not at all old, a piece of rough, brick-like pottery, and a small square of gleaming brown and gold. This is exactly like the pieces of mosaic in the museum there, and nothing would convince me that it isn't Roman. Figures I could imagine in their togas came raucously out of their friezes and became human creatures of flesh and blood, noisily driving cattle to market or buying pots.

I am holding the small gold and brown piece in my hand now. It is a double-edged talisman, and reminds me more sharply than a medieval *memento mori* of the transience of our bricks and plastic.

But to feel the concertina quality of time, go to Tong. This lies on the road from Newport – which still has a good deal of the air of an unspoilt Georgian market-town – to Wolverhampton.

'There are some marvellous marble monuments at Tong,' a friend told me.

'Oh,' I said. Marble monuments are cold, and dusty; things of wet Sunday afternoons.

But not in Tong church. From here too you can see the Wrekin, misty cow-filled fields. But the exterior of the church, which is the one Dickens describes in *The Old Curiosity Shop* and which has been called 'the Westminster Abbey of the Midlands', is not to me prepossessing. It was built in the reign of Henry IV by Lady Elizabeth de Pembrugge. She lies inside beside her husband, Sir Fulke. At her feet is a faun. He wears chain mail; she is very slender, and her dress has deep narrow ridged pleats, which are carved so simply, so without artifice, strongly cutting through the marble, that they seem to me more effective than the most voluptuous Greek folds.

On another, early fifteenth-century, tomb lie Sir Richard Vernon and his wife. He is in armour, with his feet on a lion. She has seven rings on the straight medieval fingers of one hand, six on the other. Her hair is held in a beautifully-beaded marble net which is held across her brow with a band worked with fifteenth-century art-nouveau leaves.

Sir Richard's great-grandson, Sir Henry Vernon, built the Golden Chapel here in the reign of Henry VII. It is a lovely warm, intimate chapel which can't be much bigger than twelve by eighteen feet. Its comforting atmosphere glows as you go in. The ceiling is elaborately fan-vaulted, with hanging clusters of painted and gilded fruit and flowers. There are old flowered and patterned tiles on the floor. Sun streams in through pale gold windows edged with violet, and rests on the painted gold and red of the stone figures of Sir Henry and his wife Lady Anne Talbot lying in an archway. She has long hair flowing round her shoulders and a gold cap-like net with a thick rolled border. She wears a red cloak, a white dress starred with black petals or jewels, gripped firmly at the ankle in the teeth of two little dogs. The monuments seem almost alive, as if they might smile or speak. There is no cold finality of death. I understood why the friend, whose brother had recently died, had told us of this place.

Another tomb proclaims:

> Ask Who Lyes Heare, but do not weep,
> He is not dead, he dooth but sleep . . .
> This stony register is for his bones
> His fame is more perpetuall thèn theiss stones
> And his owne goodness Himself being gon
> Shall Lyve When earthleie monument is none.

In the doorway another notice refutes the dying of the feudal era. It states:

THE GREAT BELL
The Great Bell shall be Rung on the following occasions
On Christmas Day, Easter Day
  ,, Whitsunday, St Bartholomew's Day
On the birth of a child to the SOVEREIGN
  ,,   ,,   an heir to H.R.H. the Prince of Wales
  ,,   ,,   ,, to the Earldom of Bradford

THE BELL SHALL BE TOLLED
On GOOD FRIDAY, NEW YEAR'S EVE
On the Death of the SOVEREIGN, HEIR APPARENT
or any Child ,, ,,   ,,   or PRINCE OF WALES
On the death of the Earl or Countess of Bradford
  ,, ,,   ,,   ,, ,, VISCOUNT NEWPORT OR HIS HEIR
  ,, ,,   ,,   ,, ,, BISHOP OF THE DIOCESE
  ,, ,,   ,,   ,, ,, VICAR OF TONG

1892

> I believe that nowhere in England is anything to be found which
> can approach the variety of Staffordshire.
>
> Phil Drabble[1]

Staffordshire, which lies largely to the north of the West Midlands conurbation, is very different from Shropshire, and very varied in itself. A county which includes within its boundaries areas as different as Dovedale and the Black Country, Cannock Chase and Burton-upon-Trent, is clearly a visual stimulant. But the differences lie deeper than this; are a mixture of elements derived from rock and soil, race and tradition.

Phil Drabble takes Cannock Chase as the dividing line. As one goes north with the ridge of Cannock on one's right, the country becomes flatter and superficially less lush, meaner; with cattle browsing in water-meadows, and trees, sometimes oaks, which look more stunted, and sparse. The lack of lushness is deceptive, because this is good dairyland, based on clayey marl which doesn't dry out easily. Farther north still comes the moorland grit and limestone, an area which was in fact more densely populated in the days when South Staffordshire was covered by impenetrable forest, and where burial lows, as on Biddulph Moor, go back to primitive times.

The Angles settled mainly in North Staffordshire, the Saxons to the south. Possibly one can attribute partly to that the difference in character, in appearance, that one notices as one goes northwards. Faces become more open, freckled, fairer; there seems more pleasure in the softer, less harsh aspects of life; hospitality becomes proverbially abundant.

To me the town of Stafford, the county town, is epitomized by Mrs Alice Chesters, who has a fine, strongly-formed face, white curly hair, dark eyes, country cheeks. We called on her soon after we had come to the area, when we were househunting, to ask her about a derelict cottage we had seen at Church Eaton, a village which has an old rectory standing in front of its spired church, which, seen across fields, makes a perfect vignette or print of an English village.

'You can come and live with me here, I've got plenty of room,' said Mrs Chesters, thinking we were homeless. We had only been talking to her for half an hour. And when I wrote to her this summer, and went to visit her, she said, 'I knew it was you as soon as I saw the letter,' with that country mixture of superstition and knowledge, and hugged me roundly.

Mrs Chesters told us the strange story of her husband, which haunts me like a fable. He was the son of a girl who had left Church Eaton to go and work in Chester, where she married a man whom we all agreed must have been a blackguard. As she had to work extremely hard and had little to eat, she and her small son soon both had consumption. She felt she must get back to Church Eaton. 'I know I'll die – but he'll be all right there.' So she made the journey, which one can imagine being like one of those instalments from a Victorian novel, to her mother's house at Church Eaton. The girl died. After the grandmother's death the little boy was taken in by the woman who then lived in the derelict cottage, a Mrs Machin. The doctors said, 'Let the boy run about, he'll die anyway.' When he passed out in the garden, Mrs Machin made him walk up and down for hours in the fresh air, and he survived, to help her when she in turn became frail and old.

'It was like that in those days, if you hadn't enough to eat, you got consumption,' said Mrs Chesters. Her own grand-daughter was getting married soon at Castlechurch, Stafford, and her daughter told me about Stafford market, which I later discovered for myself, spilling over with ginger cakes and 'family fruits' and butter and poultry and jerseys. It is reassuring that English country life goes on sunnily and happily despite economies and disasters, goes on not only or especially in Polperro or Suffolk villages, but in the modern houses of county towns, in Midland counties. I like to imagine the wedding procession following the same route that Queen Elizabeth I took on her way to Stafford Castle from Chartley Castle, down Crowberi Lane (Crabbery Street) and across the river at Broad Eye, followed by a vast retinue to the junketings in pitched tents.

The Earl of Richmond, later Henry VII, visited Stafford too, on his way to Bosworth Field; but the castle owes its origin to that dauntless woman Aethelflaed (or Ethelfleda), Lady of the Mercians, daughter of Alfred the Great. She built forts here and at Tamworth and Wednesbury (wooden stockades with surrounding ditches), from which to fight the marauding Danes, and also Welsh raiders. (Castles at Chester and Warwick have been attributed to her too.) Coins from her mint at Stafford, carried off by Norsemen, are in museums in Stockholm and Copen-hagen.

Nothing of the later Norman castle remains, but there is a (recon-structed) part of the baronial castle of 1350. The town was a wool and cloth town in the later Middle Ages, and from the eighteenth century a shoemaking town. Hides from the pastureland, oak bark from Cannock Chase with River Sow water for tanning, made this choice obvious. Lotus Ltd still have a factory at Stafford. It was Sheridan, MP for Stafford for twenty-six years, who made the toast: 'May the trade of Stafford be trod underfoot by all the world.'

The GEC group is the major employer today, with about 8,500 em-ployees. The town has rather the air of a county and market town than an industrial one, however, although it is less elegant than that other agreeable Staffordshire town, Lichfield. The river seems unexpected so close to the traffic of the main street – rush edged, with waterlilies, and a derelict windmill. Victoria Park has a pretty bandstand, and the river is crossed by a white ironwork bridge. The long thoroughfare of two main streets can look ugly, grey in rain, although it opens on to a beautifully proportioned Shire Hall in the Market Place. Off to the sides are baroque county buildings, old buildings in Mill Street and Water Street, including a little old people's home where I was assured flats on the ground floor are £1 a week, 'and our new places won't be standing in three hundred years' time, will they?' Rose-hung houses in Church Lane to quicken the tourist's pulse, a narrow thatched fruit stores (1610) wedged between shops in Mill Street. In the main street a famous timbered 'High House', the GPO, where Sheridan stayed in its pre-mail days, and a 'Royal Brine Baths' of 1892 with clock tower and arcades on to the river. It's a long street, and one dives thankfully into the Swan Hotel, modernized without being spoilt, and a hub as it was in George Borrow's day, when he wrote of it in the *Romany Rye*: 'Truly a very great place for life and bustle was this inn. And often in after life when lonely and melancholy, I have called up the time I spent there, and never failed to become cheerful from the recol-lection.' There are few evening eating places in Stafford, but again some-what surprisingly, it has good shops, with Italian and Greek imports, and even a patio café – unusual for Staffordshire.

*

Stafford is the place to go to delve deeper into the county's history. West Midlands Arts have their office here also. In the museum are neolithic and bronze-age tools of this and other regions. In the William Salt Library are the books which his widow tried to sell at Sotheby's in 1868, and then later gave to the county, possibly at the intervention of the then Lord Lichfield. William Salt not only bought books, but also had public records transcribed, and sent artists to make drawings in every parish of buildings of interest – 1,800 items. There are also engraved portraits in the library, and colour sketches of topographical scenes (over 3,000 prints and original watercolours in all), and Salt had an eye for contemporary ephemera such as Grand Junction Railway timetables. It seems an amazing bonus that this library is so accessible; there is no fee for copying or note-taking.

An attractive piece of history, I thought, was a cobbler's seat in the octagonal-towered St Mary's Church. The verger told me what it was. I had found him polishing poppy-heads on stalls to a mirror gleam. 'You can do it standing on your head if you programme it properly,' he said (there are several hundred of them). He told me that few people in Stafford looked at their church, and I was glad I praised a particular window. 'No one's ever noticed that one particularly before, but an expert was here last week . . .'

He was very anxious I should see the stool. It was curved in a shallow dip and shaped like a tortoise, with the head of the tortoise protruding to make the cobbler's last, to put the shoe on – in the days when crafts were crafts. There is also an altar table which a saddler used for many years, wearing away the beam where he rested his feet to a narrow strip.

'My wife is from the Midlands, so we moved back here,' said the verger. One could see why they wanted to. It is a town which would evoke loyalty.

Born in this parish, baptized in this church, was Izaak Walton, father of fishermen. His bust in the church is decorated with bulrushes – shows a very sensitive, mobile face. A photograph of a portrait, in the museum, again shows this intelligent and refined face, with irony in the eyebrows – Piscator. When he died in 1683, he bequeathed a house, Halfhead Farm, at Shallowford, to the town for charitable purposes. It is now a museum.

Why does wood represent history more poignantly than stone? It is certainly more vulnerable. In 1954 excavations outside the church revealed the foundation stones of a chapel, and five feet below that the remains of a wooden cross were found, which may have been the preaching cross of St Bertelin, who founded Stafford in about AD 700. A prince of Mercia, he renounced his position to become a hermit. During the process of excavation, the wooden remains disintegrated badly. A photograph of the shape they left in the earth reveals the faint traces of this mark left by one man, in the ground of his territory.

*

Religious or not, one can't ignore these legends of saints in Staffordshire. It was a pagan area long after most of the country had become Christianized, just as it was always an area for fugitives and rebels. The last stands against Christianity gave rise to intriguing stories, one of the most bloody and romantic of which concerns the origin of Stone, to the north of Stafford. According to the legend, St Chad lived in a cave in the Mercian kingdom of King Wulfere, who had had to become a Christian in order to marry Princess Ermenilda of Kent, daughter of a Christian king. One need hardly add that as soon as he had got her he reverted to his slummocky pagan habits, according to the legend anyway. His wife left him, taking their beautiful daughter Werburgh with her.

One day, while out hunting, Wulfere's son Wulfad was chasing a white doe, when it took refuge in St Chad's cave. It was in fact *his* doe, and he drank her milk. While the doe was recovering by a cool spring in the cave, Chad talked to Wulfad, who spent the night there, drank some of the white doe's milk and opted for Christianity. The next day he brought his brother Rufin to be converted too. Unfortunately one Werbode, who was not allowed to marry the virgin Werburgh, told the boys' father all, and he rushed out and slew them as they were taking communion at the cave. Their mother the queen exhumed their bodies later and had them buried under a monument of stones – Stone. Legend doesn't relate what happened to Werbode. Werburgh founded nunneries, and when these were later plundered by the Danes, the nuns took Werburgh's remains to Chester, where St Werburgh's Cathedral stands.

A prettier legend of St Chad tells of how Wulfere went to him in remorse, and saw the saint hang his chasuble on a sunbeam. The King tried to do the same with some of his clothes, and when he could not, knew he was in the presence of a holy man.

Some tombs from an earlier church stand in the grass outside St Michael's Church at Stone looking rather desolate, but there are no relics from the time of the town's origin. Inside the church are two busts by Chantrey, which show what a cunning portraitist he was. One is of Earl St Vincent, who entered the navy at thirteen and became Admiral of the Fleet seventy-three years later. He died at the age of eighty-nine. His triumphs included assisting in the taking of Quebec, in the *Porcupine*, and the defeating of the Spanish fleet off Cape St Vincent, with Nelson. He also

1 Black Country chainmakers, Quarry Bank

2 Harry Meads, Walsall
saddler

3 St Matthew's Parish Church, Walsall, from Harry Mead's workshop

4 Black Country whippet racing

5 Barclays Bank, St Paul's Square, Birmingham

6 Chamberlain Memorial and New Central Library, Birmingham

7 Pike Pool, Dovedale

8 Gallery of the market hall, Burton-upon-Trent

9 Sudbury Hall, Derbyshire

10 Wholesaler's window, Fenton, Stoke-on-Trent

11 Bottle ovens, Stoke-on-Trent

12 Canal basin, Stourport-on-Severn

13 View from Offa's Dyke Path towards Llanfair Waterdine

15 Turfcutting at Whixall Moss

16 Telford's Aqueduct at Pontcysyllte

17 Dom Hubert van Zeller at Chester Cathedral

18 Choirstalls, Nantwich

19 The River Severn at Atcham

tightened up things at the Admiralty, and introduced reforms. But although all his great qualities show in the marble face, in his profile Chantrey has given him an irascible and meanish chin – the chin of the man who opposed Emma Hamilton. The other portrait is of George IV, looking very noble and un-Prinneylike, in a toga.

Stone has obviously seen greater days. It has an ornate brick station, and the Crown Hotel in the High Street was designed by Henry Holland. Small plaster-decorated houses on the outskirts remind one of the town's nearness to Stoke. There is a flourishing Canal Cruising Company, with old and new dry docks where boats are repaired or built to order, and hired out. It is a good centre for travel on the Cheshire canals, the Llangollen Canal and to the south. The greatest depredation is in the High Street, where John Joule's Brewery, until lately independent, stands with its bow-windowed offices empty and with a red Bass Charrington label on the gate. It has been taken over. Next door, in a mock bow-front with bubble glass – the Joule's off-licence or 'outdoor' – wine is sold to housewives, the final insult. Monks were brewing here in the twelfth century, and beer jostled with Wedgwood's earthenware on the canals in the eighteenth. In the twentieth century members of the Campaign for Real Ale held a day-long wake outside the brewery on the day it closed, mourning the end of what some claim was the oldest brew in the country.

Richard Barnfield, the sixteenth-century poet, who had a great love of flowers, birds, the countryside of Staffordshire, was born at Stone. So was Peter de Wint, possibly the greatest English watercolourist of the nineteenth century. The wide skies, golden fields, grey water, the feeling for light and space in his paintings, must stem from his home region, although he found the same elements when he later painted in Lincolnshire. Staffordshire has this great feeling of light and space, in its uncloying variety of scenery. The flat fields, windswept or whitely blossoming hawthorn hedges; the rivers and uplands; the forest areas such as Cannock Chase. Each area distinct, none of it dull.

*

'I like to think of Shugborough as an island in the middle of industry . . . When I was a child Cannock Chase was a wonderful wilderness.'

The house, Shugborough, is vast: a little severe outside, faced with stucco since the 1920s, and with alterations of the same date clouding the effect of Samuel Wyatt's earlier, graceful alterations – portico, verandahs, added symmetry – to the house, which was itself an enlargement of the original square brick house of 1693. But there is an Edwardian elegance in the echoing of verandahs by richly looped curtains, pretty rose arbours, gardens in the grounds which slope down on the West Front to the River Sow, where swans swim past gothic ruins.

The speaker, Lord Lichfield, seems compounded of equally complex elements; in spite of his trendsetting life, the speed of his eleven motor-bicycles, he is deeply committed, tied, to this island in Staffordshire. His face is very English, very sensitive but with more solidity and wisdom in its lines than gossip-columnists would want to allow, and eyes which seemed initially very sad and weary. (Not surprisingly perhaps, as we were talking to him on a weekend which included an evening presentation at the NUJ, the unveiling of a plaque, a ceremony at the German War Cemetery in Cannock Chase and three photographs for charity on the Monday.)

'*They* take me seriously, even if my trustees don't . . .' In fact he has had to limit his commitments to causes about which he feels particularly strongly, to prevent his programme being hopelessly overcrowded.

Shugborough was offered in part payment of death duties in 1960 to the Treasury, which transferred it to the National Trust. An endowment fund towards the upkeep is provided by the family trustees, and in addition Staffordshire County Council have a lease of Shugborough, using part of the estate for educational purposes, administering the farms, with the County Museum in the stable block. Patrick Lichfield, the Fifth Earl, himself lives in an upper wing, which is furnished with soft colours – pinks, greens, gold – with flowers growing and blooming everywhere, trails of ivy from tall stands. We talked in a room which in the old days had been used to keep stuffed birds in, because it was not thought grand enough for anything else. His own childhood bedroom is now a small circular dining room. One case of stuffed birds still stands in the drawing room; the walls under the candelabra and Wyatt ceiling are covered with hessian, with oil paintings of hunting scenes and Meissen china ('I hadn't any paintings when I first did the room'); over the fireplace a modern painting by the American painter Latham. 'I'm the first person for two hundred years to have put a picture in the house.'

I asked Lord Lichfield if he felt a conflict between himself as a photographer and his life in Staffordshire. He had said he was the first member of his family within living memory to do a job. 'The conflict is largely financial,' he said briskly. Although he is about the most travelled photographer in Britain, eminently successful (he modestly says 'I'm not as good as some photographers'), taxes are so crippling that it is hard to keep his part of Shugborough in the style to which it is accustomed.

'Do you realize that if I took you two out to lunch in London it would cost me £1,000.' I hadn't. 'Privilege,' he said, 'is something people basically don't like.'

I suggested could he, or his descendants, live more simply at Shugborough.

'I could live here uncomfortably – but I feel for the house's sake it shouldn't be scruffy. I have a bed-sitter over the studio in London, but here I like things to be pretty and make fusses about things like dirty bath taps.'

As he spoke, the house became real to me, a breathing entity, something to be protected. Not a thing of trusts and mortar, but a web of lives, of its own life. The house . . . its people. Admiral Anson the famous circumnavigator, Thomas Anson MP, traveller and lover of Greek classical art, associated with Brindley and Wedgwood in industrial projects; Lady Anson, with her dressing room fitted up with 'very prettiest Indian paper of the Landskip kind with figures'; Thomas Anson who was created Viscount Anson in 1806 and who married the daughter of 'farmer' Coke, Earl of Leicester; Thomas William Anson created Earl of Lichfield in the coronation honours of William IV and Postmaster General at the time of Sir Rowland Hill's Penny Post, and who was also, although 'a fine fellow . . . liberal, hospitable . . . quick and intelligent', 'extravagant and imprudent' and who auctioned off the entire contents of the house in 1842. Lady Anson, Lord Lichfield's great-great-grandmother, who with her dogs and children was often painted by Landseer. 'The children always seemed to arrive nine months after he painted her. I have a strong feeling that Landseer was my great-great-grandfather . . .' Then, later, the house Lord Lichfield knew as a child, freezingly cold, with thirty-five indoor staff. And he knew the house from every angle, because in traditional manner he was not allowed in the dining room until he was fourteen; spent his first seven years in the nursery and the next seven in the servants' hall, understudying each man in turn, living by day with the keepers on the estate, so that he would never need to ask how a job should be done – 'But by that time there were no servants.'

They had had to cut down, although his grandfather's idea of cutting down is illustrated by the story of his father coming home from Dunkirk to find the Fourth Earl writing glumly at his desk. 'Things don't look too good,' he said, and made the warrior pour his second glass of sherry straight back into the decanter. His father continued, 'Yes, we'll have to make economies.' 'What economies?' 'I've just had to sack the third chauffeur and cancel my subscription to *Punch*.'

The place, Shugborough, is in his grandson's bones. A great lover of every outdoor activity, Cannock Chase is to him the centre of the estate. 'My love of Staffordshire centres on Cannock Chase. In my grandfather's day, he could shoot 150 brace of grouse in one day. Now it is being harmed by public access, with soil erosion and 80 deer killed, 80 stolen last year.' The solution, Lord Lichfield suggests, is to have larger motorless zones, true walkers being more careful of the countryside. He told us that each child who stays at Shugborough plants a tree in the grounds; and at another point he said: 'I always knew I would marry a girl from the country.'

Shugborough, with its museum, housing among other things a collection of traditional saddlery tools, coaches, oatcake-making equipment (also an early health poster 'How to Bathe' – Warm Water and Soap 3 min, Cold Water ½ min, Rub Down with Coarse Towel, 4 min); Lord Lichfield, a photographer doing a job, a worker in a modern world, seems to have solved the stately home problem to some extent, making the place a living part of the community, of modern life. But I wondered what the cost was to the person. Being an artist is never easy. 'My family cut me off when I decided to be a photographer not a land agent . . . I had started by doing cheap leaving photographs at Harrow, undercutting the official rate . . . It's natural that I should know people in the world I work in, the people of the age. I was best man at Mick Jagger's wedding; David Bailey stays here; I boxed for Sandhurst so it's natural I should know Henry Cooper, and so on . . . When gossip-columnists reported something my mother used to ring up and say, "You're so common, I'm not going to speak to you . . ."' Did he find Staffordshire philistine? 'People don't know where Staffordshire *is*,' he said evading my question. I phrased it more diplomatically – would he like to see changes here in Staffordshire, in the social order. 'I hope things won't change too much,' he said. The dichotomy; the new and the old; the artist and landowner. There must be a conflict other than financial.

We walked down to the drive, for John to photograph the photographer. They joked over the exposure – 'That's the trouble with having two assistants,' the maestro said. It was very cold. 'I don't feel the cold,' he said. We walked past snowdrops just coming out and the gravestone of Jumbo the British Bulldog, d. 1937. Past the eleven motorbikes. His words were picked up by the wind.

'I have a certain conviction that I'm the last of the Ansons who will be able to live here in this way.'

*

Recently, Lord Lichfield has made an appeal to Staffordshire people to support the Staffordshire Wildlife Appeal. 'Conservation is really all about people . . . Of what use will increased leisure be, if we have no countryside in which to spend it?'

At the same time, planes are spraying the bracken in Cannock Chase which is threatening to stifle the heather. In the autumn, when the heather burns with colour, the Chase is at its best. At other times, it has the chilling aspect of hills covered with conifers, but within an Area of Outstanding Natural Beauty there are pockets of the genuine product – at Brocton Coppice a remnant of the natural oak forest which existed before charcoal burning took its toll, some deciduous trees planted to add variety by the Forestry Commission, and natural regeneration of trees such as thorn or birch or Turkey Oaks. There are good views. At Womere, for instance, which is said to be a bottomless upland bog. Here it is remote and still, with rushes and sedges, bell heather, and hare's tail cotton grass waving white in the hazy summer heat. Spotted orchids and marsh violets can be found in the boggy areas, and bog pimpernel in cushions of sphagnum moss. On the heathland areas grow bilberries and cowberries, and Cannock Chase Berry, a rare hybrid between the two. Even on a hot July day the pine woods are surprisingly uncrowded. In the green shade it is cool and silent, and a strong scent of pines distils a mossy woodiness reminiscent of the old forest, as the chimes of the ice-cream vans fade.

Beside the Commonwealth Cemetery in the Chase is the Cank Thorn. This is a mysterious tree which marks the meeting place of the ancient manors of Cannock, Penkridge and Rugeley. It has never been found growing wild anywhere in the world. A tree of 1796 lasted until 1971. Luckily a forester had lifted a rooted sucker, and this was planted on the site to replace the old thorn, and grows valiantly on amid the roadside litter. The Chase is crammed with history – Castle Ring, an Iron Age hill fort; our own more prominent GPO tower; to the north the hauntingly ornate Tixall Gatehouse, standing houseless in fields, once a gateway to one of Mary Queen of Scots' prisons; obelisks, temples and monuments; the fourteen arches of the Essex packhorse bridge leading to Shugborough Park, where my favourite monument is that of Admiral Anson's cat, sitting smug-pawed on a tall column surveying the estate.

In the German War Cemetery, another monument of our times, German soldiers lie in the precise formation of their grey gravestones, as if marching still: 2,143 soldiers of the First World War, 2,786 of the Second; 95 unknown soldiers among the Erichs, Ottos and Werners, mostly only in their twenties or thirties. A wreath from the Birmingham British Legion lies by a statue by a Bavarian sculptor; a thin white cross reaches skywards. There is a simple walled garden; the plain serried gravestones reach away, marching silently over the hillside.

★

Cannock Chase was originally a much larger forest, covering an extensive area. In medieval times it was thickly wooded with oaks (which had in fact grown through the primeval conifers of the time when England was attached to the Continent – a hopeful sign for conifer haters?). This was the hunting ground of kings, and both the Danish Cnut and Norman William had laid down their game laws. But the depredations began, first for charcoal for the ironworks, and later with coal-mining, which has made its mark, as settlements grew into towns. Today we have our motorized hordes.

A long tradition of poaching began in William 1's day.

'One of the skills that have largely been lost,' said Phil Drabble when we visited him at Goat Lodge, on the land he owns in Bagot's Wood to the north-east of Rugeley, near Abbots Bromley. (Here the Abbots Bromley horn dance takes place each September in the village and at Blithfield Hall. It took place in medieval times and probably started much earlier as a pagan celebration of successful hunting expeditions. A set of reindeer horns on crudely carved sixteenth-century heads, not allowed outside the parish, hangs in the church; they look eerily ancient, strangely sinister. I was glad when rain stopped the performance we had planned to see last year. I felt it stood a good chance of being either ridiculous, or else uncanny.) Phil Drabble is completely unsentimental about the passing of more recent customs, although he may regret their passing. Born in Bloxwich and a one-time production director for the Salter spring works in West Bromwich, he has a fierce admiration for the Black Country, preferring South to North Staffordshire people. 'A Black Country bloke would bawl you out and give you a mouthful, but you could do the same and he wouldn't take offence . . . At the works, we wouldn't touch a Brummie . . . I spent the worst three years of my life in London . . .' But when he was writing his first book on Staffordshire, in 1946–7, the Black Country area was, he says, beginning to disintegrate. People were being moved to council estates and the traditional areas were being broken up. The character of the place has changed. 'There was such intense local patriotism . . . now it is an amorphous mass of industry . . . and there aren't the skills.' He agreed that there can be a certain self-consciousness, desire to look backwards, in some of the present cult of the Black Country, but although a great deal of the Black Country feeling has been lost, he clearly still likes the area and the people there wholeheartedly.

He spoke of remaining skills, in glassmaking for instance. 'There are cabinets in glassmakers' homes of the things they are most proud of having made (their "friggers").' Then the traditional sports. 'They've even started using traps' – in whippet racing, and he explained why the 'ondler had been so important. Black Countrymen love to 'ondle or feel anything, testing it with craftsman's hands. Cockfighting still occurs, he said. 'Where?' we asked eagerly (I have heard rumours of plush-lined wagons, on moonlit nights). 'Never in the same place twice.' And of pigeon racing, he said no one realized what an intensely cruel sport it could sometimes be. 'They are unimaginative chaps . . .' A system is sometimes used in which the cock is kept in sight of the hen pigeon while she is coming into prime condition for mating (having had her once), and he is then taken away and will kill himself, literally, flying back to her. Or a hen is taken from day-old chicks. Big money is involved, a man perhaps laying £60 a week on his birds and standing to win £500.

Phil Drabble's own work, of which he is more proud than of his writing, and for which he was awarded one of only four Countryside Awards to private individuals in 1970, is very well known from his radio and television broadcasts. He manages his 90 acres as a gamekeeper would, but for the benefit of species that are under pressure. He does not go into half the area at all, to give the animals and birds a chance. From an artificially high density of species the surplus can spill over into the surrounding areas, and into amenity areas where the wildlife can be enjoyed by people. The heronry, for instance, has increased from 14 to 47 nests.

Outside the window of his study is a stretch of grass, then three rides lead into the woodland, bisecting it, so that he can see things as they move across the gaps. A white deer crossed before we could spot her. Mallard ducks and a silky white bantam with her chicks were waddling happily around. He has also done much work with badgers, and deer; has found that deer don't fear arc lights, a useful tip for wardens in Cannock Chase with whom he works closely, as so many deer are killed on the roads there.

It seems the conservationists must win, in the long term, particularly in an area such as Staffordshire, which although so near industrial sprawl, indeed part of it, has areas which have long been private estates, some footpathless, which have a head start on more overworked regions. Where there *are* linking footpaths, the Staffordshire Way is being shaped as a walkway from the north of the county down to Uttoxeter, across Cannock Chase, and down to the rocky outcrops of Kinver Edge.

Already one dire project in the area has died an ignominious death – plans to create a popular site of 'houses through the ages . . . the Midlands' answer to Disneyland'.

8 Lichfield, Wall and Tamworth

> We are a city of philosophers.
>
> Dr Johnson

Lych Field – the field of the dead. The town's name may be derived from a massive slaughter of Christian martyrs by decree of the Roman emperor, Diocletian. But nothing of this darkness hangs about the city, which is also the city of the Ladies of the Vale, the three spires of the delicately ornate cathedral which rise from the flat valley of the Trent and its tributaries like spears of soot-grimed lace.

The country as one approaches Lichfield from the west suddenly becomes open arable land – one is after all moving towards the East Midlands – and Lichfield is an open city, which appears to have no tower blocks at all and which has retained the elegance of its coaching days to a large extent. As a young executive from Tamworth said to me a little despairingly, 'Lichfield – you could live there.'

The profane hub of the city is the market place. Here Dr Johnson, who was born in the house he now faces, sits looking down a little more mellowly than one might expect on cobbles and veg and nylon nightdresses. Sycophantic even in death, Boswell stands in stone a little way off. Possibly it is not Boswell's fault that his life of the genius and *The Journal of a Tour to the Hebrides* are thrust down the maws of schoolchildren so that in after life they can summon little enthusiasm for the heavy figure casting his aphorisms across the rainswept Scottish isles. I don't think I am alone in this reluctance to come to closer grips with the great lexicographer.

I moved closer to his statue, however, as it has graceful relief carvings of his schooldays here in Lichfield (at the grammar school where Addison and Garrick were also pupils) and of his penance at Uttoxeter, for scorning his father, a bookseller.

'Nice, isn't it?' I said to a florid man in an Indian cotton shirt, toting crates.

'It's been there long enough.' Then, seeing my interest, he added, 'Awful old creep he was . . . you know . . . queer.'

'What about Mrs Thrale though?' Irrelevant to the argument, but I had to know.

'Queer . . . He used to feed his cat oysters . . . *and that was only one of the things.*'

I could feel Boswell's sword twitching.

*

Part of the old grammar school buildings where Johnson was a pupil still stand, including a seventeenth-century headmaster's house, but the school is now amalgamated in the King Edward VI comprehensive school. The original school was the earliest founded after Eton and Winchester. Other famous citizens of Lichfield include Erasmus Darwin, doctor and scientist, grandfather of Charles Darwin, who lived there from 1756 to 1781, and Elias Ashmole, who in the previous century gave his collection of rarities to Oxford, so originating the Ashmolean Museum. Erasmus Darwin's biographer, Anna Seward, was a magnet to Lichfield's literary circle in Darwin's lifetime, living in the Bishop's Palace in the cathedral close. She corresponded with Sir Walter Scott, and with Mrs Siddons, who was her friend, never married, and was somewhat before her day in asking to be buried beside a churchman for whom she had formed a romantic attachment – although his widow was still alive. Her prose was convoluted, and her verse no better. 'Insatiate worms the lingering likeness chase', is one line of her epitaph to her Vicar Choral. But a painting by Opie shows her as beautiful (her eyes were auburn, according to Scott), and she was known as 'The Swan of Lichfield'. She detested Johnson.

Samuel Johnson himself, after schooldays and Oxford, set off for London with his friend David Garrick, with four pence [2p] between them. He had married an older woman, Elizabeth Porter, his 'Tetty', whom he greatly mourned after her death. Like other Midlanders, he felt the draw of the capital. Of all his achievements, the wisdom which thunders in his writings and sayings comes through to us most clearly, unvarnished, scrofulous and solid as himself: 'Books without the knowledge of life are useless; for what should books teach but the art of living?'; 'Sorrow is a kind of rust of the soul'; 'I look upon it, that he who does not mind his belly will hardly mind anything else'. Charitable, and valued by his friends, one of them said when he died, 'Johnson is dead. Let us go to the next best: – there is nobody; – no man can be said to put you in mind of Johnson.'[1]

*

The centre of Lichfield is traffic-free. New buildings are particularly well integrated with the old, a modern Midland Bank echoing the arcaded style of the old Earl of Lichfield Arms, for instance. The chimneys of St John's Hospital still stand in their oddly tall row along these small early almshouses, and there are many late eighteenth-century houses, the Georgian houses referred to by the Victorians as 'bootboxes'. The delectable uniformity of design and proportions could be copied in houses of every size, because books of design were available to even small builders, and as many shopkeepers lived above their shops, these were equally elegant. Several bow-fronted shops are still operating in Market Street. Although not a spa, Lichfield had its seasons, its race weeks, concerts and assembly rooms. Landowners such as the Marquis of Donegal had a town house there and patrons of the county balls were the Countess of Shrewsbury from Ingestre, the Marchioness of Anglesea from Beaudesert, or the Countess of Lichfield from Shugborough. Girls came out at the race week balls, and their admirers came down from London by coach.

The setting for the opening scene of George Farquhar's *The Beaux' Stratagem*, the George Hotel, still has its Regency ballroom, with a curved carvel-built ceiling, and cloudy chandeliers, Corinthian pillars and Egyptian friezes, a typical mixture of styles which followed Napoleon's forays into Egypt and Nelson's triumph at the Battle of the Nile. There are no minuets now over the old polished floorboards, but, set out for a party, the room is very splendid.

A famous annual event was the Greenhill Bower, a carnival with dancing and booths round the Bower House on Greenhill, to the east of the city where the Tamworth and Burton roads meet. (This and the Sheriff's Ride, another local custom, still take place.) Outdoor celebrations were the rule, and memorable occasions were those after Waterloo (toasting in particular the future Marquis of Anglesea who, so the story goes, had a leg shot off as he rode beside the Iron Duke – 'By Gad, Paget, you've lost your leg,'; 'By Gad, Sir, so I have') and again when Prinney was crowned George IV. On this occasion 150 sat down to dinner at the George, while 3,000 ate at tables set out down the middle of Boar Street.

The Swan is another famous inn. Travellers may well get their snacks now at the (genuine) Tudor café. Girls dance at discos, if at all, not at country style 'dances'.

The last London coach ran on 11 April 1838. Lichfield's prosperity as a staging post at the junction of trunk routes ended, and to a large extent the Industrial Revolution passed it by.

*

'In 669 St Chad with 8 companions established his cell on the site of the church near the well here. Here he died on March 2, 672.' So short a time. And a millennium or so back. Within it St Chad, created Bishop of Mercia, established a measure of friendship between the Angles and Britons, the conquerors and conquered, in his diocese, in a largely pagan age. A remarkable achievement for those or any days, by a man full of humility, who travelled about on foot until the archbishop told him to ride. But he had the advantage of being known and loved in the area, from the time when he had worked as a missionary priest there, in the footsteps of his brother Cedd.

The church is at Stowe, across Stowe Pool from the cathedral. Twenty-eight years later a church was built on the site of the cathedral, and the body of St Chad was taken there. The little well, now housed under a vine-covered canopy, is in a garden by the site of St Chad's own cell. It is surrounded by the sweet smell of honeysuckle and roses and pinks, which I am sure must last on into winter. In spite of bits of paper and plastic in the water, it is a place where miracles hover gently in the air. Perhaps the gentle saint has a sense of humour too, because after I had visited the cell, a barmaid in a pub showered me with unwarranted change and refused to take it back.

From here you look back across Stowe Pool – an angler busy under a green umbrella – to the spires of the cathedral. On the Stowe side there is also Stowe House, where the father of Maria Edgeworth lived. This pool and the Minster Pool are relics of the time when this whole area of the town was filled with swampy patches known as moggs, crossed by the changing courses of streams and brooks, with the Curborough Brook on the east running eventually into the Trent. In Chad's day his cell was on an island; to this day there is a street called Frog Lane. Because of this swampy belt running through the centre of the city, on which one can't build, Lichfield has a built-in green oasis. (Another theory on the town's name is that it comes from the Anglo-Saxon *liccian* – water.)

The cathedral stands in its own calm precinct – quiet, graceful houses; unhurried ducks swimming on green water beyond. I see I have shied away from describing the cathedral for half a chapter. How does a writer do justice to a stonemason's work?

I have to admit that to me, the interior, with its high vaulted nave which I had admired in photographs, somehow lacks light. It didn't seem superlative, as does King's College Chapel, Cambridge, for instance. For me it is the exterior, the West Front, that is Lichfield. A totally feminine cathedral, carved over like thick knobbled lace, which even its soot enhances. Worn sandstone, encrusted with statues, pointed and crenellated, buttresses flying like bird-tendons, doors flower spattered. There is something Moorish in the arches over tomb niches on the exterior, the canopied West Door.

This exotic quality is there inside in clusters of foliage on the capitals of pillars, in ornate clerestory arches. In the Lady Chapel there is blue and brown stained glass of the sixteenth century from the abbey of Herkenrode near Liège. Some faces are erased, others still exquisitely drawn as in an old master painting, so that you could spend a day reading their characters. A tender Flemish mother holds a Holy child. Some of the finest glass in England, the original donator paid only £200 for it. There is another window of glass brought over after the French Revolution, which lay forgotten later in Christie's cellars. Kempe restored the gathering of little brown-limbed cherubs who spill over a fountain like Renaissance water babies.

Childhood is also, most movingly, portrayed in the trustful pose of Chantrey's sleeping children. The two children died in 1812, one shortly after the other (the first because her frock caught fire at a party). It is not surprising the sculptor was said to come and look at them every year.

Interesting, but less beautiful, is the choir-stall carving by George Eliot's uncle, the original of Seth in *Adam Bede*, and a cat and mouse on a pillar in the chapter house, representing the cathedral's ancient link with Chester.

Above the chapter house is a brick-floored library. The day I had arranged to see it, an archivist showed me the Chaucer manuscript of about 1420 housed there. Some initials have been replaced, but most of the original flower border decoration is there, with its delicate trumpets of colour. (The Duke of Devonshire recently sold a perfect Chaucer manuscript of this date for £90,000. I can't vouch for my facts here, as the archivist was highly erudite, and spoke, apparently, a mixture of Latin,

Old English and Welsh.) I was also shown the St Chad Gospels, written about 720, probably at Lindisfarne in Northumbria. With the books of Durrow, Lindisfarne and Kells, it makes up the foursome of celebrated Celtic manuscripts, in the style of decoration which reached Northumbria via Iona, perhaps some of the loveliest manuscripts ever illuminated. It is written in a strong, square hand, and has survived many vicissitudes, including being sold with its second volume for a horse in the ninth century, and having its pages cut and gilded in the nineteenth. Its brother volume is lost.

Downstairs are memorials to Bishop Selwyn, and to Bishop Hacket, who was largely responsible for restoring the cathedral, including the missing central tower, after Cromwellian troopers had done their worst. He helped to cart away rubble in his own carriage, worked to get sub-scriptions, and saw the work completed in only seven years. Then, 'exceeding old and feeble', he is said to have exclaimed on hearing the bells chime again for the first time, 'It is my knell.' A few hours later he died. A great work completed in so short a time; and half a millennium, more or less, ago.

*

'They gnu how to pick their sites, didn't they?' said a bronzed Scan-dinavian – archaeologist? – leaping out of his red sports car. He cast an expert eye over the Roman baths at Wall (Letocetum), and at some men disconsolately shovelling earth off a villa site, and leapt back into his car and off down Watling Street, and on, who knows, to Rome. I climbed up the hill to a small church which overlooks this site, once a Roman town of at least twenty acres, one of the main posting stations along Watling Street, near its junction with Ricknield Street. The roar of traffic from the A5 thrummed up to the hill, where the fort from which the town sprang was built in the first century AD. I could see up the road away to the west, towards Pennocrucium (near Penkridge), Viroconium (Wroxeter) and Deva (Chester). Any enemy formations coming over the brow of the hill some way off would have been spotted at once, and this sunny slope seemed ideal for lounging in hot baths or recuperating in one's barracks after a march. It is interesting that in the official handbook, Graham Webster draws the conclusion that the Romans sometimes built baths before the native population were ready to use them – as at Wroxeter, where they were demolished before completion to make the forum.

The bath house is one of our most complete examples. It is sad that pavements and walls of the town, which Dr Plot saw in the seventeenth century, are no longer in evidence, although crop marks reveal sites – you can see shifting light in the pale corn – and pottery and building débris have been found in the fields around. To the south, near Shenstone, is the site of a Roman farmstead. I saw one bit of walling which seemed to have the typical red-tile layer of Roman walls, and one feels an urge to dig and delve for hours in plough and banks to find artefacts or coins, such as the enamel duck brooch, gaming counters, phallic pendants or cheese squeeze in the museum here. So Trajan looked like this, one says, seeing the lifelike head on a coin.

I asked a gardener if things were still found in the village. 'Some bits and pieces,' he said, when the foundations for a house were dug. A story is recorded of workmen finding an earthenware figure: '. . . but a woman's figure in a strange dress with a man's cap like a soldier's helmet.'[2] Minerva. The men broke her up and used the pieces to mend the bank of a drain.

*

Also near the A5, Tamworth has come down in the world since it was the site of Offa's Mercian palace. It is, if you like, a coaching city in the modern sense, since at the old Castle Hotel or Peel Arms plump matrons or intrepid senior citizens from Glasgow may call in for a wash and brush-up or – charabanc permitting – a sit-down meal. It is a town where countless roads meet, and through which traffic thunders with a swirl of dust and grind of brakes. It is hard to imagine anyone laying a head on a pillow there. As an 'overspill' town for the West Midlands built-up area, Tamworth's population has grown from 14,000 to 49,000 in ten years. Its industries are long-established, such as E. B. Hamel and Sons, narrow fabric manufacturers since 1837, or new ones such as the Reliant Motor Company, or newer ones still in the council's Amington Industrial Estate. There are indeed some attractive eighteenth-century houses, and an outstanding town hall built by Thomas Guy, founder of Guy's Hospital. In front of it is a statue to Sir Robert Peel, father of the great statesman, who was MP for Tamworth from 1837 to 1850. (It is pleasing to note that electioneering in those days was more honest and vilifications more open. 'Beware of the Speeches and artifices to which Sir Robert Peel is resorting. He is adopting his old tactics . . . Electors, be independent, and vote for the man who treats you as *men*, and not as *dogs*.') The church, St Editha's, is unusual in having an excellent modern public library in the large churchyard with glass and pebbled concrete matching the pebbles round tombstones.

Tamworth Castle is built on the mound on which Ethelfleda built a stockaded fortress in 913, reinstating the settlement which had been destroyed by Danes, to the prominence it had known in Offa's day. She may have built the herringbone curtain wall, which is the most striking feature of the castle, a beautiful slab of masonry (dated by others to the late eleventh century). From the battlements there is a wide view of the rivers Tame and Anker, and inside the castle are many collections: Victoriana, coins from the Tamworth mint, mining tools of 1800 from when it was a mining town, and objects from the time when textiles, papyrus, jewellery and perfumes were hurrying from Londinium to Wroxeter and lead was being humped on mules from Wales for shipment to the Continent (there is a pig printed with Roman numerals). In 1971 a strikingly preserved Anglo-Saxon timber structure was excavated in Bolebridge Street, a water-mill which may have been attached to Offa's palace. Offa was a good European in his day, writing to Charlemagne to complain of the quality of the millstones from the Rhineland being sent to him.

It is good that, in this town, one's faith in present-day exports, British industry, is renewed by the Reliant works. I was driven there in a three-wheeler Robin. They were working on reduced production because of the depressed state of the trade, but the public relations office was humming, kept in efficient order by the flick of an eyelash by a girl out of the Avengers, but less solidly built. A healthy-looking managing director glanced in before catching a plane to Greece. Reliant does a 'package deal' for the motor-manufacturing industries in less industrialized countries – Israel, Turkey, Greece. The firm's experience as Europe's largest user of glass fibre in the motor industry makes this service – including supply of 'KD kits', Knock Down Kits, with the importer building their own body – highly successful. Robins are also exported to Austria, Switzerland and the Netherlands on a limited basis. Scimitars are exported on a personal export basis.

'That's Princess Anne's old Scimitar in the yard. Without her special grey-kid interior trim.' In other respects her cars have been the same as others, off the line, not specially built.

In the works, the atmosphere is of unhurried, careful work, oddly quiet for a factory. The production is of necessity low volume, and they have their own market nicely tied up. Pieces of fibreglass bodies are cut from wooden templates like dressmaking patterns, 'with a bit of hosepipe stuffed over the end of a hacksaw blade – it says a "high alloy steel knife" in your leaflet but it isn't – but it works'. The mats of glass fibre are fitted into a mould, painted with resin and a catalyst and left to dry (Robins go into an oven for baking), at which point the moulds can be knocked off to leave the finished pieces, which have holes drilled for fitting. The process is of course more complicated than this, and bodies are in fact made from two mouldings, an inner and an outer, welded together with fibreglass.

After sanding and cleaning, bodies are spray-painted. 'A rotten job', I was told by my guide, who as an apprentice had done it. The smell from even where I stood was horrible. The operator wears an anti-toxic mask to stop plastic paint getting – irreparably – into his lungs. Even so, whatever his wage, he earns it. So do the men on the assembly line.

'How long do they stay on one operation?'

'How long? Oh for ever . . . until they leave . . . or retire.'

An eternity. They looked cheerful. 'They're not rushed. Not like at —. There's time to have a chat with your mate.' The line moves one foot a minute.

My confidence in the strength of the bodies was greatly reinforced after seeing them made. In a slow-speed crash they should crush and spring back. In a bad crash the impact is localized and taken by the chassis. I was shown some wrecks sent back to the maker for repair, and the tears looked neat and mendable. In a fire they smoulder. 'It gives you time to get out.' Good. Unlike invalid cars, I was told, the centre of gravity in the three-wheeler is below the wheel centres, making them much safer.

Reliant are much more self-sufficient than most manufacturers, making all their own soft trim, for instance. The workforce as I write is approximately 2,500, and the three factories have been involved in a modernization scheme, which has also taken environmental factors into consideration. An old mill building has been preserved as part of the headquarters development for instance. A small four-wheeler, the Kitten, has just been developed for this country, and in design and production they seem on top of the job. (There seems to me very little room for legs in the back seats though.) There does seem pride in the product. The first prototype Robin stands in the yard and they almost pat it affectionately as they pass.

The company has come a long way since T. L. Williams, of the Raleigh Cycle Company, decided to produce his own three-wheelers in a workshop in his garden at Tamworth, because Raleigh had discontinued production of three-wheelers and he had faith in them. His first van was licensed on 1 January 1935. He died in 1964 and the company, by then greatly expanded and with fibreglass mouldings introduced in 1956, was then directed by Mr Raymond Wiggin, who is still managing director and who increased turnover ten-fold during the 1960s. The Reliant Motor Group, of which the Reliant Motor Company Ltd is the main trading subsidiary, is independently owned, the largest car manufacturers to be so. It is part of the Hodge Group (with an international banking organization as the ultimate parent), whose founder Sir Julian Hodge controls it from the fourteenth floor of a Cardiff skyscraper (having set up business in a small office thirty years ago).

Blocked in the rush-hour congestion in Tamworth my guide turned to me and said, 'There are two roads above Tamworth and two below, with one road in the middle and no traffic lights. I live in the road in the middle.'

And the town?

'Dead,' he said.

And roared off in his Robin.

9 Burton-upon-Trent; Tutbury, Rolleston; Uttoxeter; Dovedale and the Manifold Valley

> Oh, my beloved nymph, fair Dove,
> Princess of rivers, how I love
> Upon thy flowery banks to lie,
> And view thy silvery stream
> When gilded by a summer's beam.
>
> Charles Cotton

The small River Dove joins the sturdier Trent just above Burton. The Trent and Mersey Canal runs parallel to the larger river, which in its turn sprawls and divides, so that Burton becomes an island, or a series of islands, set in its flat, watery plain.

Burton – the home of beer. The first thing which assails you as you leave the railway station is the smell of it – a warm, heady smell of mashing beer. It pervades the whole town and the townspeople seem so used to it that they no longer notice it; when I asked what the smell was, I was met by puzzled looks and the suggestion that it might be meat pies. I was immediately intoxicated, by the smell, a half of best bitter, and by the town. It is unspoilt, perfectly Victorian. Why isn't it packed with tourists? But there are none, and there are few hotels. Yet this *is* England, one face of England; a thriving town, not a museum.

The streets are wide, many of the houses nineteenth-century brewers' cottages, one up and one down, with a picket fence in front and joining terrace gardens at the back, bright with flowers. There are other, more imposing streets of eighteenth-century frontages, but it is the Victorian which triumphs and gives the town an unusual unity. A Baptist church of 1882; a Salvation Army building in Mosley Street (did the 'Tutbury Tup', a racy Mosley of long ago who appears to have been the local bounder, drink at the Roebuck Inn in Mosley Street?); the old LMS Railway grain warehouses with wooden grain chutes; the palatial Bass brewery buildings with their gateways and mounting blocks (and un-expectedly the gold and blue paint proclaiming B. Grant Ltd of St James's near by); the 1873 public baths down by the river; a pinnacled Co-operative Society building; the Town Hall, presented to the town by its first MP, Michael Arthur Bass, the first Lord Burton. This has a clock-tower, and a white ironwork balcony; the interior is the apogee of delectable Victoriana – delicate white-and-gold ironwork balconies, tiles, ferns, a stained-glass ceiling letting in the light. It is perfect; fit for kid gloves and large gold chains on heavy mayoral stomachs, stately officialdom and reassuring prosperity.

The Victorian spirit seems to live on in Burton. The borough buses are cream and red, the lettering on shop fronts is innocent of modern typography, and notices on the Town Hall exhort the inhabitants to use the public baths – swimming and sauna. Since there is only one cinema and a Bingo, it seems likely that they may do so for amusement. On Thursday and Saturday there is the market. Oh let the fainthearted who fear that England is dead, that the old customs are dying out and that the flood of plastic and convenience foods will drown us all, come to Burton market. There is hope yet. Under the great dome with its bull's head outside and delicate green pillars within, are mounds of rounded fruit surrounded by cauliflower borders, stalls of pale yellow or striped slab cake, glistening brawn, bowls of home-made potted beef topped by butter, gargantuan joints and fresh oatcakes. There is no rush, no grabbing. The pace is slow and old fashioned, voices contented. The best bitter still merry in my head, I bought oatcakes and asked my landlady to fry them for me, which she did, with pursed mouth, in silence amid her patio tiles and Cosy Karpets. They tasted ambrosial, of warm heather.

In 1004, Wulfric Spot, son of Wulfruna of Wolverhampton, built the Benedictine Abbey at Burton, of which little remains. A market porter tidying up his trestles proudly showed me the remains of a wall, the parlour doorway. He also pointed out the recently cleaned bull's head on the market hall – 'Nobody knew it was there.'

There is clearly a ritual to market day. After shopping, pensioners – of every class (one feels there are still classes in Burton) – and others go past St Modwen's church in the market place to the old buildings of Friar's Walk Grammar School, founded by an abbot of Burton Abbey and now used by the parish. The lawns outside run down to the river, and inside there is coffee and unlimited biscuits for 7p; anyone can sit and have a good talk and rest their feet. The two church cleaners shared their biscuits with me hospitably. Gay old pensioners reserve places for their lady friends, and it would seem that it would be impossible for a citizen, however senior, to be lonely in Burton. This is surely how the church should be in our century – extending unselfconsciously and warmly into

148

daily life. Talking to the vicar with his rosy-cheeked face, and one of the readiest, most appealing smiles I have seen, one could understand part of the reason why this meeting place seems a natural successor to the smoking concerts and Sunday School treats of the old days in Burton, when over 1,000 children were taken round the town in brewery floats before their tea and games. But the church is lucky in its setting and the use of the old Friar's Walk buildings; most church halls with their public-lavatory architecture would cast a blight over the proceedings. Here, I was strongly reminded of Cambridge, in a beer city instead of a city of learning, since grass runs down to the river on both sides, with trees and gardens, and an elegant iron bridge decorated with rosettes.

*

Across the river a white-haired Negro gardener is sweeping up leaves in an avenue of trees and nods deferentially in greeting like something out of *Boy's Own Paper*. Here is Andressey Island. 'But when St Modwen had come to the river called Trent, which flows past Mount Calvus, which in English is called Calvecliff, they built there a church consecrated to God and St Andrew, which place is called Andressey, because it is a small island. It was desert at that time . . .'[1]

This was in the seventh century. Modwenna, daughter of Mochta, Prince of the Clan of the Conalls, had founded a convent in Louth, Leinster, in AD 630. Aelfrid, illegitimate son of Oswin, King of Northumbria, pillaged her convent, and she followed him back to England, to Whitby, to demand redress. He promised to repay all and installed her at Whitby with his sister Elfleda. Later she visited Burton and built her church. The water of her well on Andressey was said to effect cures.

There is no one on Andressey Island. There are roses, and syringa, and beech trees. Untroubled cows crop grass in the fields; silver-leafed branches blow across the gently clouded sky; the sense of rush ebbs from your shoulders and you are constricted to rest and be tranquil. Yes, England does still have a heart. You can hear it beating here; in the clank of the brewery fork-lift trucks; in the lapping water; in the wind in the trees; in the silence. The flag flies on the romantic Victorian water tower perched like a castle on its hill above the town, and the roses bloom in St Modwen's desert. I feel at peace and reassured. Something I had feared not to be able to find, had feared would be spoiled in our lifetime, certainly that of our grandchildren, is here and seems likely to continue. We are lucky to be living in the 1970s, not a futuristic world. The clank rises prosperously from the breweries; the river flows calmly on.

A city . . .

　　blue-massing clouds; the keen
Unpassioned beauty of a great machine;

And washen stones, gay for an hour; the cold
Graveness of iron; moist black earthen mould;
Sleep; and high places; footprints in the dew;
And oaks; and brown horse-chestnuts, glossy-new;
And new-peeled sticks; and shining pools on grass; –
All these have been my loves. And these shall pass

　　But the best I've known,
Stays here, and changes . . .[2]

'It's a dreadful place . . . but I've bought the café . . .' said the Cypriot café-owner. By now, after more best bitter owing to the hospitality of the Bass Charrington brewery, which I had not liked to refuse, I was momentarily inclined to agree with him. If he could be persuaded to keep his café open a little later, I thought he ought to do remarkably well, because there are few eating places in Burton and virtually none except his where you can get a meal after seven o'clock. This is fairly universal in unsophisticated places in the Midlands, and has caused John and I to race like hungry terriers along the streets of small towns, too late for tea. There are three other people in the café, looking gloomy. The pubs are empty in the evenings, too, which seems surprising, but perhaps beer gets on top of you if you are with it all day long. When times are quiet free beer has been known to pass hands, and brewery employees have been seen to 'go home staggering'. When offered a drink one licensee accepted tonic water. It is not a very ebullient atmosphere for the young, or for visitors. A boy sits glumly on a doorstep; in the suburbs the television screens flicker behind lace curtains, and outside the bed-and-breakfasts the landladies' commercial gentlemen, up from Kent for a six-month stint at one of the large firms – Marmite, Pirelli, CEB – look fat and bored and rev their cars.

A young German traveller, visiting Burton in 1782, recorded his impressions.

I had intended to stay the night, but soon gave up that idea. Although the houses were as grand in appearance as those of London the Burton people had such a small town mentality – pointing their fingers at me – a walking stranger. I passed down a long street where all the people were standing at their doors on both sides, and I had to run the gauntlet of their curious gaze, and hear behind me the sound of their hissing . . . nowhere have I found such hated concentration on a passer by as here in Burton.[3]

Things have not entirely changed. I noticed here again the difference between the people of various parts of Staffordshire. There are more beady eyes and fewer smiles in the streets of Burton, and the people tend to be dour and uncommunicative. They will not be charmed; their stares can be unnerving. Walking down the streets of Burton in jeans I felt much as the German traveller had felt, and yet once they have accepted you one feels they would be true friends. It is difficult to get to know them. A classic moment in a bar when John offered a drink to a woman licensee whose face looked interesting, even dramatic. 'I'll have a Britvic Orange,' she said, 'thanks,' and walked, with it, firmly away from us.

Montague Smith, who now lives in Wolverhampton, confirms this. He comes from Burton, and when he was at art school, there were only eight students at the school. Wolverhampton seemed a very friendly place after Burton, he says.

He showed us sketches of the town he had made in those days, and told us how he remembers the little red brewery trains which used to cross the streets. Bass had a red engine with copper funnels, Worthington a sapphire blue engine, and Marston's was dark green. The Statutes Fair took place in the market place, with cakewalks and coconut shies. On Saturday nights, the colliers from south of the river, who were a different community from the brewers, would come into town and there would be terrible fights.

As a child Monty was taken on excursions to Tutbury Castle, and out into the countryside to the west of Burton where the brewery barons had their large houses – Rangemore Hall, Dunstall. One of them rented Sudbury Hall from the Vernons, and drove to and from Burton in a gig. The 'barons' were still powerful during the war years; they had not always been noted for good relations with employees.

All Monty's family except his father had been in brewing. One of his aunts, however, worked in Faulds, the community of farms which was wiped off the face of the earth in the terrible explosion (the fourth largest ever known) of bombs stored underground, in November 1944. Two large farms were completely obliterated, with people, cattle, sheep. Trees were uprooted and flew through the air. Buildings in Burton, six miles away, were damaged. Church spires split. Now all that remains is a barren crater, covering 172,000 square yards.

*

The history of Burton was built round beer. The drink may have been introduced into the Trent Valley by wandering Neolithic tribes; the Romans found it here in 54 BC. The monks of Burton Abbey realized that Burton water was especially suitable for pale ales. This is not the water from the Trent, but from wells rich in gypsum, which makes the water ideal for fine, pale, bitter ales. (Today, from one of the wells, thirty feet deep, we were told that five million gallons a week are taken without lowering the level of the water.) In 1744 William Worthington set up his brewery and in 1777 it was merged with that of William Bass, who had sold his haulage business to one Pickford. Today there are only four breweries in Burton, the two large groups – Allied and Bass Charrington – and two others. (Bass Charrington is the largest brewery in England, turning out 50,000 barrels a week and paying £2½ million a month in tax on two breweries.) Behind the new technical college are the Soho wharves from which in the early eighteenth century beer was exported to the Baltic ports and Russia, where 'Piva Burtonski' was acclaimed. When tariffs got too high, India became their target, with India Pale Ale. A cargo of this was wrecked in the Irish Sea in 1827, and barrels were auctioned off in Liverpool to reimburse the underwriters, so starting its popularity on the home market.

In the old Bass Charrington brewery (which is the 'new old' brewery of 1863, not the original building) draught beer is made in the traditional way, in rooms sweet with scrubbed wooden floorboards and the rich smells of sugar and malt. It seems very orderly; there are highly-qualified technicians in overall coats, and only twenty-nine men are needed for one shift. In the 'Burton Union' room are great wooden barrels, and this is the only way you will see wooden barrels in Burton, because all beer is now sold in metal casks. By the Union process yeast can be recaptured to be re-used for the fermentation process in the great frothy tanks, so that the same strain of yeast used in 1777 can be used today. A famous brew was that mashed on 22 February 1902 by King Edward VII for Bass and Co. Called the 'King's Ale', bottles of it are collector's items. Monty Smith showed us a bottle of it he treasures.

If draught beer dies out, and I am assured in Burton that it will, we will no longer drink the drink so loved by Peter the Great and the Empress Catherine of Russia. In the new Bass brewery, built to a German design, one man sits at a vast control panel and undertakes the whole process. Hop pellets are used instead of hops (and hops are now picked by machines instead of happy holiday hop-pickers), the beer is pasteurized and 'polished', which in other terms means 'taking the guts out of it'. So why will draught beer vanish, why will we no longer be able to drink Falstaff's barley broth? The main argument seems to be that landlords and owners of large clubs can more readily cope with keg beer; it is ready for use directly, while draught beer, a friendly licensee told me, 'has to be handled like a baby'. He gave it three more years only. A sad day for England. When will people realize that work is more enjoyable if it involves skill, if it involves a pride in the craft itself as well as in the product?

There are many other industries at Burton. Spare yeast goes to the Marmite factory (and beer in fact produces few waste products, no pollution). There are the large Pirelli works, engineering firms, and the vast Drakelow power station. The town has made a tilt at modernity with a hideously ugly shopping centre – with, the town guidebook assures me, 'eye-catching murals reminiscent of Aztec culture'. I prefer the fishing-tackle and bicycle shops, the stores for sports goods and fertilizers, but it is a satisfyingly busy industrial centre.

Two boys in fashionable wide trousers from the technical college play darts desultorily in a deserted pub. I ask if they can study brewing there (you now have to have a degree in brewing to be a 'brewer'). 'Brewing?' one queried. He didn't know what I meant. The Central Electricity Board pays towards his course, as do other big groups for other students. 'I shall be earning £60 a week by the time I'm twenty-one.' I should have asked what he will spend it on. Will he spend it on barley broth and go fishing in the silver streams of the Dove? Will he say with Izaak Walton, 'As for money . . . neglect it not: but note, that there is no necessity of being rich; for I told you, there be as many miseries beyond riches as on this side of them . . .'

*

The road from Burton to Tutbury goes past the Pirelli works, then Stretton with its bungalows, and on through flat but pretty country to Rolleston with its water meadows where cattle feed among elderflower bushes and willows, and poplar trees. This is some of the most fertile land in the country, famous for its hard corn.

Tutbury is a remarkably attractive large village, with a wide High Street where stands the Dog and Partridge Inn, in striped sixteenth-century black and white, with nostalgic photographs of the meet inside, c. 1939. There are two antique shops selling oak furniture, muffin dishes and cobwebby lace; the Webb Corbett Crystal works where the famous Tutbury cut crystal glass is made; the curved front of F. J. Gane Iron-mongers with its grain chute and pale-green paint; no tourists. Indeed so tucked away is Tutbury Church on its hill above the village that I was surprised to see one other person there besides the organist and myself; and yet the small square church, for its size the oldest building in Staffordshire, already old when John of Gaunt built his castle near by, has in its west front one of the finest pieces of Norman architecture in England. The wide arch of the doorway is repeated six times in six inner arches, the sixth, since the church stands on an alabaster hill, being made of alabaster. The arches are elaborately carved with tigers' heads and flowers; above is a window with the same wide arches echoing the pattern. The broad lines make the stubby church warm, almost homely; the ornate carving makes it ethereal.

At the top of the hill is the ruined castle, mainly built by John of Gaunt, Shakespeare's 'time honoured Lancaster'. Here he bred warhorses, held his magnificent and cosmopolitan court, was the patron of minstrels, of Chaucer. Here his second wife Constantia laid out the Queen's Garden of vineyard and arbours, wild geranium, lilies, mallow, sorrel and columbine. Here later, the unlucky Mary, Queen of Scots, Ronsard's 'belle et plus que belle et agréable Aurore', spent years of her imprisonment, her plight in the rheumaticky castle only alleviated by hawking on Hanbury Hill, hunting in Needwood Forest, 'sixteen dishes at both courses', and casks of Burton ale, in which her letters were also smuggled during the Babington plot. 'I am in a walled enclosure on top of a hill, exposed to all the winds and inclemencies of heaven. Within the enclosure there is a very old hunting lodge, built of timber and cracked in all parts . . . the sun can never shine upon it . . . nor any fresh air come to it.'

In spite of illness, she had not lost her dangerous charm. Nicholas White wrote: 'very few should have access to or conference with this lady, for besides that she hath a goodly personage, she hath withal an alluring grace, a pretty Scotch speech, and a searching wit clouded with mildness'. He also remarked on her many coloured wigs, which she wore at random.

Now sun shines into the dip within the ruins. Local residents buy season tickets; their children toboggan there in winter, play cricket in the summer. But when the castle grounds are empty the tall North Tower rears hauntingly against the hurrying clouds, its slit windows – were they so to her? – reminiscent of the fleurs-de-lys of Mary's beloved France. From the walls the flat plain stretches away on all sides, endlessly bleak, indomitably English. She couldn't win.

*

John joined me to go to Rolleston. This was by way of being a pilgrimage, because he had never visited the place where members of his family had lived since 1614. The Mosleys trace their family back to

'Ernald, a Saxon', Ernald de Moseley who lived in a hamlet four miles from Wolverhampton, in the reign of King John. Later members of the family moved to Lancashire, but in the seventeenth century Rolleston was added to the houses at Hough End and Ancoats, and it was around Rolleston that the adventures during the Civil War of a Captain Nicholas Mosley centred – the hero of a highly-coloured but romantic historical novel *Nicholas Mosley Loyalist or 'What's in a Name?'*.

Why do we have this nostalgia for our ancestors? Perhaps, like one small facet of our affection for children, it is part of the wish for immortality, to be part of a thread if we can't see its end. (By the Dove I was reminded of my own ancestor Sir Henry Wotton – the poet and diplomat who wrote of the role of a diplomat that he was an 'honest man sent to lie abroad for the good of his country' – who was a fishing companion of his biographer Walton. Did the two friends spend sunlit days there together as well as at Black Potts below the Eton playing fields?)

Our decision to move to the Midlands had very little, except in an undefined way, to do with the fact that John's family on both sides came from there. He had only lived in Derbyshire for four years as a child. We were, however, eager to see more of this part of the world.

The Rolleston estate was sold in 1928. It is now an estate of a different kind, with superior but ugly villas filling the area between the pretty black and cream lodges. John could hear the clopping of hooves in his mind's ear, but said it was a happy sound. I walked down to a dank tangled wood – the spinney and fish pond – where trees lie hazardously at an angle of 45 degrees to the ground, and the water is filled with overgrown rushes. It seemed very sad. A mother was walking her child in the wood. 'I believe there's a lot of history attached to it,' she said.

In the village they said 'there's a book on it in the library', and added, '*he* comes here sometimes'. But the Mosley eagle still spreads its wings on the pub, on gates, and in their chapel in the church under a Kempe window, memorials to many Oswalds, Nicholases, Edwards and Tonmans quietly line the walls. There is an alabaster monument of the Edward who bought the house, but his nose is broken, one can't trace likenesses.

> These eyes, these brows, were moulded out of his;
> This little abstract doth contain that large
> Which died in Geffrey, and the hand of time
> Shall draw this brief into as huge a volume.[4]

But I like to think there are closer resemblances between John and the 'John Bull' Mosley of whom Sir Oswald Mosley has written movingly in his autobiography. John Bull, like John, had diabetes, but more importantly was 'in every sense a child of nature . . . he was immediately and entirely disarmed by any appeal to compassion and suggestion of friendship. He was completely a man, and I greatly loved him. His simple and generous nature made him a most likeable person, and he evoked almost universal affection from all who met him . . . His life and being were rooted deep in English soil.'[5] He appears to have been unafraid of his emotions, and burst into tears when his grandson Oswald joined the Royal Flying Corps in 1914. Although not so immoderate as his father, Sir Tonman, who had a large area cut out of the table to accommodate his stomach, John Bull died after a heavy dinner, topped up with his favourite combination of walnuts and port, which seems a splendid way to go.

By the small remaining part of the house a balustrade still stands, some urns lie in the grass. Another villa is going up a few yards away.

*

From Rolleston, which must have been an idyllically pretty village, we went on towards Uttoxeter. Large cars sailed through the summer afternoon, homing towards well-tended acres. Much of the tenor of life goes on as it always has.

The road runs through flat country, with fields of wheat shifting like green velvet in the wind; past Sudbury, a mellow brick village where the Meynell hunt has its kennels. Beyond is Sudbury Hall, built by Mary Vernon in the early seventeenth century. I think this is the loveliest great house I have seen, and it is not yet as much visited as other National Trust houses. It is brick, but the bricks are criss-crossed by a pattern of darker blackish bricks, like wickerwork; the windows and portico are surrounded by curling stonework. It is utterly unremote, unpretentious, among its oak and beech trees. The architecture sings; if she only did this, Mary Vernon did enough.

Uttoxeter itself has nothing very remarkable about it. It is a market town. It looks a prosperous market town. There is a caravan park down by the racecourse. There is a somewhat melodramatic carved monument commemorating the famous penance of Dr Johnson, who stood with bared head in Uttoxeter market place in 1780 to atone for refusing one day as a boy to help on his father's bookstall. 'Pride was the source of that refusal . : . I went to Uttoxeter in very bad weather, and stood for a considerable time bareheaded in the rain.' The town seems self-sufficient, self-contained. There is nowhere for a traveller to get a cup of tea. But in a very English way there is life going on in an unadvertised corner if you know where to find it. Every evening the sports cars draw up and the White Hart Hotel becomes a magnet for the youth of what seems like the whole county. Walter, the genial head waiter, shows them, in their denims, into the immaculate, ancient, panelled dining room, and afterwards keeps a happy eye on the proceedings as the bar becomes crowded with farmers' sleek sons and landowners' unkempt sons and pretty blonde girls with wide eyes and mouths ridiculously and promisingly agape, waiting for a stranger – from London? – to walk through the door and take them from their small provincial town to somewhere where time doesn't stand still in the afternoon, where there is something other than munching cows to look at. The Tutbury Tup might have been delighted with them.

In fact the White Hart seems to have changed little over the years. There is a notice advertising 'brakes, wagonettes, dog carts and every description of carriage on the shortest notice for fishing, shooting, private or pleasure parties', and in 1806 they were meeting at the 'White Hart Assembly Rooms' to listen to a young lady giving a piano recital. It certainly seems merrier and more friendly here than in the Kings Road.

*

From here you can drive across the Roman road by Rocester, to the ruins of Croxden Abbey. This is another place where peace, by a dappled sycamore tree, is almost palpable; but there is also something more electrifying in the atmosphere. The shell of an immensely high West Front still stands, with three tall lancet windows pointing to the sky, following the line of the empty stone coffins of monks, lying in a field, rounded out with hard stone pillows for their heads. Where are their bones lying now? Clouds move behind the soaring arrows of the windows, which reach into a white infinity.

The coffin of the founder, Bertram de Verdun, is also here, the twelfth-century crusader who also built Alton Castle, a little to the north. A turreted nineteenth-century convent now stands on the site, perched on a precipitously rocky height above the River Churnet like a castle of the Rhine. On the other side of the valley are the famous gardens of Alton Towers, once the home of the Talbots, the 'Muriel Towers' of Disraeli's novel *Lothair*.

There are greater literary associations in Ellastone, once more by the Dove. This was the Hayslope of *Adam Bede* (George Eliot's father, on whom she modelled Adam, lived here), and Loamshire is Staffordshire.

In this, as in her other books, her piercing but generous portrayals of human nature seem to stem from the countryside she knew, so that a Victorian surface vapour is unimportant. Writing of the seduction of Hetty, her 'fallen' heroine – 'Such young unfurrowed souls roll to meet each other like two velvet peaches that touch softly and are at rest; they mingle as easily as two brooklets that ask for nothing but to entwine themselves and ripple with ever-interlacing curves in the leafiest hiding-places.' Surely she was thinking of the valley where the Manifold River meets the Dove, the valley which is nicknamed Paradise?

Dovedale stands in danger of being spoilt; the planning board of the Peak District National Park within which it lies is aware of this, and is organizing meetings and asking for public participation in plans to prevent it. Even on a wet day it is packed with walkers and hikers. Walkers are usually quiet and thoughtful people, but their presence in hundreds is bound to alter the appearance of what is after all a small fishing river, *the* small fishing river of Izaak Walton and Charles Cotton, whose little fishing house stands in an overgrown tangle of trees in Beresford Dale. However, one can still admire the deep, winding valley, and the dramatic jaws of the fish-like rock rising out of the tree-enclosed Pike Pool, and if one is lucky hear local lore from the water bailiff. The Izaak Walton Hotel holds fishing rights for two miles; it is an exclusive type of hotel, with the atmosphere that that implies. The day we called in, there was a high-powered head waiter, and a cross couple in the car park were trying to salvage their illicit weekend.

At Alstonefield, in a church that is the epitome of an English country church, there is pomander-like carving on rich oak pews, one of them Charles Cotton's. Outside, the hills stretch away, sheep feed; a farmer walks up a rounded field; the line of a grey limestone wall goes up a hill like its backbone. One becomes aware here that it is these drystone walls which make this part of the Peak District so light, so warm in colouring. There are no dark-green hedges. The light catches on the edges of the carefully-stacked walls, on the sides of the stone houses; everything is softly grey, and yellow with buttercups. A line of white sheep move across the horizon marching in single file like soldiers. Bees and a solitary curlew. At Milldale a field is as vertical as a cliff, with shorn golden grass reflecting the evening sun. This, or something like it, must be the Sunny Bank or Shining Tor marked on the map.

By comparison with Dovedale the valley of the Manifold is virtually unspoilt. It is overlooked by Thor's Cave, a primeval cleft in a cliff-face, with a ceiling ribbed like a fish's mouth. Adam Bede's remark on Eagle-dale (Dovedale) applies: 'I never had a right notion o' rocks till I went there'. With a cow bellowing overhead on the roof it is not difficult to feel like a caveman there, and remains have proved it was such a home.

The Manifold runs underground in this part of the valley in summer. By the riverbed are clouds of dark blue cranesbill flowers, and dog roses so large that they seem like another species. Derbyshire is famous for its roses, and this is after all only just across the border. I will swear that birds sing louder here.

The Leek and Manifold Light Railway used to run along the valley, but it was closed down for lack of use. A farmer's wife who has lived at Wetton for forty-six years remembers when she was the only passenger on the train, going to school in Leek. She confirms that the Manifold Valley is unchanged. We stayed with her, and watched her cook for her four men – husband, son and two grandsons, round the kitchen table. In the next room hang antiques which she will not sell to the antique dealer who comes sniffing round to buy; the sheep castrating tool is more brightly polished than the fine gun; there are copper skillets and a shepherd's crook of nut wood. 'There's not much to shoot now – only hares. The wood's full of *couples* – you disturb them if you go there and they've disturbed the wild life away.'

In the winter she cooks oatcakes twice a week for tea 'to get the kitchen warm for when the men come in'. Then, the snow is on the ground, and 'the nights get long'. A peak of the summer is the Royal Show; this year it rained and she got rheumatism which will stop her digging in her garden. 'You have to keep going, haven't you?' Amusements in the village have perhaps lost some of their blood. There was a wedding, and it was said there would be 'beer stirring', free drinks. After closing time the landlord brought out a glass drinking-horn and offered its contents free to any man who could drink it in one quaff – 'You pay me if you fail.' None of the crimsoning young men ventured. Time was when a man drank half a gallon without lifting his mouth from the horn.

They have television, 'but there's a lot of rubbish, isn't there . . . a lot of filth . . . We're great readers, all five of us.' And at the door looking out to the fields: 'You've got to count your blessings. If you look around there's a lot to be thankful for . . .'

How pleased Izaak would have been.

I could there sit quietly; and looking on the water, see some fishes sport themselves in the silver streams, others leaping at flies of several shapes and colours; looking on the hills, I could behold them spotted with woods and groves; looking down the meadows, could see, here a boy gathering lilies and lady-smocks, and there a girl cropping culverkeys and cowslips.

And this, and many other like blessings, we enjoy daily. And for the most of them, because they be so common, most men forget to pay their praises: but let not us; because it is a sacrifice so pleasing to Him that made that sun and us, and still protects us, and gives us flowers, and showers, and stomachs, and meat, and content, and leisure to go a-fishing.[6]

In the Five Towns there was nothing. You might walk from one
end of the Five Towns to the other, and not see one object that
gave a thrill – unless it was a pair of lovers.

Arnold Bennett, *These Twain*[1]

'You wouldn't think Staffordshire could be so different,' said the owner of
a small café, as he continued drying up in a sunlit back room, having given
me my tea. I had said I came from Wolverhampton, and that the people
there were very different from Stoke people. He knew what I meant at
once, and continued talking about his town, about the old days when it
was 'terribly smoky from the coke'. 'But this sun can be a bit too hot,' he
added, as if unused to the brave new world.

In our conversation lies the difference. In South Staffordshire, gleaning
the human content for a book can be like trying to chip flint with a
butter knife; people seldom talk to you unasked, and when asked, offer
the bare minimum of information. Conversation does not flow; extrovert
behaviour, let alone a mood of euphoria, is strikingly absent. But walk
down a street in the Potteries, or go into a pub, and the feel of the place
laps round you warmly, promisingly. A mood of expansiveness grips you
because here man actually seems anxious to speak to man; hospitality
assumes giant proportions.

I don't think one person spoke to me on a recent visit without ending
the sentence with 'love'; or if not that, 'duck'. A woman, seeing me come
away from a potbank, ran after me in the street to offer information,
gripping my arm with a smile; a church caretaker also ran after me with
her trolley of cleaning materials to ask if I wanted to see inside the locked
church, threatened with demolition ('Well, we fought, duck'); a man
walking his dog in the park was so brimming with anecdotes that we
walked three times to Hanley market square and back together, regardless
of time. 'And that's where the old Port Vale football ground was, you
know Port Vale? I was born over there in Sneyd Street (he pronounced it
Snee) – that's where the Sneyd colliery was where the colonel, or lord, I

forget which but a gentleman anyway, got all his money from . . . looking down from these hills over the town pre-war you could see nothing but black smoke down there . . . that on the hill at Cobridge is the Little Sisters of Mercy home for the aged, very nice . . . and (with pride) that will be the new Tesco.'

Football, coal, the grime from bottle-ovens, a large proportion of elderly residents, new town planning; old and new threads in the strand that makes up Stoke, itself made up from the six towns of the Potteries.

In Josiah Wedgwood's day lonely farms, muddy lanes and hawthorn hedges lay round Burslem and separated it from his new works at Etruria; overhanging tree branches shaded the path from Etruria to Hanley and women returning from market travelled together after sundown for fear of ghosts.[2]

Before the war, a woman who lives in the country told me she used to be brought by her parents to the hills overlooking Stoke and was shown the black inferno of smoke and belching chimneys. 'And we were frightened, because we thought Hell would be like that.'

After the war –

'The phrase "planner's nightmare",' David Sekers at the Gladstone Pottery Museum told me, 'was coined for Stoke.'

And now –

'It's your future we're planning,' recent posters advertising structure plans told the residents. 'We need your help.'

Bulldozers are at work round the modern City Museum and Art Gallery with its outstanding collection of pottery and porcelain; near by the ground is razed for Tesco, C & A being already there; in the new parks sapling trees stand like wands in the wind, a modern echo of the little forest planted by the great Josiah to beautify his works; there is little smoke now; the small houses of the Five Towns can stretch in the sun; yet in some indefinable way the place seems not so much changed as unchanging. Or is it that, although so traditional, Stoke is what we may be going towards?

*

The six towns, since Arnold Bennett's Five Towns omitted Fenton – Longton, Fenton, Stoke-upon-Trent, Hanley, Burslem and Tunstall – are incoherently coherent. A long road links them from north to south. The city, Stoke-on-Trent, was formed in 1910, and the original town of Stoke is the administrative centre – and also the home of the Stoke City football club. Coming from Stafford by train, through flat farmland

and water-meadows, beside the River Trent and the Trent and Mersey Canal, you arrive at Stoke station. This is a listed building, in the same style as the North Stafford Hotel facing it; mellow brick with diamonds of black, white crenellations, towering above the little houses near by. In front of the hotel is a statue of Josiah Wedgwood. Three giants in a desert they seem at first glance.

I had felt anxious and keyed-up approaching Stoke. I had never been there, but had heard much about it. I love beautiful china, and the names Minton, Spode, Copeland are to me the stuff legends are made of, as evocative as the words Parthenon or Delphi must be to some people. And at Stoke, surely, they would be mixed with something more earthy, in this home of mankind's first craft? the craft shaped from earth. Could the place live up to such expectations?

Gradually, and then overwhelmingly, I saw it could. Local maps were out of print and I had no idea where to go from the station. Almost at once I was outside the North Stafford Polytechnic, with students hurrying past, music sounding loudly from the buildings and 'Fight for Grant' and 'Student Occupation' painted across the windows of a new office block. Purposeful, anyway. I retraced my steps to find the large Town Hall, and St Peter's Church, which has plaques to three Josiah Spodes, to William Taylor Copeland – Master Potter – and, above two little vases, a monument of Wedgwood with a face to which one can apply that odd term 'speaking'. Not surprisingly, as it was shaped by the great sculptor Flaxman. Less mentioned by guide books are the warmly-coloured tiles all round the church: on the floor, in the apse and chancel; as diamond-shaped brown-and-yellow memorials round the pink plaster walls; even outside, on tombs. As I wandered back through the streets of seemingly tiny houses, each row with different scrollwork or decoration on the plaster above windows, as if cut by a potter's thumbnail, I could say, it *is* a pottery place. It *is* different.

By the station the canal is much in evidence; also blue-and-white Wedgwood vans; derelict gaps. Also, and I must let it speak for itself, the large sign, 'Jones and Shufflebottom Ltd, Sanitary Specialists'. John will be delighted, I thought. He had told me 'Stoke isn't just your fancy china you know, I want a shot of a street full of lavatories piled up.' (The Shufflebottoms must be a family, or families of substance; in the museum a cannier one had made a bequest under an adaptation – 'beothom', I think – of the name.) Stoke is china, sanitary ware, hotel ware, fireplaces, tiles, mementoes and 'fancies', as well as Queen's Ware.

*

The most northerly of the six towns, Tunstall, has been described by Mervyn Jones in his book *Potbank* as the prettiest. His descriptions of Stoke are marvellously apt and witty. Of the houses:

All are built in brick . . . deep red brick . . . The colour is invincible; it has not been blackened by the smoke of ages, like stone or brick of a softer colour. It has only been darkened to a solemn shade of maroon – crimson in sunlight, near to blue in the rain – the colour of old scars or of a drunkard's cheeks.

Of the people:

They had the type of face which I kept seeing in the Potteries – a face which appeared to have been put in a vice and squeezed from above and below, making the flesh ooze out in soft pink bulges of cheeks and chins. In this face, the eyes and mouth were diminished and a pair of spectacles was the only distinguishable feature.[3]

I recognized this face at once; it is also a remarkably sensitive face, often with blue or grey eyes, even more often with fair or gingerish, frizzy hair, in marked contrast to the dark type of Staffordshire man. Is there a Celtic outpost here, in these wide-browed, pale faced, musical people?

Tunstall was the home of another writer, C. Shaw, whose book *When I Was a Child* gives a picture of the horrendous conditions in which children worked in the potteries in the 1840s. It is a most moving book. Bennett used it as source material for his novel *Clayhanger*. Shaw tells how as a child of seven he worked, or rather literally 'sweated' from five in the morning until six or eight at night; of small children heaving and pounding clay and lifting moulds on to shelves in the burning hot stove-rooms, while older potters drunkenly abstained from working on Mondays and engaged in orgies; of indifferent works' owners; of the pottery riots in support of the Chartists and families reduced to starvation by the Corn Laws, with only Shaftesbury and a few like Carlyle and Mrs Barrett Browning raising their voices for better conditions. He quotes Lord Brougham for instance as saying 'charity is an interference with a healing process of nature, which acts by increasing the rate of mortality and thereby raising wages'. An attitude perhaps applied by some in our wider world to distant, unseen places – since there are always people who want to keep their eyes closed. Strangely, this book in many ways could have been written today. There are personal passages, as when he tells heart-breakingly of how on a day 'full of sweet stillness', a day 'when you feel that that is the first spring day, even though it may come long after spring time has gone' he saw a boy walking along reading a book and realized for the first time his own condition. 'I had acquired a strong passion for reading, and the sight of this youth reading at his own free will, forced upon my mind a sense of painful contrast between his position and mine . . . I can remember, though never describe, the acuteness of this first sorrow.' Other passages are on general themes, true now as then. 'We glibly talk of "better times", but this hurrying and superficial generation seldom thinks that these times are richer for the struggles and blood of those who went before them, as the early harvests of the plains of Waterloo were said to be richer after the carnage of the great battle fought there.' ' "Knowledge comes, but wisdom lingers", and no wisdom seems to linger so much as that of statesmanship where vested interests are in the way.'[4]

*

But there was pottery in Stoke long before Victorian days. South of Tunstall lies Burslem, where the trade was flourishing in the seventeenth century with the making of butter pots by farmer-potters. (The pots were long cylinders holding about 14 lb. Burslem was called 'Butter Pottery'.) Kilns dating from the thirteenth century have been found near there, and a Roman potbank, the only one found in England.

It was in Burslem that Josiah Wedgwood was born in 1730, and his great achievements coincided with and enhanced the impetus which made the region a booming centre for the supply of fine tableware, with services for the newly fashionable tea and coffee. In 1730 there were under 4,000 people in the modern Stoke-on-Trent area; the number had nearly doubled in a little over thirty years.

A bad attack of smallpox when he was twelve left Josiah with a painful knee, and he had to abandon the thrower's bench and turn his attention to other branches of the trade. But one can't doubt that he would have been a great man even if this turn of fate hadn't forced him to study the potter's art in its entirety. Great in every sense. He read voraciously, and once wrote, 'My wife says I must buy no more books till I build another house'. (A remark constantly being made to us.) He had many friends; was generous, very seldom doing accounts; loved plants and shells and in later life spent much time on his garden at Etruria Hall, growing rare fruits and plants in beautiful vases. He wrote lively and witty letters. To his partner Thomas Bentley, advice to give to one contesting an election:

RECEIPT. Bullocks roasted whole – Quantum sufficit. 6 small Cannon to be fired at every vote gained from the Enemy. A Fighting Captain to be made use of occasionally with the wavering & timerous. Get the Scaigs (a person well known in Tamworth) to make *quere faces*. A Poet is absolutely necessary and may be heard of at Birm^m.

Besides being an artist, inventor and administrator, he worked to promote turnpike roads in a roadless region and played a large part in the planning of Brindley's Trent and Mersey Canal, the vital new artery of the area, bringing it the life blood of expansion. He was farsighted in seeing the American Plantations as a promising export market. Yet possibly he was greatest of all in his championship of the Society for the Abolition of Slavery. The design he commissioned for the society, with the famous inscription 'Am I not a man and a brother' was made into seals to be sold and given away. It was worn as rings, shirt-pins, coat buttons, ladies' hairpins. A sharp reminder among the tinkling teacups.

A visit to the present-day Wedgwood works at Barlaston, and the museum there, enables one to see the range of his art. Green-glazed and mottled ware made when he was a partner of Whieldon, jasper medallions (Garrick and Sarah Siddons: amazing how much character in the small pieces), jewellery, friezes, vases, 'piecrust' ware used instead of pastry when flour was short during the Napoleonic wars, a bas-relief made by George Stubbs, who visited him, and toy coffee pots made by a later Wedgwood for the children of Charles Darwin (one of Erasmus Darwin's sons married Wedgwood's daughter Susannah). Also examples of the famous cream-coloured earthenware, named Queen's Ware when it received Queen Charlotte's approval: pieces of the 952-piece service made for the Empress Catherine of Russia, and, to my mind loveliest of all, early cream ware with very simple designs of grasses and leaves, from his interest in botany.

The factory is set in the middle of fields. It seems very rural. I was directed through frozen plough by a commissionaire, and on my way back was given a message to take to the level-crossing keeper at the railway halt to say his granddaughter wouldn't be coming to stay as she had measles. Here girls from Wedgwood's wait for the bus to go back to the boutiques in the town. They are pretty, as are the things in the dress shops. There is a gracefulness here, lacking in much of the Midlands. Some of the girls wear china medallions on their coats. In the decorating shop you see them bending studiously over the cups and plates, their hair often tied back round a George-Eliot-like face; there seemed to be a lot of Roman noses. Each girl makes her own mark on ware she has painted; the brushes are very long, hands unwavering. They come straight from school at sixteen and are trained for two years without previous art-school training.

This is of course the most glamorous department. 'It depends which department you are in,' an older woman told me heavily. Others press, carry and hump, or painstakingly fit on transfers or raised motifs. But the factory seems very quiet after those in the Black Country. A thrower will work on about six shapes a day. They have the faces of craftsmen, and hands which dart and grow like sea creatures, with delicate fingers flattened out to spatulas. There is clearly great skill even in the more modern casting techniques, or throwing on to moulds. It is difficult to gauge the tedium involved in the more repetitive jobs. At another manu-facturers it seemed hotter and more dusty, faces less happy. A little sixteen-year-old with pasty white arms was rubbing a transfer on a patterned pot lid with soft soap – lid after lid. I asked her if it was boring and her little yawning eyes filled with tears as she nodded yes, and tried to look bright as she told me she would learn how to do the next stage up, which appeared marginally less tedious. But the guide was delightfully friendly and uninformative, and seemed most preoccupied with whether we wanted to wash – 'We can't come back this way'. In marked contrast to the more highly organized Wedgwood visits, which would delight Josiah: coffee from beautiful white pots and, an eye on the American Plantations, a black bust of Dwight D. Eisenhower at £38.50, in the seconds shop among stylized oven-to-table, detergent-and-washer-proof ware, and attention drawn to the plate 'our Queen Mother has'.

'My,' said a smart couple from the United States, 'you can't think what a thrill it is.' They were watching the service they owned being painted – one of the more ornate designs. 'Thank goodness we bought it then, it's £30 a place setting back home now.' It had tripled in price in a year.

The Wedgwood group are planning to double their capacity with a long-term expansion programme costing some £9 million, hoping the market will keep up.

'It's all right for you,' said a man as I walked away from the factory past clay-dusted hedgerows. 'You're going and I'm having to coom.'

*

Stoke is classless, if anywhere in England is; a warm, working place; as Bennett pointed out 'the people of the Five Towns have no particular use of half-measures in any department of life'.[5]

I am sitting in the snug small wine bar in the Queen's Head in Burslem and can see this is true. I am staying at the George Hotel where once there were bloody riots but now are modern bricks and comforts, have eaten warmly and well at an Indian restaurant, the only restaurant it seems, after that wild, cold dash through deserted, restaurant-less streets. They must have taken home their oatcakes from the two women smilingly flipping them from iron slabs, or potato cakes from Hanley market, or possibly – such is my nostalgic mood – after a game of billiards beneath the fringed lights in the fourteen-table saloon (a nice place for a sit, too) be eating grilled fish caught with the aid of supplies from 'A and A . . . Everything for the Angler' where the sign sports a gilded fish and an Edwardian fisherman. Or be at the Burslem public library behind its ornate pink Wedgwood Institute friezes, or watching *Elvira Madigan* at one of several Stoke film clubs.

They come and go at the pub. Plump, innocent faces smile. They open the door and beam and say hullo to the room at large and talk cheerfully and without self-consciousness about national insurance and graduated pensions and football and the cinema. The woman sitting opposite me, plumper and more smiling even than the others, under her flat hat, begins singing softly and musically to herself. We shout across to each other. 'There are too many Bingos,' she says. 'I never go.' And she tells me how lovely Roger Moore was at Screen 3, which is very nice because small and you can't hear Screens 1 or 2. And Moore visited the countries out where her son had been. And she had loved the film so much and become so excited that she had lost her silver bracelet, had worked it off her wrist in her excitement and never noticed for a week it had gone. 'Well, you don't wear bracelets every day.' Her enjoyment, and the fact that she hadn't noticed that a possession of value had gone, both struck me like thunderclaps, here in the Midlands. Well, you don't see them every day.

*

'Arnold Bennett Novelist and Playwright was born here 27 May 1867.' The plaque is on the wall of what is now the Five Towns Café, which is definitely a caff – small, with plastic much in evidence. How Bennett would have hated it. It represents in its bleakest form all that he ran away to London, and to success, to avoid. Because like so many talented provincials his one idea was to get to London, and in his first novel *A Man from the North* he gives a picture of such an escape. John Wain, another native of the Potteries, echoes the feeling in his autobiography *Sprightly Running*,[6] speaking of himself 'coming straight from the most provincial of the provinces', and describing Longton where he once went to school as 'one of the most squalid and depressing of the Pottery towns'. But Bennett, for all his yachts and Grand Hotel inclinations, admirably, almost despite himself, shows the other side of Stoke. It is there in all his Five Towns novels, and particularly in a short story 'The Death of Simon Fugue', in which an inhibited Londoner comes to the Potteries, and is amazed at the mud, the oblivion to outside events, the wholehearted hospitality and intoxicating sense of friendship, the generating of local myths, idiosyncratic habits, and even – artists. Unrecognized locally, of course.

It is a two-way process that one perhaps doesn't analyse often enough. It certainly never occurred to me in my twenties to work anywhere other than in London, although I was not born there. It is a process which Margaret Drabble has used as a theme in her work, and her biography of Arnold Bennett stresses it as a starting point. She has beautifully pinpointed his quality as a novelist – 'deeply moving, original, and dealing with material that I had never before encountered in fiction, but only in life'.[7] I hadn't read his novels before, and they strike me as amazingly suited to present-day taste: his inability sometimes to understand people, his feeling that women in particular can be unpredictable and mysterious, has resulted in him letting characters speak for themselves, act unexpectedly so that one has all the interplay of life, seen from different angles, and not that quality so beloved of the English in their fiction, the portrayal of 'real characters'. His depiction of a marriage in *These Twain* is a case in point. The quarrels are sublime. He would also have understood our irritation, I feel, on finding on a wet Saturday afternoon that number 205 Waterloo Road, where he lived as a young man, now a museum and shabbily Victorian and small, was shut, at least half an hour after the specified opening time on one of the few opening days.

*

We had in this instance ignored that first law of exploration, that you have to discover a place for yourself. Then you will get the authentic tightening of the throat, head expanding with excitement. Which I experienced looking down the long road between Hanley and Burslem across at Cobridge Church on its hill, and narrow parallel rows of red-brick houses like a child's toy world. Or walking along this long road, the view from Bursley Road to the west, with the sun going down in white mist, pierced by a spire, and below the skyline pierced again by tall chimneys – the Shelton Steel works – and more rows of houses, just emerging through the whiteness. The Potteries can be beautiful. I was very glad to have seen them first on a misty day, with the haze lapping round the dark bricks, the curve of a bottle-oven solid and small and changeless in a smoky landscape under the yellow ball of the sun. In the past the fog would have been black, but it must still have been dramatic.

There are not many bottle-ovens left. There were 2,000 in existence after the last war; now there are only about twenty. There is one, not used as a kiln, in the works of Dudson Brothers of Hanley – potters since 1800 – makers of vitrified hotelware. Here you get the atmosphere of a traditional down-to-earth potbank, with wheelbarrows of clay scurrying past and tougher conditions. 'You can't get the young ones into it,' a woman who works there told me (referring to the smaller works). 'They'll do decorating but not the heavy clay work. There aren't the facilities like at Wedgwood.' And there is also the health hazard of the trade, from clay dust, partly eradicated in Stoke but not entirely. I saw sore eyes in various works, also. But she was very cheerful and roundly content. 'It's hard, heavy work, but I enjoy it . . . I like it because I've been in it all my life.'

Which doesn't seem such a bad reason, when you think about it, and is typical of the Potteries.

But Stoke isn't entirely traditionalism, or pottery. There are the coal mines, now mostly on the outskirts, as at Trentham and Longton. There is an inventive streak which one can see back in Josiah Wedgwood's day and in the experiments of his son Tom, whose discoveries foreshadowed the first principles of photography – he could throw objects on paper prepared with nitrate of silver from 'light produced from different bodies by heat and attrition', but could not find the way to fix them there. (This was nearly half a century before the date usually applied to the discovery.) There is in the centre of Hanley, the next town going south after Burslem, a model of the Spitfire invented by Reginald Mitchell, the designer born at near-by Talke, usually surrounded by eager schoolboys and fathers. The old Hanley Theatre has been pulled down, but there are many concerts, and the Victoria Theatre at Stoke is one of the most lively and successful in England, often putting on plays with local themes.

Hanley provides the inevitable shopping centre for the six towns, and suffers thereby. But it still has a flourishing flower and plant market, and one of those enviable indoor markets. The modern building of the public library is a smaller but no less comfortable or well-stocked version of the new Birmingham library. The town's lodestone is the Museum and Art Gallery, with a collection of pottery and porcelain hardly rivalled in the world. Josiah Wedgwood's throwing wheel is here; there is clay in the crevices of the wood; I couldn't resist sitting on its bench with my hands in the lead trough round the wheel, challenging time. There are early 'toys' or figures made by Ralph Wood (the firm of H. J. Wood is still manufacturing in Burslem); New Hall teapots; canary lustre ware; a large vase painted for Wedgwood by E. Lessore, as fine as any painting; examples of Staffordshire blue china, which was later brought to perfection by the Josiah Spodes – the first of whom was hired as an apprentice by Whieldon for 7/-[35p] a week, 'hired Josiah Spoad for night martlemas 1 week 0-7-0', and whose 1770 site houses the lovely old factory buildings of the present factory. In those days master potters worked alongside their men with sometimes as little as 10/-[50p] a week profit.

There is Italian maiolica, Japanese raku, Turkish and Persian pottery. John called me over to a small blue and white piece of china, a Persian gravestone. The inscription to a heavenly maker touchingly reads: 'Since I am nothing at all it were best if thou wouldst swiftly take my hand . . .'

There is an equal simplicity in huge brown and yellow platters and mugs by Ralph and Thomas Toft. I don't think any ware can rival this seventeenth-century Staffordshire slipware; naïve, golden, smiling, with childlike designs and disregard for inessentials – names are sometimes spelt Ralph Oft, or Ralpph Toft. And there are tygs, a pleasing name for burgeoning multi-handled Kentish mugs.

*

In Fenton and Longton, the two most southerly towns of the six, you can get the atmosphere of the Potteries well. Longton is also known as 'Neck End' and is said to be a bit rough. Here there are narrow terraces, with pensioners standing outside their doors, a game of football going on at the end of the row. Small and large pottery works abound. In a window in King Street, Fenton, we saw an assembly of pudding bowls, earthenware breadbins, chamber pots, a china phrenologist's head and souvenirs or 'fancies'. A bottle-oven rears its head by Longton Parish Church. Beyond Longton town centre is the Gladstone Museum, which is the product of co-operation between preservationists, industry and planners (but not Wedgwood, who 'have their own show', and who have 'let the eighteenth-century factory at Etruria go'). After the war, when Stoke had to be replanned, the city wanted a clean sweep, which also meant pulling down the obsolete bottle-ovens. A few are preserved here at the museum, which is a working museum showing how a Victorian potbank was geared. There is a steam engine, slip is mixed by the old method and pottery is made. 'A man in a pub asked me to sign Toft on one of my plates,' said a potter working there, as he turned out a brown slipware Toft-like plate. 'He was serious, too,' he said in a shocked voice.

David Sekers is the museum director, very approachable and informative. 'We've just bought an 1840 lavatory; it's out in the yard if you want to have a look.' It was a two-tier contraption, aptly called, someone thought, the 'tripper' or 'tipper'. Eventually the museum will also have Victorian potter's houses, and will include a science museum of ceramics, the first to be created.

*

Stoke is showing great imagination in planning and reclamation. In 1968 when the reclamation programme began, Stoke-on-Trent had more derelict land than any other county borough in the country – about 2,000 acres – caused by coal-mining, the extraction of marl – for pottery, bricks and tiles – steelworks, and the railways. Now it has an unbeatable record in the field of reclamation. Great efforts are also being made to clean up the River Trent. In 1970 the Upper Trent was the most polluted river in the country, but now it is hoped that there will be fish and swimming again. Tips and waste land are being reclaimed, nature trails and green walkways created.

As at the new 'Forest Park' at Hanley.

'It's all grass and cinders,' said an old woman disgustedly, about this. 'Very rough walking, but it doesn't seem too bad if there are two or three of you, does it?' (Trentham Gardens are Stoke's traditional pleasure ground.)

But the grass and saplings will grow, in time. Some of the planners' plans will succeed, without, probably, over-streamlining the city. In the old potter C. Shaw's day he was able to make the interesting observation that the lack of machinery to be set and regulated in the pottery trade, and therefore the potters' freedom to come and go, made it difficult to organize the workers and streamline them into trade unions. This no longer applies. The ceramic union is well organized, but because the pottery trade was traditionally composed of many small family firms as well as the larger concerns, a family feeling and sense of community have given the place a very good record for the low number of labour disputes. Yet an independent trait seems still to be there in the people of this conglomerate city – a city which reminds one sometimes of a painting by Lowry or Grandma Moses. Conditions have changed, new suburbs have sprung up, but character goes on. Possibly many of us would like to work more independently, near our homes as many potters do, see our towns and our work linked more naturally and vitally, providing a sense of identity and freedom for individuals.

'Some MPs think that there should be many more other industries here,' a spokesman for the British Pottery Manufacturers' Federation told me. He didn't agree. He saw the industry holding up well, although orders are not what they were, in this difficult economic era. Manufacturers have long order books, however, and the strain has not been felt yet, although there is some short time in tiles and sanitary ware to date. There is and has been a shortage of labour in some of the grades of workers.

In tableware and domestic ware, 50 per cent of the trade is for export. (35 per cent in tiles and sanitary ware.) The EEC is the largest market after the US and Canada for porcelain and china household ware, and 1974 showed an increase in both of these markets over 1973. In 1975, figures in money terms for porcelain and china household-ware exports were again up.

It is fascinating to peruse the export lists, and imagine porcelain sailing or winging off to Laos and Bangladesh, Saudi Arabia and even £150-worth to Vietnam. Oman seems to import a huge amount of china. 'Electroceramics' are of course an important line. Ornamental ware is on its way to Qatar and Hungary, Venezuela and Gabon. 'Sanitary ware' is no doubt being trundled to Germany, Western, and the PDR of Yemen, St Helena, the Faroes and Tonga. Are they using our plumbing in Sao Tome-Princ?

*

'I have constantly pressed in the House of Commons for new modern industries to be attracted to Stoke-on-Trent,' said Jack Ashley, Labour MP for Stoke-on-Trent South. 'There are three staple industries (pottery, steel – the Shelton Steel Works – and coal – the Hem Heath and Florence Collieries being in his constituency), but they are not expanding in terms of manpower. To have the future of the city resting on so few industries and contracting in the sense of manpower is highly dangerous. It could be affected by world conditions at any time . . . there's no point in waiting until we're ruined.'

He said his first speech in Stoke had been on the need to diversify industry, to attract new modern industries and promote training schemes. When the Michelin factory came, they had no trouble in finding workers and it is now a very profitable concern. 'The value of an amiable work-force is invaluable these days – Stoke has had very few labour disputes.' He would even like to see civil service departments moved to North Staffordshire, and felt the employees would appreciate living in such a beautiful area.

He speaks as one who knows about labour disputes, having become a member of his union's national executive council at the age of twenty-two, when he was working at a copper factory in Widnes. I had read about this and his work as a labourer before going to university, in his autobiography *Journey into Silence*,[8] which is beautifully written. Knowing that he had, for instance, wheeled heavy copper bars to the furnace on a truck, I was surprised that he is quite slight in appearance. He is extremely quick and volatile – even his hair, though fine, looks full of determination and energy – and he has a tremendous sense of humour.

I asked what year he was awarded his Companion of Honour.

'What year was my CH?' he called to his wife, Pauline.

It was 1975. 'Jack's terrible about years,' she said.

In 1974 he was elected West Midlands Man of the Year, by radio, television and newspaper editors. I suppose to most people he seems, as he does to me, to be the conscience of Westminster. 'I happen to be interested in the underprivileged,' he says, simply.

He began his political career campaigning for better housing conditions in Widnes. His constituency in Stoke contains some of the poor areas and some of the best areas (such as Trentham). He has fought in the past for better pensions, and one scheme which he started in Stoke was named 'Operation Snowball', because MPs elsewhere adopted his tactics. He wrote a leaflet of which 10,000 copies were distributed, setting out the benefits such as heating allowances and entitlements to bedding and clothing to which the elderly are entitled, in an attempt to safeguard anyone at risk against hypothermia. Stoke, with a largish elderly population, is active in helping pensioners. At Longton there are lunch clubs, and Jack Ashley would like to see these extended to daily events, as places to meet over a hot lunch. As I write he is campaigning for more help for unemployed school leavers, and also suggesting temporary public work for them, to 'help bridge a dangerous and dispiriting gap'.

I asked him if he would like to see more power given to the regions. His reply was definite, affirmative. 'We've got to fight for what we get as a region and area . . . if we don't do it, no one will do it for us . . . London thinks of London by and large . . . if they think of Watford, that's a miracle.' He also felt that North Staffordshire should be regarded as a special region. It has its own industries, doesn't necessarily benefit from the prosperity of the West Midlands in prosperous times. It was clear he appreciates the region. 'In London, people don't have this rich local culture.' (Of which the *Sentinel* in Stoke gives the flavour very well, combined with national news.)

Had he ever lost faith in the working class? I asked.

'I was born into the working class, you know . . . My faith in them is as firm as ever it was . . . more realistic perhaps.' He said some problems were exaggerated, our strike record for instance being four times better than that of the Americans. That 'when I had setbacks', when he became totally deaf, they showed him by their willingness to help that they had the right values. 'I don't want to generalize . . .'

'What would you most like to achieve for Stoke?'

'To fulfil the potentialities of the people I represent. They have a tremendous potential for happiness and skill.' To create a better environment and improve educational facilities and social services. To achieve a better and more mixed economic structure. He would like to see more training schemes, so that people could be retrained and the younger ones acquire new skills.

A very positive answer. He has a very positive outlook. He seems to have that rare trait, a belief in the quality of happiness, that it is everyone's right, possible of achievement. One feels that for him it is not enough just to endure stoically – that he would ask of himself and others, and for others, an active enjoyment and optimism.

'A tremendous potential for happiness . . . I happen to be interested in the underprivileged . . .'

The 'stinking ditch'

Kidderminster is a town of carpets, Stourport of canals. As regards charm, the canal town wins hands down. Bewdley, which in the eighteenth century declined to have the Staffordshire and Worcestershire Canal built on its doorstep, calling it a 'stinking ditch', had the edge over both for some time, but today traffic sweeps through the streets of the happily situated Severn-side town.

Kidderminster had been a cloth-weaving town since at least the thirteenth century, and carpet weaving was introduced in the mid-eighteenth, and still goes on today. The small factories of the nineteenth-century family businesses are the most striking feature of the town – there is a proliferation of tall chimneys and decorative warehouses, which give character to otherwise ugly streets of small houses or soulless super-markets. But undoubtedly you have to dig for it in Kidderminster. The tall church has been cut off from the centre and from the Georgian Church Street by a ring road, in what seems a mood of wanton perverse-ness. There is a hum of industry from the carpet works, but suntanned Worcestershire people who are not working seem to be hurrying back to the outskirts. Outside the door of a tall multi-storey housing block I saw an old woman in long skirt and apron, her white hair neatly pinned back, her cheeks rosy, looking out wistfully at the urban daylight, misplaced without her cottage as in one of those pictures in which you have to spot the wrong element.

Below Stourbridge one is emerging from the Black Country, leaving behind a certain harshness for something more rural, leisurely. One begins to notice the plump, unhurried faces of farmer's wives out shopping; middle-class couples out on a workday in pale clothes and large car, driving far more slowly than anyone in the Black Country would deign to do; a certain retirement from the gritty nub of things.

Many of the large cars pull up at the Tontine Hotel in Stourport, which is one of those towns so attractive that they survive their own popularity.

To date Stourport is relatively unspoilt. Created as a canal town, when Brindley (the great canal engineer of the first, Bridgewater, canal of 1761 and of 365 miles of inland waterways) brought the Staffordshire and Worcestershire Canal to the junction of the Stour and Severn, in 1771. Bewdley, a centre for the earlier Severn river traffic, had refused to become part of the canal network. So round the basin at Stourport were built the fine canal buildings: Georgian red brick terrace cottages and wharfs, the Tontine Inn which was originally five houses used by hop merchants, and a red-brick warehouse with a white cupola, which is now the Stourport Yacht Club. It is uncluttered as if still in the canal era, a superb arrangement of low buildings and white lock woodwork, surrounded by a maze of locks, then streets of Georgian houses spreading from the town centre, with the rush of the Severn water below the sloping lawns of the Tontine.

I asked a woman who lives in one of the early cottages in Mart Lane what it was like living in 'An Ancient Monument ... Of Special Historic Interest'. She smiled broadly and said 'these will be up when the other ones are down' waving at her elegant bay window. Like most of the canal-side people I have talked to, or those working on canals, Mrs Brown doesn't at all regret the coming of pleasure boats and holidaymakers. They seem to have brought back colour and life to the dying waterways, and there is a pleasing lack of overnostalgic whimsiness. Boat people are practical, and even amateurs need to be professional on the water.

'I was nine months old when I came to live here,' she told me. 'I've lived here ever since. These were the very first houses. They belong to British Waterways. We've had some really good fun really ... All the carpets and vinegar used to go by canal; there were barrels banging, and the boats. Then the cows and sheep and pigs used to be driven down this lane to the slaughterhouse and they often fell in the canal ... the pigs would be trying to swim ... they cut their own throats with their trotters when they swim, you know.'

Clearly modern life can't quite match up to that. But there must be watery disasters enough. By an arcaded barn or warehouse on the canal, I met a couple standing disconsolately by their boat (most of the craft here are motor cruisers, not narrow boats as at the Birmingham Gas Street Basin, and there are many firms hiring and building boats, such as the Severn Valley Cruisers or Canal Pleasurecraft). 'We should have been on the river by now,' the couple said, and pointed to a boat moored to theirs. 'But our friend's engine ...'

I have a hollow feeling that if I ever indulge in a canal holiday, it will be like that. I remember John asking an enthusiast at a canal regatta if he often had to dive in to free the propeller. 'Yes,' he replied, fixing us with a testing eye. 'Even for matchsticks.' How many matchsticks there must be in those 2,000 miles of waterways.

Beyond the Tontine Hotel, where holidaymakers were recovering beerily or downing a quick noggin before the off, in a bar with a skylight and glowing glass painted with Victorian moss roses, I found a more experienced hand, who had been living on his boat there for several years and working in a chainworks. He told me it was very quiet during the week, and it was a beautiful mooring, on the wide river. He was just about to sail to Cape Town, with one crew. He pointed out that this was a more risky venture than on a yacht (his motor cruiser looked very small) as there was no ballast, for a start. He wouldn't be coming back to Stourport, but obviously it has been a workable existence there, and preferable to a commuter's lot for anyone wanting to take stock or amass funds, or exist contemplatively as the fishermen on the opposite bank.

I wandered on, down the towpath, through alleyways between old factory walls as narrow as towpaths. Stourport is a surprisingly busy place, with metal clanking and timber piled in yards. A tangy, cool smell of vinegar was wafting down to the river. It must be one of the best smells on a hot day, a complete antidote to heat. When I went round the factory, I was given a taste of the fermenting liquor, a frothy, heady cross between beer and vinegar. 'By Thursday it has that warm, new-milk taste,' as my guide said appreciatively.

The factory, now owned by British Vinegars, incorporates Sarsons and Holbrooks and vinegar has been brewed here since the 1780s or '90s. Alf, the last of a team of nine coopers at the works – one of the few remaining coopers in the country – still works there repairing casks for Holbrooks Worcestershire sauce. Vinegar is casked in plastic, as oak is too expensive now, and 'shopkeepers won't waste time drawing out of a barrel. It's all supermarkets now.' But the ingredients for Worcestershire sauce are stored in the barrels for two or three years in advance, to mature.

The process is much like the brewing of beer, but vinegar is cooled into fermentation. The wort is acetified by the addition of bacteria, until the alcohol becomes acid. All this takes place in huge cylindrical vats, which at the fermenting stage give off gases so powerful that they can kill – no one must go down into them until they have been tested for safety. The wooden vats, scrubbed boards, look pleasantly old-fashioned, but the process is obviously streamlined, and in the spirit vinegar section there is specially imported German plant. The Worcestershire sauce gives off a powerful smell of lemon oil.

The foreman told me his father had been in vinegar before him. He showed me the junction of the Stour and Severn right by the brewery, and told me that the vinegar had gone by boat to Wolverhampton until the end of the last war, the malted barley coming up by river. Barrels were also loaded on to smaller boats to be taken to Holbrooks' manufacturing depot in Birmingham, for chutneys, sauces, pickles. The care that goes into the old Worcestershire sauce recipe seems rewardingly anachronistic (sauce is exported to Sweden, Germany, Italy). Shallots from Holland, matured in casks for two or three years; 'secret' ingredients. But pickling, he assured me, was 'building up'. 'People are going back to doing their own pickling.' A very healthy sign. He always did his own, he said, and had a lovely patch of horseradish roots on a lot by the factory.

*

By comparison, Bewdley, which had equally attractive features, seems a less workmanlike, more holidayish place. This may be partly due to traffic to the near-by West Midlands Safari Park. (Another attraction not too far from both is the Avoncroft Open-Air Museum of buildings, at Stoke Prior, Bromsgrove.) Severn Side, the street in Bewdley with seventeenth- and eighteenth-century houses separated from the river only by a narrow street, without railings, is incomparable as a waterside setting. There is a bridge by Telford; across the wide river from the seventeenth-century River House and row of merchants' houses, an unbroken line of trees comes down to the banks. More old houses lead away up other streets, Load Street running up the hill to the eighteenth-century St Anne's church. In Lower Park Street is the house in which Stanley Baldwin, three times prime minister and MP for Bewdley from 1908–37, was born. Yet Bewdley, now besieged by cars, and with many courtyards and alleyways converted into commuter residences, all patio and little peace, probably had its prime in the fifteenth and sixteenth centuries. Prince Arthur, elder brother of Henry VIII, lived here for a while during his short, tragic life, at Tickenhill Manor. Later this house became one of the homes of Sir Henry Sidney, father of Sir Philip Sidney, while he was Lord President of Wales and the Marches. From the sixteenth to eighteenth centuries, much of the carrying trade on the Severn was centred on Bewdley.

The barges used on early river navigations were of many sizes. The first two industrial canals, the Sankey Brook (St Helens) and the Bridge-water, could accommodate broad boats. But when Brindley went on to make the Trent and Mersey Canal, the central section was built for narrow boats, for reasons of economy. All the connecting canals had the same dimensions, Brindley being the consulting engineer. So his Staffordshire and Worcestershire Canal, the Birmingham and Coventry canals and their branches, all had narrow boats, not barges. Brindley worked tirelessly, often against opposition, and died at only fifty-five. Josiah Wedgwood, who was one of his supporters, wrote that he was 'a real sufferer for the good of the Public'.

Thanks to him and others, Birmingham, unenviably situated for water navigation on a plateau, became the centre of the country's canal communications – canals from the north-west, including the Staffordshire and Worcestershire, running into the Birmingham network through Aldersley Junction and the Wolverhampton locks; with the Birmingham and Fazeley Canal linking those from the north-east; the Grand Union and Worcester and Birmingham running in from the south-west via Worcester Bar. By 1840 there were about 4,000 miles of inland waterways in Britain.

A gradual decline only came with the consolidation of railway traffic. The narrow canals were not enlarged. Then the First World War and growing road transport between the wars increased the decline. After the Second World War the canals were nationalized and the government no longer used them for carrying coal. But the bigger canals were modernized and there has been great encouragement of pleasure cruising. There has also been a policy of co-operation with canal societies and volunteers to restore stretches of canal. There are over forty canal societies. Two in this area are the Staffordshire and Worcestershire Canal Society, and the Birmingham Canal Navigation Society, the latter founded in 1968, to preserve waterways, but also to promote boating, walking, and industrial archaeology.

*

'I hope it goes on for ever and ever . . . after I'm gone.'

Fred Moore, whom we first met at the Calf Heath marina near Four Ashes on the Staffordshire and Worcestershire Canal, where he now works, is a boatman through and through. From four generations of boatmen. His father was born on a boat at Macclesfield in Cheshire, and he was born on the *Woodcock* in 'A' Basin, at Broad Street, Wolverhampton, in 1907.

'I've never seen a doctor in my life.'

He has a healthily pink, sincere face, and when he talks about the canals, his eyes light up. There are about 2,600 miles of canal navigable at present, and he knows every inch of them. His mother of ninety no longer lives on a boat, and misses the life. It was she who taught her son to paint the bright castles and trees and traditional designs on cans and dippers and spoons, which are now sold to holidaymakers, but which were part of the equipment of the working narrow boats. 'She would stand at the side of the boat with a paint-brush in her hand, and a fag in her mouth. Fag after fag after fag. And always her umbrella hanging there, in case it was needed. She always had her umbrella. She's very intelligent, never went to school; she still signs her name with a cross. And she would paint a tree as we went past, or a castle. That was how they painted them – real castles like Leamington – and the pictures got better and better.'

Fred taught himself to write, and showed me his script, a beautiful curling idiosyncratic script which has its own style of letters but which is perfectly clear. School for him was a floating school on a boat, to which children went while their own boat was being loaded. 'When our boat was leaving they called to us and we had to go – it was only an hour or two in school – but it learnt some of them something. I regret no proper schooling in a sense.'

Before working on cruise boats for the last seventeen years, he worked on coal boats, on tugs and the narrow boats of Ernest Thomas Ltd. 'A grand life – I'd live it again. I think myself now, that canal life – it can come back with the cruising – I'd like to see it come back.'

He told me about the horses, and how a boatman with his horse was like a man with a dog. 'He loved his horse. A good horse could do thirty-five miles a day, carrying twenty-five tons. They gave their horses oats, molasses, meal, hay, condition powders, everything.'

At his cottage at Old Birchills, Walsall, by the Top Lock where the stone of the bridge is scored deeply by the horses' ropes, Fred Moore has a little shed where he makes rope fenders for the boats, and Turk's heads. He is going to teach the art to a blind school, so that they can profit from the present interest in such things. 'This is a craft, this is,' he rightly says. (I have included him in this chapter because, although his cottage is at Walsall, as a boatman he knows the canals of the whole region, and beyond.)

He showed me his scrapbook of photographs and cuttings. Photographs of his father, a very fine looking man, in a jacket with a velvet collar and pearl buttons, with a double-breasted waistcoat with pearl buttons, silk scarf, straight, turn-up trousers, and soft, good-quality shoes. Always smartly turned out, Fred said, and always the pearl buttons. Had he been quite well off then? I asked. No, Fred said. It was clearly a brand of pride which has largely vanished among other types of worker today. The boatman's traditional working wear was a beautifully pleated white shirt, which the women would iron in the cabin, with braces made of wool and a tie tied round the neck and then tucked under the braces on the shoulder. Even in a photograph of 1923 during the boatmen's strike in Birmingham which he showed me, the women all had shawls round their heads. They would wear, like Fred's mother, a white apron edged with lace they had made, and white bonnets. Crochet was another art, and in their cabins by the stove were hung pierced hanging plates and crochet work.

'Tnis girl, look you . . . I was courting that girl before I married my wife. And that's my wife with me taking coal to Cadbury's. And my old dog on the working tub. And there's Joe Shaw, the union man. Myself on the *Maverick*. And talking to Wynford Vaughan-Thomas.' Fred Moore has advised the BBC on television programmes about canal life, and has also given advice to *The Archers*. 'I've had a grand life.'

He works immensely hard at the marina in the holiday season, and in recent weeks the low level of the water has been a problem, since now water is no longer pumped back up the eight locks. 'If it had gone another week without rain, we'd have been finished.' But, 'It's a grand life – I'd live it again.'

> Wise men there formerly were among the English race . . . and
> what happy times those were . . .
>
> King Alfred

On travelling farther into Worcestershire, one is very conscious of approaching the south of England, although strictly in the Midlands still. Despite the Malvern and Cotswold hills which frame the county on either side, and are beautiful in their own fashion, there is nothing wild about Worcestershire. It is close to the soft underbelly of the south – paler, mellower and less unexpected than its northerly neighbours. The darker sandstone has been bled out of the earth; the fields stretch golden and calm, drowsy with hops and poppies, peopled with cottages, ripe with fruit. The soft notes of civilization sound from the cathedral city.

Unfortunate Worcester. Sacked by Danes, Saxons, Welsh. The city, faithful to the Stuarts, that was torn and hacked by Cromwell's troops. Surviving all this, it is in our century being pounded and suffocated to death by traffic – and enervated tourists. Driving through Worcester is infernal (there is no ring road); walking through it is a dusty, more prolonged form of torture, which only its remaining features of undeniable nobility make at all worth while. There is one compensation, in the shape of numerous cafés; where there are tourists there will be cafés, in a chicken-before-egg situation that must pose headaches for tourist boards. (Another indication of whether a town will be spoilt or not is the number of public lavatories. At a place such as Leominster, where at the station there is only a – firmly locked – door saying 'cloakroom', one's heart lifts at once in the expectation of empty streets.)

If you can ignore the traffic in Foregate Street and the High Street, there are memorable buildings to admire. The elegantly pillared and corniced Lloyd's Bank, the Berkeley Hospital almshouses with plaster figures, a superb guildhall with a statue of Queen Anne in a brocaded dress, with Charles I and II in niches below. Off in narrower side streets are quieter, more appealing areas, as in Fish Street, or in the St Swithin's area, where the Community Health Department is in a particularly pleasant house, with Venetian windows at the back. The fifteenth-century Commandery was shut for restoration when I visited it, but there are many timbered houses in Worcester, particularly in Friar Street, which has however at one end a spiralled multi-storey carpark that could only have come from a nightmare. It crushes the little timber frames in spirit if not with the weight of its concrete.

In Friar Street the Tudor House Museum is a growing venture. It has correctly-and sparsely-furnished Tudor and Stuart rooms, complete with part of the Boscobel oak in which Charles hid and a huge trunk covered with nails like a porcupine, which bears the initials of Thomas Habington, who was associated with the Gunpowder Plot. In the courtyard are farm implements and a hop-pickers' canvas crib, into which hops were picked before being measured in wicker bushel measures. In the late Middle Ages Worcester was a clothmaking town. After a decline, trade flourished again in the eighteenth century with china, glove and carpet making, so well that four churches were built during the century. But the city was, and is, also the centre of an agricultural area, and hop-picking one of the most important of its rural industries. The old Hop Market in Foregate Street has been converted into small shops, but down a side street is a plaster frieze which prettily represents hop-picking in the nineteenth century.

A second station in Worcester, and the canal, have made the Shrub Hill area an industrial suburb, which has however early Victorian factories in red and yellow brick. Worcester today is not primarily an industrial city. It is a cathedral city, through whose streets clerics stride with faces of faint distaste for the modern bustle, noses questing heavenwards like those of affable pointers; the city of the Three Choirs Festival, with *The Dream of Gerontius* performed in the cathedral, concerts, and special performances at the versatile and successful Swan Theatre; the city of the County Cricket Ground, territory of famous cricketers such as Basil d'Oliveira. Visits by international teams are commemorated on special plates by the Worcester Royal Porcelain Company. It is the city of china and Lea and Perrins sauce, and clean middle classes, and culture, and schools such as the Alice Ottley School, where the girls wear navy blue boaters tip-tilted on their fair heads – 'A bit of an old-fashioned place,' a small freckled rebel told me.

*

It takes more than road drills to crack the spirit of a town. It is still there in Worcester, although not particularly evident if you look at the outside of the cathedral, with its flat, rather lifeless sandstone, in spite of a precinct which is hollyhocked and porched, with cats under mulberry trees. Possibly one gets closer down by the river, through the Watergate which leads to a quiet riverside walk, and where the tidemarks of past floods are marked at disturbingly high levels. Or in the enclosed cloisters (the Friends of Worcester Cathedral have chosen this good spot for a tea bar). Possibly looking at the outstanding monuments inside the cathedral, of rich Elizabethan clothiers in stiff ruffs, or a comely sixteenth-century mother remembered by her son, or Sir John Beauchamp the first baron created by patent, Lord Beauchamp of Kidderminster, in 1387, with his wife whose head lies on a black swan's soft back; or, among all these richly black and red and gold effigies, the simple plaque to Edward Elgar, OM. When I was there a plain green laurel wreath lay under it.

King John, who often visited Worcester, and directed in his will that he should be buried here, lies here too in stone, above his tomb, with a seal in one hand and a sword in the other. In a chapel near by is the tomb of the young Prince Arthur, who brought his bride, Catherine of Aragon, to Ludlow Castle, and who died there a short while afterwards. The centuries when courts were held as richly in these distant towns as in London crowd in on one; how much the country was then characterized by diversification of wealth and pageantry and dramatically clashing wills, lineages. Modern town 'festivals' are greasepaint affairs by comparison. Could some more vital pomp and circumstance ever return to the provinces, something less fleeting than visits from a hard-worked monarch or smiles from Miss Cheese 1984?

In the crypt you are closer still to the past of Worcester. Built by St Wulfstan, the last Saxon bishop, it is the earliest part of the cathedral, and pure Norman work. Over a hundred pillars, partly blocked in since the thirteenth century, form an ambulatory round a central area – a cool cavern of graceful curves, a northern Cordoba. By one of those lucky chances which travellers can seize if they don't rush at a place but let it come at them, I caught an exhibition in the crypt showing the history of Worcester. During it, the underground vault was flooded with recorded singing by the cathedral choir, some of the chants being from the thirteenth-century antiphonal belonging to the cathedral which contains pieces of the oldest church music used in England, chants going back to the time of St Oswald in the tenth century. It was glorious, spine-chilling. It is not surprising that music has a special place in the cathedral today; besides the choir there is a voluntary choir, which takes over in school holidays and on other occasions – an extra link between cathedral and city.

The first settlement at Worcester, by a ford near the cathedral, dates from the fourth or fifth century BC. Later, it was the camp of the Hwicce, a West Midlands tribe, and a charter of Uhtred sub-king of the Hwicce grants land at Salwarpe to the cathedral in AD 770. This is written in a beautiful script. Another, and particularly firmly and finely written manuscript is that sent by the great Alfred to Waerfrith, Bishop of Worcester, after invasions by the Danes and Norsemen, appealing to him for help in rebuilding education and religion for his people.

This book is for Worcester.

Alfred king commandeth to greet Werferth, bishop, with his words in loving and friendly wise: and I would have you informed that it has often come into my remembrance that wise men there formerly were among the English race, both of the sacred orders and the secular; and what happy times those were throughout the English race . . . and how foreigners came to this land for wisdom and instruction; and how we should now have to get them from abroad if we are to have them . . .

The wise words have lost none of their punch.

*

'Look at it, isn't it lovely! *Look* at the gorse . . .'

A small bullfinch of a housewife eyeing one of the porcelain birds modelled for the Worcester Royal Porcelain Company by the late Dorothy Doughty.

The woman's husband (sheepishly), and I, were looking at two cider mugs on the shelf below, the Abergavenny Cider Mugs made in 1813 and painted by Humphrey Chamberlain, regarded by many as the finest paintings on Worcester – sporting the 'Power of Love' and 'Bacchante' with inimitably abandoned bosoms.

'Look, defying gravity – *isn't* it marvellous.'

They were. There is a type of Englishwoman, and possibly American woman, who if presented with the most beautifully portrayed nude in the world would prefer birds. Or puppies. Anything but human flesh at its most innocent and peachlike. And if one thinks of Royal Worcester at its best one probably thinks of fruit, velvety purple plums, moss-like peaches, cherries, smoothed with invisible brushstrokes. In fact it was characteristic of Humphrey Chamberlain of the cider mugs, that his brushstrokes couldn't be seen and when examined by present-day painters, they agreed that his flesh areas were done by a process of oiling and dusting with powdered colour, a very difficult technique.

This porcelain, and countless other rare pieces are in the Dyson Perrins Museum next to the Worcester works. There are early blue-and-white examples of the Dr Wall period, including later onglaze printed ware by the process now interestingly thought to have been brought to Worcester by Robert Hancock, whose knowledge of transfer printing was learnt at the Bilston and Wednesbury enamel works. There are pierced baskets (cut out with a knife, not made from strips as at Leeds), early figures, later highland-sheep-type plates, scenes from Byron and fruit painted by Thomas Baxter, other treasures too numerous to list. One is also struck by the variety of articles that have vanished from our tables – roast chestnut baskets, sweetmeat holders, asparagus servers (Worcester still make egg coddlers). My favourite service is the Blind Earl service, which was first made in about 1760 for the Earl of Coventry, who had lost his sight in a hunting accident. He had loved fine porcelain, and asked for a pattern to be reproduced which he could feel, as one can feel the raised leaves and curling rose stalks of this design.

The sharp-beaked Dorothy Doughty birds were initiated at a time when the company's fortunes were reviving in the 1930s. A few years previously times had been hard in the trade. An entry in the official history reads: 1930 'Factory in hands of official receiver'. The popularity of porcelain models helped to turn the tide. There have since been many other limited editions by a range of designers, while artists such as Harry Ayrton, who is semi-retired, paint fruit as beautifully as ever – a recent edition of three bone china plaques, one of a set of fifteen sold for £2,400 in 1973, was recently resold for £4,000. Worcester porcelain is widely exported, and there is also a thriving electronic components division. In some years 250,000 visitors see the factory. The oldest for the manufacture of porcelain in England today, its origins go back to 1751. There have been guided tours since the eighteenth century, and part of the Severn Street works is a curving building of about 1860. Inside the painting shops there is a heady smell of aniseed or lavender from the painting oils used to wet the powdered paints. It seems an ideal situation in which to work, but the girls, who each paint their initials on every finished piece, still have to wear radio headphones to ward off boredom and keep themselves awake. The work is bound to be repetitive, however skilled and pleasant it may be.

'The brush keeps slipping off the moulding,' a girl tackling a Blind Earl plate told me (she preferred thimbles), but Mrs Appleton, who was gilding pieces of this service, said it was her favourite too – 'There's nothing to touch it . . . anywhere'. She explained the intricacies of gilding. 'What we put on Wellington is the very best . . . not watered down.' I could see no models of Napoleon, but there was another horseman who possibly fared less well.

It must be oddly satisfying to feel that your initials could be sought after in antique shops by future generations of collectors, or your name worn on a little girl's china thimble. But, for birds, I would choose the soft-eyed Worcester canaries of 1770.

*

'It's very well signposted.'

'Yes,' said John. 'Our road signs drive Americans mad. They're always being told they're on the right road to Lower Tollpuddle when they need reassurance that they're on the Bristol road.'

We followed clear notices from the A44 (alternatively from the B4204) to 'Elgar's Birthplace' in the village of Lower Broadheath three miles from Worcester. Luckily the composer was spared a recent crop of neo-Georgian pillared fronts. But from the tiny cottage, with a coach-house and stables built by Elgar's father and elder brother Henry, there is still a wide, unchanging view of the Malvern Hills, with which so much of his music is associated, in particular *Caractacus*. He was a man of his landscape, and in 1921 he wrote: 'I am still at heart the dreamy child who used to be found in the reeds by Severn side with a sheet of paper trying to fix the sounds and longing for something very great. I am still looking for this . . .'[1] While working on *The Dream of Gerontius*, based on Cardinal Newman's poem, he wrote '. . . the trees are singing my music – or have I sung theirs? . . . It's too lovely here.'[2] During his time in London he wistfully named a Hampstead house 'Severn House', and when later an old Severn Bridge was taken down, he bought two lengths of the iron balustrade to put up in his Worcestershire garden. W. H. Reed wrote, 'I thought they looked rather crazy in the garden, but took care not to say so . . . I think he used to go out and imagine that the Severn was flowing under them as of old.'[3]

By this time he was an old man; his companions, Marco and Mina, two dogs whose grave is at Lower Broadheath. The graph of his creativity seems only to have arced fully during his wife's lifetime: 'All I have done was owing to her . . .'[4] Proponents of women's liberation might be scandalized that she gave up her career as a published novelist to foster his talent, spending hours ruling bar lines on his paper for him or writing in choral parts. Would we have seen his full genius without her help? (Judging from her published poems, she was right in assessing his talent as the greater.)

Elgar's nature attracts as powerfully as his successes. Unlike Dr Johnson, he did not scorn his father, owner of a music shop. There is a touching account of the old man, too feeble to attend the ceremony at which his son was given the Freedom of the City of Worcester, watching from his old room as his son turned from the dignitaries to salute him. When he was made a knight, Elgar at once bicycled over to tell his father – a grand-daughter photographed the two together, with the old man clutching a handkerchief, as if just having wiped his spectacles.[5]

Like many other creative searchers, Elgar seems to have been spurred on by a sharp desire for fame as well as by the vision of elusive symphonies. When he was young, he once told his mother that he wouldn't be content until he received a letter from abroad addressed to Edward Elgar, England. Such a letter would certainly have reached him; but he could equally have said, Edward Elgar, Severn-side, England.

*

There are other noteworthy houses in the area – Berrington Hall, a late eighteenth-century house with a fine view laid out by Capability Brown; Eye Manor; Eaton Hall farmhouse near Leominster, the home of the Hakluyts, including Richard Hakluyt of the *Voyages*. The weary tourist might do well to visit Droitwich or Leominster instead of Worcester. Droitwich, named by the Romans *Salinae*, because of its salt springs, is intriguingly named a 'spa' in brochures. Leland, who can bore with his 'towns knowne for' clothiers and nailers, called the town dirty. It is a little ramshackle, even lopsided, because of the extraction of brine. But the streets with their crooked houses have space and an unpretty, unpainted casualness. Undeveloped until the nineteenth century, the town was set up as a spa by John Corbett, who built a salt works, several hotels, and the St Andrew's Brine Baths. His own industrialist's palace, Château Impney, built outside the town by a French architect, in steep-roofed Louis XIII style, is now an hotel, the mecca for twentieth-century businessmen who hold dinners and meetings there in a style of luxurious détente. A little simpler, but still imposingly bell-towered and turreted, is the Worcester-shire Hotel opposite St Andrew's Baths; and then there is the Raven, sixteenth-century timber embraced by nineteenth-century additions, with genuine stained glass and fifty-five bedrooms all with colour television and bathrooms 'en suite', as they say in advertese.

Signs of un-spa-like life on a late afternoon in Droitwich are few. I asked a woman the way to that ubiquitous focal point the Town Centre. She looked blank. The market?

'Market? Shops? They wouldn't be open now. Not in Droitwich.'

I found the brine baths. The building is absurdly full of promise even from the outside. In woodwork, with Austrian-style gables and windows and with a hint of the cricket pavilion. The water is green, heated to 97 degrees, 40 per cent more salty than the Dead Sea, and smells of Badedas. The atmosphere is hushed, nannyish. In fact the baths offer a complete return to the nursery, the jangled businessman's womb. Plain wooden chairs painted in cream enamel; tufty nursery rugs on the polished floor; no turnstiles or impatient notices; private cubicles with green curtains which are just public enough to be upper class.

A white-coated nanny, guardian, came towards me with a welcoming mixture of smiles and tut-tutting pursed mouth. 'We've got plenty of costumes, no need to worry about that.' The businessmen were wallowing like heavy, happy seals. A few women growing quietly pink from the warmth in their corners. 'Go away,' one seal shouted, like a rude school-boy. Conversations were quiet, interrupted by lazy submersions. Does one say 'See you in the Brine Baths at six' at Droitwich? (And for how much longer will one say it? The baths are threatened with closure, I later learnt.)

'It's very relaxing. Good for arthritis. You don't rub yourself dry, we bring you a hot sheet and you wrap it round you and sit until you're dry. Then you have another towel round your feet.' Warm white yards of towelling seemed to be draped everywhere. I gathered my courage.

'Time for the last ticket's just gone,' she said. No treats today.

I had a stiff drink in the Raven, where the seals obviously go to flex their muscles afterwards.

*

In more cerebral mood one should visit Leominster, in Herefordshire, one of England's most beautiful counties, which seems to have the wildness of Wales without its rainswept scragginess. Down through the Shropshire hills into a countryside which appears entirely devoted to sheep and cows, the red-and-white Herefordshire cattle ousting the black-and-white. There are few fields of cabbage or beet spinach for the hungry conurba-tion; the landscape is on a different scale, with smaller fields, many thistles, dilapidated mansions suddenly clinging to hillsides. There are small church spires and colourwashed farms, and willow trunks lean away from the rainfilled wind from the west.

The country comes right up to the station at Leominster, in a sprawl of grasses and willows. It is a large town, from its days, spanning the thirteenth to eighteenth centuries, as the great wool centre for the Welsh borderland, when the fine wool named 'Lemster Ore' was far-famed. This is mentioned in the plays of Ben Jonson, and Herrick wrote of a 'bank of moss more soft than the finest Lemster Ore'. Drayton, too, sang its praises:

> Where lives the man so dull on Britain's furthest shore
> To whom did never sound the name of Lemster Ore,
> That with the silkworm's thread for smallness doth compare.

A large town that has kept its size but has not been filled with modern traffic and industry. In its streets you can see what towns such as Worcester must once have been like; the Priory Church is vast enough to be a cathedral, and more than beautiful enough. Looking on to fields, as churches used to do, it has an immense west window, and on the south side five windows in Decorated style thickly studded with flower-like knops. It is immediately attractive from the outside, and inside, on a lower level of floor, are gigantic Norman pillars sixteen feet in circumference, in the nave of the former priory which lies parallel to that of the main church. On the same site there was also a nunnery, endowed by Leofric of Mercia, and when the chancel floor was re-laid in 1950, many female bones were found. The town very likely has its name from the Mercian earl.

The huge church was empty except for two Frenchwomen when I was there (the only tourists I saw in Leominster). In a bucket was a mound of arum lilies, with their yellow pollen spilling over white silk petals, their clean scent filling two naves. Lemster Ore. In the museum in Etnam Street there is a golden-white silk wedding dress worn by a girl in 1704, with a ribbon-edged cape; fluted and immaculate as the lilies.

The museum was shut. 'Won't be open until tomorrow. The lady who runs it is bad.' It is that kind of town. Hanging baskets of flowers hang outside the pubs. Old men carry shopping in baskets from the blind shop. Girls pack up Welsh cakes in small shops and in soft voices ask 'The iced one, is it?' There are dark Welsh faces and these curling Welsh voices; agricultural merchants; a long stretch of main street and many other streets, curving or narrow with timber frames. Sadly, Alexander and Duncan Ltd (garden tools, billhooks, axes) have moved from their imposingly-fronted shop with a great plaster lion on top, but other buildings sport colourwash, or bright purple or green woodwork.

The town's character is self-evident. There is time to stand dreaming. A man with very blue eyes, and white bristles on his brown chin stood leaning on his bicycle, unhurried. 'Yes, there's farming round here, like,' he said, and waving his hand round proudly, 'It's a big town.'

Although not gimmicky, there are many antique shops in the town. This is an advantage, I was told by Helen Vine, whose husband concentrated on selling antiques until recently. If there are a good many shops, the dealers find it worth while to come round.

Helen Vine herself sells hand-printed and dyed fabrics. 'Aprons and smocks for butter money, and so that I can buy silk for batik work.' Her scarves and lengths of silk are soft in colour, with patterns that often have a striking leaf-like structure. She sells to the West Midlands Arts Shop in Birmingham – 'I'm amazed how much money there must be in Birmingham' – and in towns such as Hereford, where there are a very active Guild of Craftsmen and Society of Craftsmen. With a large window for displays, she works in their house in Leominster which is pleasantly un-done-up, showing bare plaster which they intend to cover with raddle later; full of bunches of flowers and kittens and with bricks showing in a fireplace they have just discovered. One of those couples who have not so much dropped out as shaped their own life style, which clearly can work in a district such as this. Helen's husband now does silkscreen printing for an electronics firm; with one daughter, she has enough orders, does not want to become a big firm but plans to pursue her individual line.

A way of life which is enviable, which many would envy. But besides the hard work involved, and an outgoing nature (which helps ward off loneliness), one gets the feeling that places rub off on such craftsmen, that they are right to choose places which have escaped the mainstream, the slick.

'It's a bit cheaper living round here . . . But there's a lot going on. I don't regret leaving London . . . Here, you think about things like the Ludlow festival, so you actually go to them, do the things. In London it is all there and you never do it . . . Leominster is a very friendly place . . . I like being involved in this street . . .'

One hopes that the size of Leominster will prevent it getting spoilt too soon. That craftsmen, not tycoons, will buy up the houses for sale. But in this borderland you need a cool head, to keep your feet firmly on the ground. Listening to two men speaking Welsh perhaps, or whistling a tune so haunting that it makes you want to run up the nearest mountain and never come down again, you might fall under the spell of the ancient magic that is palpably close here. Like it or not, you are near to the primeval faery element in Wales.

> Clunton and Clunbury,
> Clungunford and Clun,
> Are the quietest places
> Under the sun.
>
> A. E. Housman, *A Shropshire Lad*[1]

Some critics take a donnish delight in pointing out that Housman was *not* a
Shropshire lad; that he was born near Bromsgrove in Worcestershire, and
later lived in London and Cambridge. But I think they miss the heart of
the matter; the spirit of these poems about places which he must have
visited as a boy; the essence of travel for us all, to places seen on the
horizon and later remembered. It is this longing for *el dorado*, the remembrance of a loved place when one is somewhere else, the gleaming,
misty presence of the Shropshire and Welsh hills which all West Midlanders must be aware of, that comes across so poignantly in his poems.

> Into my heart an air that kills
> From yon far country blows:
> What are those blue remembered hills,
> What spires, what farms are those?
>
> That is the land of lost content,
> I see it shining plain,
> The happy highways where I went
> And cannot come again.[1]

He must have gone to Ludlow market, as people still do; he knew the
boys of Knighton town downing their beer, the golden broom by Wenlock
('Oh tarnish late on Wenlock Edge, Gold that I never see;'),[1] the valleys of
Ony and Teme and Clun, their villages and spires. And I find this 'minor
nineteenth-century poet' has a good deal to say to us today; he is so stoical,
and possibly derived from the classics (he was Professor of Latin at both
London and Cambridge) some of his philosophical ability to consider
death as a welcome sleep after endurance of what is often, he found, not a

particularly pleasant world, certainly not one with a cosy patriarchal God putting things right.

*

Are Clunton and Clunbury, Clungunford and Clun still the quietest under the sun? Strangely, we found that they were. We approached them along Wenlock Edge, the long limestone ridge which stretches westwards towards Craven Arms, and which in the distance looks like a hairy backbone leading from the Wrekin to the sleeping monster-like mounds of the Long Mynd and Caer Caradoc, with the two Clee Hills to the east. On the very end of Wenlock Edge is a hill fort, and near by, Craven Arms, and Stokesay Castle, a little castle which is one half grey stone fortress, one half timbered house, complete with weathervane. Craven Arms was built as a railway town, and looks it. Like people, most places have at least one thing to recommend them, but I was unable to find it in Craven Arms. It was developed on a grid system round the junction, with mean little houses to accommodate the railway workers, and a grid it remains. I had gone there a week previously, nosing out the ground, to one of the autumn sheep sales, which are among the most important in the country, and to which generations of farmers have flocked to buy top-quality two-year-old Clun ewes and Kerry sheep.

It is an amazing sight to see about 5,500 sheep neatly penned in their adjoining pens, then trotting up the gangway to be auctioned, leaping up at men's chests in the jostle. Grown sheep *do* leap, it seems. There are no sheepdogs; men with long sticks with a forked top, 'out of the hedge', prod and whistle. The unwary spectator, who has to climb over pens anyway, will be stampeded if in the wrong gangway. It is definitely a man's world, and a little dour, I found. Slit-mouthed, prosperous looking farmers hit their legs with sticks (you even see a gaiter or two), and I got more information from the friendly Clun Forest Sheep Breeder's Society representative than from them. Hardly surprising as they were intent on business. Do the slit mouths twitch or forked sticks quiver to make a bid? One can't tell. But the auctioneer is far more jolly, and knows every flock and its home. Black-spotted-faced Kerrys, 'the oldest flock in the book'; Cluns 'like peas in a pod'; ewes (Cluns are famed as good mothers) who have 'got some room there, they'll bring you some sort of lambs – from up above the castle there', and even 'a bit like their owner these, Jo, don't look very bright'. The slits grin. The sold sheep rush off to waiting vans, and the new owners occasionally grumble when they have time to see what they imagine to have been slipped in with the others. 'There wasn't one like that in the ring.' The two-year-old ewes were sold for about £15 to £20 each that day, and may finish up anywhere in Britain, in the hills of the north or lowlands of the south.

We later went to another sale at Church Stretton, hoping an injection of Welsh hill farmers would add some *joie de vivre*. There was a strong smell of whisky in the air (it was a cold day), but otherwise it was sober, although the auctioneer really had them by the ears – 'Gentlemen, how low have I got to go?'. 'That's the most he's ever given away in his life.' One small white lamb sat alone and bewildered in a pen, with its brethren all round staring at it from their 40-strong enclaves. One knew how it felt. In an old-fashioned chemist's shop were traditional packs of 'scar powder', 'worm treatment' and twenty or so sheep cures and veterinary products. The farmers usually no longer dye their sheep saffron or pale yellow or red for fairs, but we saw two coloured golden orange here.

*

So on, out, to the country which gives these sheep their name. Soft, wood-filled country, which in the autumn as we first saw it instils one with the belief that no scenery could be lovelier. A tufty proliferation of trees of many varieties, golds merging with green, with bitter ochre, with willow green, and between the woodland, rain-fresh Shropshire grass, and beyond, more hills. There is nothing enclosed, oppressive, over-sleepy about this countryside.

Towards Bishops Castle it becomes difficult to drive because of pheasants skittering over the road. The signs denoting cattle crossings seem to have taken on a different aspect, showing a wild, woolly prehistoric-looking beast with aggressive jaw, instead of the uddered English cow.

Off to the left is Walcot Hall, built for Clive of India. A half-mile plantation of trees on the hillside used to spell out PLASSEY, but was cut down during the last war in case it gave enemy pilots their bearings. This brilliant soldier and administrator, or tyrant, as he was later regarded by many, ended his days in gloom, opium and suicide, but memorials to him dot the region, and his son became the Earl of Powis.

Bishops Castle is built on a steep hill, running up to an eighteenth-century town hall and lock-up, and, more welcoming, the Three Tuns Pub, which has its own little brewery adjoining, and whose landlord Mr John Roberts is the third generation of brewers. The bar sports notices such as 'Drink Roberts' Home Brewed Ale, No Doctors Wanted'. It tastes good, anyway.

Thus fortified you can roll down to Clun, which has also been known to have been called the 'drunkenest under the sun', and does seem to have quite a few pubs for such a small place. It is immensely attractive, in a very plain way – dark-red-and-green painted post office, grey cottages, roof tiles on which moss happily grows, a pack-horse bridge, and a beautiful crumbling, lichened castle, surrounded by sheep. The castle was built by a Norman Marcher lord, one of the lawless breed whom William the Conqueror installed, with the right to own any land they could wrest from the Welsh. Scott described it as the *Garde Doloureuse* in *The Betrothed*.

Sheep, and distant tractors, are the only sounds you hear round about. There are more tractors on the road than cars out of the holiday season, and shops don't seem to expect much trade, some only being open one or two days a week. A café owner gave us a run-down on local gossip, and said she wished they could have a street market. Later, I saw a 1906 photograph of an old street market in Clun. There is a small museum, displaying local articles, from flints to sunbonnets. One or two houses lie empty as 'weekend' places but the village is not only unspoilt: it seems determined to remain so. There are still farmyards in the main street.

*

A totally amazing experience. At the edge of the village, the Trinity Hospital, almshouses founded by Henry Howard, Earl of Northampton in 1618 for impoverished elderly men. You walk through heavily studded oak doors into a series of courtyards round formal gardens. Doors open into miniature, snug-looking houses. A man is shaving with his door open, in the sun. Through the final archway you come on the vegetable plots, a riot of marigolds and cabbages. Directly beyond them, the valley and fields. The vegetable rows run in neat parallel lines towards the distant hills.

A small figure in a green woollen hat is digging potatoes. Large, healthy potatoes with a powdering of earth, lie between the lines of cabbages.

I say good morning, tentatively.

'Hull*o*. I'm so glad you've come.' He has no idea who I am, that I would be coming.

Mr Mackie is one of those people who make you feel all's right with the world, or as he would say 'God willing'. His eyes shine with friendliness, he loves the place, you, his fellow inmates. His jacket collar is a little frayed, which only goes to prove all the rest.

He tells us the history of the place, in which he takes a keen interest. Torn between a desire to tell us everything and a sensitive fear we might want to rush away. About the West Indian curate, the housekeeper, the head gardener and his beautiful borders of pinks, the small chapel where the founder's prayer is still read, and the communicants have their own box pews. There are ten cottages for couples, six single cottages. One or two inmates are not so well, or crippled, but 'myself, thank the Lord, 100 per cent'. The walls are about three feet deep, and there is central heating. 'Yes, look at my bathroom, isn't it nice?' Inmates pay for electricity, have their own furniture. Meals on wheels visit, and in the neighbourhood all the societies, from Liberals to WI take a turn with this service. By a long refectory table are photographs of Victorian gentlemen in top hats – the pensioners used to wear uniform. Now, they are selected according to need, probably with the help of their church, as in Mr Mackie's case. Why can't every village have one of these peace-filled units, which makes old age seem as desirable as childhood?

'We'll come again in the spring, when the pinks are out.'

'Yes, there's a dear, that's right.' And then, as a smiled afterthought, 'Yes, that's right, God willing.'

And he wrote to us later, in a letter brimming with goodwill and buoyant with curlicued script: 'Hullo Dear Mr and Mrs Mosley . . . sincere thanks to your goodselves . . . some visitors do promise results of their photographic efforts but with "negative" results . . . I may be shewing (DV) these picturesque views to friends in Australia during December . . . recently the variegated colours of autumn foliage has been most glorious . . . Someone said: Oh to be in England now that spring (or was it April?) is here, whoever it was should have said: Oh to be in Shropshire now that Autumn is here . . . God bless you for the sincerity of a promise fulfilled. Yours in Christian Fellowship, Alex Mackie.'

But then, Shropshire people are the friendliest people, as different from Staffordshire people as cheese from chalk – or bull-terriers. Their voices are lilty, their smiles beam. They call you 'dear' or 'folks'.

We stayed at Springhill Farm, far out in the hills on the old Clun-Clee Ridgeway, a prehistoric track where flint arrowheads have been found (there is no native flint in the area, so these must have been imported from chalk country eighty miles away in the Marlborough Hills). We were greeted with log fires, daily roasts, scalding hot bathwater. Our hostess is a marvellous cook and sings as she washes up; some people might have thought this windswept farm caught, at twilight, between lonely hills and black, panther-shaped clouds, lonely, but it would be hard to find anyone who seems more content. Her daughter visits her and finds the village gayer than Shrewsbury where she works.

The farm has a bit of everything, cows, arable and sheep. Mainly sheep, as they do best here, until this year, when farmers are distinctly worried. (But does one ever meet an optimistic farmer?) Wool is sold to the Wool Board, but production for meat is the mainstay, although one farmer in the neighbourhood is specializing in Shetland sheep for their wool. One reason why hill country is so good for sheep is because it is cooler; in the valleys in spring sheep tend to get too hot, may lie down for a scratch and then be unable to roll back on their feet. After twelve hours on their back, they may die.

The methods of sheep farming, our host told us, have changed very little. Pens are more modern, and shearing is all electric, but at Springhill they don't contract out the shearing – 'we had the shearers but there was wool and twine everywhere and sheep all over the place'. His wife can remember her grandfather shearing with hand shears, but she said of sheep dyeing – 'it was a good thing when that mostly stopped'.

This year was a very late summer (1974), and they were trying to get the oats in on the first really sunny day for weeks. We were hoping for fine weather to walk along Offa's Dyke, but they were hoping for one more fine day to get in the oats. 'It's like stealing it in, like.' It rained. This brought home to me that even the sturdiest of long-distance walkers or most embattled of conservationists is something of a parasite compared to people whose life and the land are one and the same. And how philosophically they bear setbacks which would send city dwellers rushing for their tranquillizers. They smiled, and said 'Maybe we can rest today', as the rain soaked into the remainder of the crop. The sheep sheltered by the hedges, in ditches. 'It's surprisingly warm down there; people who cut them down don't realize this.'

We were repeatedly told that Offa's Dyke was a lovely walk *if it was fine*, but not 'if there was *weather*'. This made us nervous. 'The ones going all along it come in here . . . a bit worn out,' said our host. 'I believe "fair buggered up" is the phrase,' his wife corrected him. The dyke also seemed strangely elusive. If John Hillaby had had difficulty in finding it,[2] would we succeed? We pored over guides and maps, and learnt everything about the dyke from the fact that King Offa set it up in the late eighth century to the fact that Lord Hunt opened the long-distance footpath that runs along it or near by, in 1971. We couldn't discover how actually to get on to the damn thing. I thought I heard muffled laughter from the kitchen. A trifle grimly, we set out, armed with cameras and bars of chocolate – and gumboots, which the tourist guides had told us must not be worn on any account.

We did know the dyke and the Clun-Clee Ridgeway crossed just by Springhill Farm. We didn't realize this was an understatement. After peering at signs, and through hedges, we saw the dyke, all fifteen foot high of its green snake-like mound heading straight for the farmyard and ending temporarily smack up against a barn, giving one wall splendid shelter. We'd been sleeping over Offa's ditch for two nights.

It is a marvellous walk. We went down towards Knighton, over Llanfair Hill and the highest part of the 168-mile-long dyke. It is very exciting to be walking along the ridge, to imagine men digging it centuries ago. At times the bank is about twenty foot high, and its ditch correspondingly deep. Offa ordered that Welshmen bearing arms on his side of it should lose their right hands, and for a second offence, their heads, but as he cunningly had it dug on the western slopes of the hills, with a good view towards Wales, the sight of it must have been discouraging enough in itself.

We were walking through Clun forest, which is sweeping moorland (forest in the ancient sense of 'royal hunting ground', but probably richly wooded originally also). In fact the hillsides hereabouts seem disappointing at first glance – brown and green chequerboards. But the landscape grows on you; the light shifts over the slopes, the sun pinpoints an emerald field; it lives. Off in the distance are the Black Mountains and the Brecon hills.

This is the country of Wild Edric. Edric was a Saxon leader who revolted against the Normans. While hunting in Clun forest he got lost, but found a lighted house full of dancing fairy maidens. He carried off one of these sisters, Godda, to be his wife, but she was later reclaimed and he died of grief. Another legend tells how, after Edric was reconciled with William I, he and the golden-haired Godda were imprisoned below the Stiperstones (in Shropshire) as a punishment for their submission to the enemy. There they still dwell with their retinue of Saxon warriors. Lead miners used to hear them knocking to get out. They are only allowed to ride over the hills when war is about to break out, and were seen before the Napoleonic and Crimean wars, before the 1914 war and the last war. Godda wears a green habit belted with gold; Edric carries a great sword and is mounted on a warhorse. It is said that he cannot die until England returns to the state she was in before the trouble of those days.[3]

I gazed along the valley for his wild hunt. It was beginning to get a little misty. There was nothing fairylike except delicate larch trees, dipping their weeping arms to the ground. A far from wild, middle-aged couple in blazer and oatmeal tweed, walking their dog, smiled at us brightly, and seeing us by now a little weary and gumboot-sore, cried, 'There's a nice pub down at Llanfair Waterdine – you might just reach it before closing time.' And sped to their white Cortina, determined that they at least would get there.

Unless we had been greyhounds, it is hard to see how we could have done, as the pub was a good few miles away, off the official path. We trudged on through lanes in search of it, in a valley that is like the worst of Welsh country – mean and scrubby looking, full of water and run-down farms. A mongrel broke its cord and snarled after us. John stopped once more to tackle his gumboots; mine, the fitted kind you try not to be seen wearing in the country, are in fact ideal walking gear over rough ground.

In a hollow was the pub, shut, and a deserted Edwardian-style mansion, with French windows opening on to tangled, mysterious lawns. We found our way home through lanes, with the twilight deepening, and the mist creeping up. The green mounds of the distant hills became shrouded; then the near hills vanished too, and strange shapes loomed through the whiteness. We passed a small farm where they had clearly been using a horse-drawn rake to get in the hay. Each farm seemed miles from the next, isolated. Cut off by hills looming in the mist like rising whales. What compass do they use for survival? And in the snow? We later learnt that our farm, Springhill, gets a subsidy from the council to keep their road open – £1,000 in a long winter, November to April.

*

Clunbury is the most attractive of the other Cluns – below a flaming, bracken-covered hill and winding round a river with orchards on one bank. At Clungunford there is a prehistoric barrow by the church. Clunton seemed rather drab. It was near here that we saw the only flash of sophistication in the shape of Harry Hotspur, speeding with a friend in a red sportscar, no doubt returning from getting the mood of the Welsh Marches, the haunts of Owen Glendower. We had seen him in both parts of Henry IV in Wolverhampton that week, grappling with a moody Hal and an audience of schoolchildren.

Near here too was a line of golden, feathery poplars. The woods of this area are spectacular. The Forestry Commission own six areas in Shropshire hill country, and many private owners also develop their woodland according to plans approved by the commissioners. There is not the usual impression of stark conifers, but of a great variety of trees – spruce, larch, oak, beech, sycamore. Driving the next day towards Anchor and the Welsh border, near an old farm called Hall of the Forest (another ancient farm near by, Lower Spoad, has a heavy carved wooden chimney beam of a deer hunt that typifies the pre-Norman spirit of the hunt in these forests), we were brought up short again and again by the autumn colours of the leaves, with Wales bluely in the distance. Scarlet hawthorn berries, blackthorns, black elderberries, golden leaves and bracken, and wild cherry trees, of which there are many in the area (again planted by the Forestry Commission), burnt a brilliant crimson.

The country alters subtly over the border, but still looks soft and fertile. Little cottages have the carved dormer windows of Wales, painted in bright colours.

Newtown has surprising charm. All year we had read in Midland newspapers about Welsh anger over the water from the Elan reservoir which supplies Birmingham. We half expected to see dark, angry faces and hear insults hurled in Welsh. But these border towns are calm and friendly, and English and Welsh seem to mix in complete harmony. There is a Welsh lilt to the voices, and shops are called 'Griffiths and Griffiths', but only one in twenty or thirty speaks Welsh, except on market days when people come in from the villages. There are fleeces in shop windows, but British woollen clothes are sold in preference to Welsh because they are cheaper at present.

The Severn flows broadly here; it is easy to imagine the floods of 1964, and the 'Night of Terror' in 1946, when a bridge was washed away. The town is somewhat like Burton-upon-Trent – red-brick Victoriana. It is dominated by the Pryce-Jones building, 'the largest retail store in South Wales'. It was established in 1859 by Sir Pryce Pryce Jones, who already had a factory. Sir Pryce sent samples of Welsh fabrics to international exhibitions, and the exterior walls are peppered with stone medallions of awards – 'Vienna 1873'. He was also a pioneer of shopping by post; in the 1880s he averaged 2,000 letters a day and was patronized by royalty and the crowned heads of Europe.

You enter the store over mosaic steps, half expecting an elephant or a nabob to appear. On the stairs is a stained-glass window with royal crests, and the motto 'Patronized by Her Most Gracious Majesty the Queen'. No name. They obviously believed Victoria would reign for ever.

The lavatories say 'disengaged' for 'vacant'.

The store is a bit more hoydenish now. 'Owned by one of those Gussies,' an employee told us (Dacca Ltd). 'No,' he said, 'I *don't* think Sir Pryce would approve. It's a different place altogether.'

My mother had been telephoning me from the warmth of Brighton, speaking to what she regards as the utilitarian and arctic Midlands. 'It's going to be a very hard winter: the snails are going underground.' I bought vests at Pryce Jones which stretch from neck to knee. Did Victoria get hers here?

On a Saturday afternoon both libraries in the town were firmly shut. We glanced hopefully at an uninspiring municipal building. 'That's the *Town Hall*,' a policeman said with shocked pride. There were also some ambitious flats in a modern Welsh-castle effect, looking like the onset of a migraine.

The pubs of course were open, also the cream bun shops. (The relation of cream buns to the wide girth of Shropshire or Welsh women must strike the most charitable observer. But then the cream keeps out the cold. 'Starving' means 'frozen' in Shropshire.)

It was the week of a general election in England, and I wondered if *Plaid Cymru* supporters would be vocal. This is much more a thing of the north however, of Caernarvon and thereabouts. Round the pub fire in Newtown, which is staunchly liberal, conversation ran something like this:

'You got in again at Carmarthen, the bloody nationalists. I suppose the beer will be full of water again.' (Speaker from Birmingham, pinching market-stall girl's knee.)

Publican: 'We'll poison it.' Then good-naturedly, 'You can have all our water and we'll keep the beer.' By the fire the grey Welsh beards nod.

The amicable atmosphere seems suitable for a town that in 1771 bred Robert Owen the socialist.

On the outskirts is a small trading estate, and a GKN works. We went on up to Welshpool, which is similar but less attractive. On the other hand, Montgomery, half way between the two, has a fine Georgian square although it is a small place; graceful paving opens almost immediately on to fields, and above is a ruined castle growing out of a wooded cliff. How pleasant county towns must once have been – from farm to market or banquet with one clatter of a carriage wheel.

George Herbert was born in this castle. His father was Sheriff of Montgomeryshire, and his mother a lifelong friend of John Donne, who addressed to her his elegy 'The Autumnall' ('No Spring, nor Summer Beauty has such grace / As I have seen in one Autumnal face'). Donne must have conceived here his poem 'The Primrose, being at Montgomery Castle, upon the hill, on which it is situate'.

The whole Welsh border country is of course a string of castles, from north to south. Chirk, Oswestry, Chirbury, Montgomery, Clun, Ludlow, Radnor, are only some of them. One of the most striking is Powis Castle, outside Welshpool, which is comparatively modern, the oldest part having been built in the early fourteenth century and much of it being Tudor. An earlier castle had stood quarter of a mile away, and had remained proudly unconquered by the Marcher lords, the seat of the Princes of Powys, who were sitters on the fence between the Welsh and English.

The present castle was called Castell Coch (the Red Castle) from the red sandstone from which it is built. Smoky pink sandstone rather, its turrets rising from formal gardens with tall yew hedges and pink stone arcading, above shrubs which in the October sun are also hazy with pink and crimson, spiked with palm fronds. It has the appearance of an Italian castle, both warm and formal. But beyond the red dragons which guard the gates, a canal winds, instead of fountains, and mild-faced bullocks crop the grass. The border country may be Welsh in part, but it is very English too.

14 Shrewsbury, Ludlow, Much Wenlock, the Long Mynd

> While Ludlow stands . . . we have an England to protect.[1]
>
> John Betjeman

The England of the Welsh Border country has always needed protection. Towns such as Ludlow and Shrewsbury, where two of the most important castles of the Marcher lords stood, and stand, have a turbulent history of battles and bloodshed. Sometimes, as in the much restored Shrewsbury Castle, this history is hard to detect; but at Ludlow Castle, and at Battlefield, where Harry Hotspur was slain, the air is cold with spilt blood and the wind seems to carry the heroic and doomed sound of trumpets.

Many magnificent heroes, or villains, besieged Shrewsbury. The town, the county capital, was an important centre by the reign of King Edgar (959–975); there is evidence to suggest that before that it lay on a prehistoric trade route. By the time of the Norman Conquest the town had five churches, and Roger de Montgomery then built the castle in the neck of the loop of the Severn within which the town of Shrewsbury lies, like an island.

Wild Edric, whose ghost roams the Stiperstones, was one of the first leaders to besiege the castle. He burnt down part of the unfinished fortifications, but was finally forced back. A century and a half later, in 1215, the great Welsh leader Llywelyn captured Shrewsbury for a short time during his campaigns on behalf of the Wales which he had welded into a single nation. He captured castle after castle, and when he grew old beseeched his lords to remain faithful to Wales and to his son David, who, however, promptly paid homage to Henry III. But Llywelyn the Great's grandson was as brave and skilful a leader as his grandfather. He ignored the summons of Edward I to pay him allegiance and Edward was reduced to capturing Llywelyn's affianced bride. Ultimately Llywelyn made peace for a while, but after a further campaign, he was killed in a skirmish by the Mortimers near Builth, and when his brother too was defeated by the English, Edward had him hanged and quartered, the four quarters being sent to York, Bristol, Northampton and Winchester. The execution took place at the High Cross in Shrewsbury on 3 October 1283. Six months later, Edward presented his infant son to the Welsh as Prince of Wales at Caernarvon. The Welsh wars were over.

But not the warfare. In 1403 took place 'one of wyrste bataylys that ever came to Inglonde, and unkyndyst' – the Battle of Shrewsbury.

> Two stars keep not their motion in one sphere;
> Nor can one England brook a double reign,
> Of Harry Percy and the Prince of Wales
>
> Fare thee well, great heart! –
>
>   – this earth, that beares thee dead,
> Bears not alive so stout a gentleman.

Prince Hal, during the encounter with Harry Hotspur in *Henry IV Part I* in which he mortally wounds him. Shakespeare's battle is not entirely historically accurate, but when one has seen the play one can see the events in no other guise. The outlines are the same anyway, and he gives us the essence. (Shakespeare's colourful Owen Glendower was indeed a legendary leader, who had waged guerilla warfare against the English for years and who seemed to have the elements on his side, so that people believed he used black magic. Prince Henry may not have been quite so wild in his youth as Shakespeare has it, but he was only fifteen at the time of the battle, and his courage on the field there was later confirmed at Agincourt.)

At the battle, Henry IV, whose title to the throne was disputed, and his son Prince Hal, defeated the Scots Douglas and Henry Percy (Hotspur), who with Glendower had rebelled against the King. Glendower did not reach the battle; Hotspur, marching from Chester, had a force of about 10,000 men, the King 2,000 more. The King was positioned on a slope three miles to the north of Shrewsbury, now known as Battlefield. A small crest of land marks the spot where Hotspur's men were attacked from the rear by Prince Hal, and he slain. The battle had lasted three hours, and a strip of country three miles long was covered with the bodies of the dead. It is estimated that on Hotspur's side alone some 5,000 died, and the proportion of knights was high; ten of those who fell on the King's side had been knighted that morning.

Henry IV founded a chantry chapel on the spot in memory of the fallen, the building being erected over a great pit in which most of the dead were buried. The little church still stands.

It is in marshy land. White daisies are scattered over the field. In a neighbouring paddock one white horse was cropping grass when we were there; in the paddock on the other side was one black horse. A few solitary crows. A warm gust of air seemed to hover round one of the three original doorways, which are very small, so that John had to bend double. Otherwise the church is cold, and on the hammer-beams on either side of the roof hang the coats of arms of the knights who fought in the battle – Henry IV, the Earl of Dunbar, Sir Hugh Stanley, Sir Hugh Mortimer, Sir Madoc Kynaston, the Earl of Stafford, Sir Richard Hussey, and others. Lions rampant, brave reds and golds and blue, black birds. The small shields are immensely moving, hanging defenceless there; brave and defiant; defying time. The trumpets sound in the cold air. The daisies grow. Is it hallowed ground?[2]

*

The people couldn't believe that Hotspur was dead, so his body, which had been interred at Whitchurch, was disinterred two days later and brought back to the High Cross in Shrewsbury. A notice there, not far from Woolworths and a multi-storey shopping centre, tells that 'the Dead Body of Henry Hotspur was here placed between two mill stones and afterwards beheaded and quartered'.

> And all the budding honours on thy crest
> I'll crop, to make a garland for my head . . .

A few people with cameras pause, but the street is busy with crowds of shoppers. Modern Shrewsbury is a great shopping centre. (Shrewsbury is 'correctly' pronounced Shrozebury, although many locals call it Shruesbury.) On Saturdays it is chaotic, and the traffic in the narrow streets assaults the ear drums. It is quieter on weekdays, but there is a general impression of shopping baskets and women piling into the cream-bun shops to regain their strength. A problem faces Shrewsbury in that although by the thirteenth century it was a big trading centre and import-ant for its wool industry, and had a great resurgence of prosperity in the sixteenth century after a period of decline, it never became an industrial town in the nineteenth century. So on the one hand there are a great many fine old buildings which have survived, while on the other hand there was little good nineteenth-century planning, and post-war re-developers had a heyday erecting monstrosities higgledy-piggledy among the brick and timber. The problem now is that the town cannot really cope with its heavy traffic, and yet how does one re-plan without destroy-ing old buildings? Shrewsbury must stand firm to retain its city centre, or the beautiful old town will be irreparably spoilt.

One can't complain too much, however. Today it is still a town of immense attractions, unexpected bonuses. You can wander from the castle-like railway station down narrow streets or 'shuts' called Grope Lane, Gullet Passage or Butcher Row, which look as they sound – black-and-white, leaning, overhanging. Dogpole, a wider street, leads down to Wyle Cop, where stands the Lion Hotel, with an arcaded balcony like a black Mary Queen of Scots bonnet on its white front, and other timbered houses. Pigeons nestle under the eaves and on the sills, their mauve grey feathers softening the scene in grey evening light. (Too many of them apparently. Recently the council was reduced to shooting some – after dark. For fear of the English bird-lover?)

Other parts of the town are Georgian. During the seventeenth and eighteenth centuries the county families had town houses in Ludlow and Shrewsbury, and often spent the season there in preference to London, an uncomfortable coach-ride away. Celia Fiennes, a traveller with an eye for the niceties of houses and elegant gardens, mentions that (in 1698) 'there are abundance of people of quality lives in Shrewsbury more than in any town except Nottingham'.[3]

It is less gay now. In spite of concerts and an experimental theatre, one gets the impression that the town is a daytime place. 'Well, there's Tiffany's . . .' said some girls I asked (described in the town guide as 'dancing to big bands . . . in an atmosphere of Byzantine majesty'). There are pink-and-white 'county' girls, but they have flats in London as soon as they can escape from Mummy and less splendid middle-class Byzantium. You see them in the train – Jane and Amanda and Lucy – chattering loudly and blinking long blasé eyelashes as the small-town life recedes behind them.

But the visitors flock in.

One small, elegant house, Clive House, has two outstanding museum collections – porcelain and military objects. The porcelain is mostly the delicate blue-and-white Caughley porcelain, and examples from the famous Coalport Company founded by John Rose in the 1790s. There is a magnificent Coalport dessert service (*c.* 1805) called the 'Animal Service', with tigers, rabbits and dogs meticulously painted within a rich border, and an equally striking botanical service hand-painted a little later. Visitors come from as far as South America on personal recommendation to see these treasures.

Another small museum: another age. Rowley's House, a sixteenth-century timber-framed house, stands in an unprepossessing area of bus station and car park (scheduled to be re-landscaped during Architectural

Heritage Year). It houses among other things, Roman finds from Viroconium. There are hammers and axes and shovels exactly like ours, and pottery which could come from any crafts shop. A silver mirror found at Viroconium is studded with Roman art-nouveau flowers. Stacks of brown soup bowls are pure Habitat (although I have seen nothing like the glossy red Samian ware, the Roman export-market dinner ware). This homeliness makes the Romans seem very near. The reconstruction paintings by a museum artist of tiled houses and markets and a pillared open-air swimming pool, make ideal material for school visits.

School and Shrewsbury; all but synonymous. The old buildings of Shrewsbury School, which was founded in 1552, are now the public library and art gallery. A statue of the distinguished Old Salopian Charles Darwin sits broodingly outside. Inside, you are in school. There is that indefinable but unmistakable atmosphere which schools seem to have – an enclosed feeling, an oppressiveness enhanced by sunny views of the outside world seen, as here, through gothic windows. Initials are carved deeply in the thick oak windowsills – but one looks in vain for those of the most distinguished of all Salopians, Philip Sidney. The top floor, the art gallery, is the school hall, with decorative ironwork. From here you look out towards freedom and the gleaming river, but cannot quite see the present school buildings on Kingsland on the opposite bank.

These seem inaccessible until you know the way. I wandered towards them across Quarry Park, Shrewsbury's pride (Percy Thrower was Superintendent of Parks in Shrewsbury until 1974). The grassy slope runs from St Chad's Church down to the river. A magnificent glass-enclosed public swimming bath (or rather baths, 'heated swimming complex' in guidese) also looks over the slope, which is alive with schoolboys enjoying their lunch hour. Are these lucky privileged creatures from Shrewsbury School? It appears not. They come from the pleasant brick buildings of the Priory School, one of the town's several grammar schools. They don't see much of the boys from *the* school, but consider them 'all right, the ones we know', and have a certain sports rivalry with them. The Priory boys showed me how to climb through a short cut on to a suspension bridge. (There are nine bridges over the Severn in Shrewsbury; the most beautiful, the Old Welsh Bridge with its gate towers, can now only be seen in prints.)

Across the river, past other, tweed-jacketed, red-cheeked boys from Kingsland Grange, to Shrewsbury School. Close to the gateway is a war-memorial statue of Sir Philip Sidney, looking very young and handsome and courtly. His successors were coming out of lunch, looking relaxed and happy. There is a great feeling of space, and of trees in the Common round the buildings; trees are carefully planted, and boys have bird boxes and are keen ornithologists. There seems to be freedom from organized sports except for one or two days a week. It is a rowing school, but there are alternative pursuits such as music which can be followed in the afternoon. A new reading room well stocked with everything from Solzhenitsyn to Saul Bellow (and, of course, *Rupert of Hentzau*) looks out over the river. I leafed through books on famous Old Salopians – Mgr Ronald Knox, Neville Cardus, Richard Hillary, and Stephen Paget, a nineteenth-century man of letters who apparently came up with the splendid maxim, 'Truth may be found at the bottom of a well; but so may a dead cat.' On a wall in the library proper was a self-portrait of another OS, Samuel Butler, looking like Dirk Bogarde. Present-day Old Salopians include 'the Private Eye Lot . . . I don't know if we are *quite* so proud of those. . .'

The librarian Mr Lawson, who is also a research historian, was busy with a lanolin preparation with which he was restoring old leather bindings. And they are worth restoring. It is a fabulous collection of books, with sixty books printed before 1500, an illustrated Boccaccio printed in Louvain in 1487, a bulky herbarium with pressed flowers collected in 1676 at Oxford – countless other treasures. The early books of before 1800 are largely those given to the school by notable citizens when it was a country grammar school, before Samuel Butler (the headmaster), and Kennedy and Moss, changed the school from its run-down state to an independent public boarding school. The books were kept on chains, and leading citizens could come to read them.

We moved on to a large safe. A strong room, but my guide threw open the doors with abandon and I felt these books were here to be handled and looked at. I can still see in my mind's eye the writing of the margin notes of a Juvenal of 1100.

'How can I describe the size of the writing?' I asked Mr Lawson. A millimetre is far too big. The letters are each the size of a pinprick, a column of insect writing beside the scribe's beautiful text.

Philip Sidney's name is entered in the old register for October 1564, when he entered the school with his friend Fulke Greville. He 'tabled' in town with alderman George Leigh, and brought with him his own tutor (for subjects such as French not taught at school, and probably to keep an eye on his religious education: the Sidneys were extreme puritans). Accounts kept by the latter show that although Sidney is known for having been a serious youth, boys were boys then as now. '. . . for mending a glass window in his chamber, 4d', 'for a stopper for his inkhorn

1d', 'given to the laundress to buy silk to mend his shirts, 4d' (as son of the Lord President he bought numerous pairs of gloves and shoes), 'for certain bird bolts to shoot at birds, 8d'.

I learnt more history in half an hour from Mr Lawson's enthusiastic commentary than in a school year. He also showed me the Moser collection of English watercolours – a Turner, De Wints, David Coxes, a surprising Arthur Rackham. Boys who had classes in the gallery progressed in one term from 'How much would you get for that one?' to 'I like this one, because . . .' What a heritage. Very English. I looked out at the sculling race on the river, gilded in the evening light. Spires rose beyond trees. Anyone would want this for their child. And yet . . . shouldn't this heritage be for every child to see, to have?

*

Shrewsbury is also churches. The old Abbey Church, St Alkmund's – by a well-restored corner of timbered shops and houses, the Bear Steps – St Julian's, and St Mary's. The last is the loveliest. Visiting churches can be a tiring business, and usually one thinks yes, that is quite nice, or not so nice, a little cold or dark, or over ornate. Reading notes later one cannot remember why a particular gargoyle was so momentous, and one's readers would wonder still more. Guidebooks which progress from 'light' to 'light' tend to leave one without it. But in Shropshire I have seen two churches which literally took my breath away, so lovely are they. Going in to the church of St Laurence in Ludlow, I was reminded of Notre Dame; its tall pointed arches rise up to infinity in a burst of light; I stood staring, rather to the surprise of an elderly lady with a stick who goes there every morning, six days a week: 'I can't manage the evenings because of arthritis'.

St Mary's in Shrewsbury is rich and warm – a broad nave with rounded arches, the royal arms in gold, a beautifully carved ceiling in squares softened by wings and leaves. The light streams in through the clerestory windows on to the pale pink stone; through a brilliant Jesse window in blues and gold and green with one spot of bright pink, the Virgin's robe. The sun shines through the Flemish stained glass so that a bright blue and red are burnt in spots of colour into the stone and hang there, in November above the war memorial with its poppies and rosemary, in a brilliant kaleidoscope round the hanging figure of Christ. There is hardly any need for the gilded organ to play.

*

Markets, too, are an essential feature of Shrewsbury. A new general market, and on the northern side of the town a 25-acre modern cattle market. The town is the natural centre of a large agricultural region. The Shrewsbury Agricultural show is a major annual event, and the cattle market, besides serving its commercial purpose, with an abattoir near by, provides a showground for other shows. It was also the scene of demonstrations by farmers during the recent beef crisis, when Shropshire farmers led calves to the market place to be slaughtered, to show their anger at beef prices.

As elsewhere, farmers in general have had a lean time in the last few years, or as one farmer put it – 'Last year it was all wet, and this year all dry. The animal side is really dicey, very up and down. Some farmers have had a very mean time.' Because of the fodder situation, 115 dairy farmers in the West Midlands got rid of their herds in one month recently. However, there are more encouraging elements also. Mixed and arable farming have fared a bit better, especially co-operative efforts. One Shropshire farmer's wife whom we know, who with her husband runs four farms for a big combine, living on one, reports that they have had a fair year, with oilseed and rape doing well, and also hops. 'The whole point about it is that you must have something to sell each week to keep going.' With other farms in the co-operative in different parts of the country, this is possible. Profits are shared, and a farm must give six months' notice to leave the venture. Combines go round twenty different farms all over the country, and are even shipped to Australia and back each year, as the co-operative have 17,000 acres of corn there, and this proves the cheapest way.

Labour is one of the major problems. 'The spare-parts bills are something shocking. That's with the younger, careless ones. The older men are not so madbrained. Students drive the tractors flat out. An older man with at least ten years' experience, goes more steady, and knows how to mend the tractor as well.'

In the Shrewsbury Smithfield market we saw the Shrewsbury Shire Horse Show and horse sales this year. It is a cheerful occasion, packed with children, ruddy faces, deerstalkers and tweed tam o'shanters, with canny whiskered farmers' faces nodding sagely. The great shiny flanks of the shire horses gleam and their hooves smack down on the concrete as they wait impatiently in the pens, with their manes and tails plaited and dressed up with ribbons. Seldom seeing shire horses in the fields now, it is a pleasant shock to see so many. Although they are mainly kept for showing, they are not at all redundant creatures. In a bad winter, after torrential rain, enquiries flood in to shire-horse owners for horses to draw carts in potato fields which have become too waterlogged for tractors. A horse can still take a plough where a tractor can't if the ground is very bad indeed.

In the old days of course, as an owner pointed out to us, 'When a horse was in a field it was feeding it. Now tractors drop oil.'

Shire-horse colts were selling for about £400 and a prizewinner had been withdrawn at £870. We photographed Hollinsgay Boy – or Prince for short – champion of his class, who has gone on to win other prizes this year. He was coming up to four years, unbroken; but shire horses are no trouble to break in if they have a good temperament. Ponies in the sales were selling for about 83 to 106 guineas (prices are still quoted in guineas), although there were no bids of even £10 for a few of the colts. This was probably due to the financial climate, as riding in the area is as popular as ever. Local horse shows give evidence of a high standard, and seem identical to those of yesteryear: a preponderance of girl riders, determined small children dressed as Indians or knights for the fancy-dress class, and even more determined mothers having as much trouble with heavy teenage daughters as the daughters have with their horses – 'Well if you must get so *tense*, what can you expect . . .' 'O *Mum*my . . .'

*

It was in Shrewsbury market that Mary Webb, the writer, sold produce on a stall to eke out her and her husband's small budget. She would walk there 'in an old coat and faded gown'.[4] She was a tireless walker, and would walk for hours, her mind on other things, once with twenty tiny pearl buttons of a dress undone. The middle-class regarded her as eccentric. Her looks had deteriorated by the time of her marriage – she had suffered from exophthalmic goitre and pernicious anaemia from the age of twenty, and died at forty-six – and one feels there is much of her in Prue Sarn, the hare-lipped heroine in *Precious Bane*. 'For indeed I loved my kind and would lief they had loved me . . . I would lief have ridden forth and seen new folk, new roads, new hamlets, children playing on strange village greens.[5]

She was born at Leighton, at the foot of the Wrekin, and after her marriage lived in several places near Shrewsbury, her last home being at Lyth Hill. Her husband worked in London for a time, but Mary could not be happy out of Shropshire, although by the end of her life she was meeting in London people such as Lady Asquith, Mrs Thomas Hardy, Walter de la Mare. She 'did her best to live in other places without success. Life outside Shropshire was to her rather an existence. Her letters from

London breathe a longing for her home, garden, flowers, hills and woods . . .[6] She was very much loved by her friends and people in the country. Such was her generosity that one day she would have £100, the next nothing. One Christmas she gave presents to all the old people and children at Meole Brace, where she then lived; a small girl wrote to her in London saying that for her present she would like a piano. She got it. 'She was like that,' commented her friend Miss Southern. And a former cook to her parents, when asked if she knew Mary had become a writer, remarked: 'Books? No, I didn't! Fancy! – she never seemed a girl like that.'[7]

I read Mary Webb's novels as an adolescent, and was entirely carried away by them. The dreamy, violent passions she evokes are just the thing to find an echo in the breasts of teenage girls. I expected to find my adult reaction very different on re-reading the books recently, but no, not entirely. To me she is a writer of some stature, and that her books are not in paperback amazes me. True, the (authentic) Shropshire dialect can be irritating, with the 'liefs' and 'times', and there is a side to her that would be too much for anyone. (When a friend asked her one day 'Where have you been to get so wet?' she replied 'the tall corn called me, and I had to walk through it'.)[6] Yet here is someone who has walked through wet corn; who knows Shropshire – and life – exactly and precisely; who has a grip on both.

She writes of the mere at Sarn, in *Precious Bane* (Bomere Pool, to the south of Shrewsbury).

I call to mind the thick, blotting woods of Sarn, and the crying of the mere when the ice was on it, and the way the water would come into the cupboard under the stairs when it rose at the time of the snow melting. There was but little sky to see there, saving that which was reflected in the mere; but the sky that is in the mere is not the proper heavens. You see it in a glass darkly, and the long shadows of rushes go thin and sharp across the sliding stars.

And again, how perfectly she describes in another instance country which could be the Shropshire weald moors, or the region beyond Ellesmere. 'There was a kind of sour laughter in the thought of it. It called to mind the blackish autumn evenings, when grouse rise from the bitter marsh and fly betwixt the withered heather and the freezing sky, and laugh. Old harsh men laugh that way at the falling down of an enemy.'

Her poetry is more purple, sentimentalized, than her prose. Fame came to her late. After *Precious Bane* had been published eighteen months, in 1926, Stanley Baldwin wrote to her 'I have not enjoyed a book so much for years.'[8] Typically she sent in reply a bunch of spring flowers – violets.

He started the fashionable ball rolling. My own sister Jancis has the name of the white-and-gold Jancis of the novel, and I see from the flyleaf that my mother was reading *Precious Bane* the spring my sister was born.

I had to see Bomere Pool, the mysterious, reputedly bottomless lake where Wild Edric's sword is guarded by a great fish – Mary Webb's Sarn Mere. We had searched for it in the dark one night, and by day it is not much less bleak. Driving from Kenley, it lies beyond a green stretch of farmland, near Condover, with a view of the Wrekin and away to the Stiperstones, Caer Caradoc. Here it is suddenly cold and windswept, however, rather treeless countryside, with a quarry gnawing into the hillside. As we struggled through the teeth of the wind past gorse bushes, and icy rows of plough, I remembered her description of the oxen ploughing through the snowy fields, their coats yellow against the frost. It is harsh, killing land.

Bomere Farm seemed rather more like Cold Comfort than Sarn. A muck-collector whirled its dangerous cargo past us. A man was asleep in a car in the yard. Meal spilt from a barn. Behind a fence lay a dead calf. A worker told us the lake was 'by t'house', but to get down to the water you have to brave notices from the Condover Estate (possibly old, or not I imagine put up by the Royal National Institute for the Blind who now run Condover Hall as a home for deaf and blind children) telling you that if you have dogs they are likely to be shot.

The rushes are there round the lake, and the twisted arms of beech trees. The sun went in as we reached it, leaving the water dark and sullen. Then a water-skier zoomed across from the far end, leaving a white wake which whipped the water into spray and made it lap against the edge, with a chilling splashing sound.

John started to take some photographs. The skier, who was an adept, instantly thought he was in demand, and circled to within feet of the camera, with a graceful swoop, utterly destroying the atmosphere and threatening to swamp us. I consoled myself with the thought that Mary Webb would have loved his swarthy good looks, and if she were writing today no doubt he would bend silently from his skis to carry her heroine off to the sunset.

*

While Ludlow stands ... But will it stand? In 1974, the beautiful Ludford Bridge which crosses the Teme into Ludlow in a swirl of water and willows (and which has withstood erosion, and wars) was being hacked about to allow the free passage of juggernauts. There was a ten-year battle between two sections of the Department of the Environment over this matter. The Ludlow Civic Society accepted the scheme on the understanding that the widening would be only temporary until the Ludlow by-pass is completed. The chairman was quoted as saying: 'Something had to be done to keep up with the times . . .' It is accepted, then, that we have to have juggernauts; that they cannot make the ten-mile diversion they were making while the alterations were done; that they will continue to cross this old packhorse bridge at the rate of one a minute (I timed them); that they assault the town on the other side up a steep hill to within one inch of the irreplaceable carved timbers of the Feathers Inn.

We must have progress . . .

Go to Ludlow to have your ideas on progress reshuffled. In buses going to the town you will see grey heads, tweed caps, raincoats for the men and tweed coats for the women. You will hear farmers saying 'Oo aye', literally, and retelling a joke of a man who killed all his calves and cut off their tails to prove the point, thus spoiling the skins. They are discussing the terrible price of feeding stuffs: 'they've got to do summat.' As you cross the street in the town, an old woman will clutch your arm: 'I'm terrified – I'm coming with you,' as lorries thunder past, probably narrowly missing drivers such as the octogenarian we saw standing be-mused by his battered car, which had just been hit by another, as a lorry bore down on him. You can go into the Feathers, with its light-brown, not black, timbering – 'that prodigy of timber-framed houses',[9] Pevsner calls it – carved with dolphins and strange faces like Pacific prowheads. Inside are panelling, embossed ceilings, royal coats of arms. There is excellent coffee instantly available for 10p. This was one of the first eight licensed houses in England, and was an hotel as long ago as 1521, in the reign of Henry VIII. A notice outside ('genuinish', I was told) tells you that in 1600 you could have had

Dinner at noone, supper at five, served by comelye and complyante wenches. Good Englyshe Beefe, and churchyarde laddes neede have no fears theyre boiled mutton come from 'Flokkes kept by moonlight'. Venyson pastyes . . . Whyte Bredde made from wheate for Gentylfolke, pure browne from rye and barley (no beans or Acorns) for Churles. Good doves. Geyse (greene or stubble fatted). Succulent bares guaranteed not to cause the Shropshyre melancholiye and subsequent throat slittynge. Home Brewed Ales. Meade.

Butchers in the town offer something of the same today. There are golden steak-and-kidney pies and pork pies, joints like illustrations in a cookery book. A supermarket is tucked discreetly away round a corner.

In spite of heavy through traffic Ludlow is still probably, as John Betjeman has said, 'the loveliest town in England'.[10] On either side of Broad Street stand magnificent Georgian houses, which if one looks at old prints one can see are quite unchanged. Even the cobbles are still there, preserved in cobbled inclines to the pavements. Recently two or three of the largest houses, the eighteenth-century town houses of leading Shropshire families, were up for sale. Few people could afford these town mansions now, and presumably there is a limit to the number of solicitors (those perennial squatters in discreet Georgian offices). What will become of Ludlow?

Beyond being the haven of the retired, which it is. There are good trains to Birmingham and Shrewsbury; Wales is on the doorstep; the people are friendly. And 'there's a nice caravan park'. Progress.

And a haven for visitors. Farther up Broad Street, towards the Butter Cross, are half-timbered Tudor houses. De Grey's café, sixteenth century, has a long room which stretches back at least 120 feet; one can imagine it filled with stylish Regency gatherings. Now shoppers scoff tea and cakes, or fish, with, as John said, enough chips to keep the fish alive for a year.

This was the old Ludlow, the setting later for Mrs Molesworth's *The Cuckoo Clock*.

Near by is the Angel Inn, with a room at the back, the Nelson Room, where Lord Nelson had his title confirmed in 1802. He spoke to the people of the town from the bow windows on the first floor. The room, fittingly, has some ship's timbers, and ravishing prints of Emma Hamilton.

The inn was a coaching inn to Worcester, Oxford and London. You left Ludlow 'every evening at 3 o'clock', stopped the night at Worcester and set off at 5 a.m. via Chipping Norton, the Bear in Woodstock, the Angel and the Star in Oxford, to the George and Blue Boar in Holborn. Or if you remained in Ludlow, you could, on 15 August 1803, have seen Mr and Mrs Siddons in *Othello*, or in *The Mountaineers* or *Deuce Is In Him*. A box was 3/- [15p] the pit 2/- [10p], gallery 1/- [5p]. (Details are given on playbills in the town museum, in the Butter Cross, which has a varied collection including gingerbread moulds, and instruments of torture.)

Not far away is the parish church of St Laurence, with its tall tower. It is one of the largest parish churches in the country, and its windows are magnificent. It also has some well-known carved misericords (the under-sides of the seats for the chaplains of the guilds, which tipped up to make a ledge to lean their behinds on during the daily service). Deer, hounds, a townsman with sides of bacon, an alewife, a fuddled drinker, a mermaid

. . . and also figures which seem to be embracing or fighting, some defaced, as being probably too much for the Victorians.

At four-hourly intervals the church chimes ring out, a different tune for each day of the week. It is a heartening and peaceful moment. You may glance at the plain memorial to Sir Philip Sidney's sister: 'Heare lyethe the Bodye of Ambrosia Sydney . . .', or wander outside to see the simple plaque on the side of the church, where Housman is buried. 'In memory of Alfred Edward Housman, M.A. Oxon. Kennedy Professor of Latin and Fellow of Trinity College Cambridge. 1859–1936.' In the bed in front of the plaque are some of the purple crocuses he loved – 'The beautiful and death-struck year . . . I heard the beechnut rustle down, And saw the purple crocus pale . . .'[11]

It also gives lines from his own *Parta Quies*:

> Good-night; ensured release,
> Imperishable peace,
> Have these for yours.

Here, surely, he has peace. And the end of the poem speaks clearly to those who have none.

> When earth's foundations flee,
> Nor sky nor land nor sea
> At all is found,
> Content you, let them burn:
> It is not your concern;
> Sleep on, sleep sound.[12]

From this peace to the castle, which reeks of bloodshed and strife. Through the market-place, and past municipal gardeners by the Town Hall leaning on their spades and tending roses in a leisurely, autocratic way. Past the retired citizens, some of them clinging here to the last of England's quietness, others aware of an age of pleasant privilege crumbling around them. Past sheep cropping in the outer bailey of the castle, to ruins which forcibly remind one of a more robust, virile age.

One of the strongest in the Welsh Marches, Ludlow Castle was made a royal castle under Edward IV and in the fifteenth century became the seat of the Lords President of Wales, who were almost like kings in these parts with their court of the Marches which ruled over all the border counties. The castle *looks* like a royal seat, with splendid windows and entrances and a grandeur that many piles of stone lack. There is a fine carved stone fireplace in the ruined banqueting room; in the inner courtyard is a circular Norman chapel with arcading, where weeds grow now from the gargoyles round the walls. In the great council hall Milton's masque *Comus* was first performed, in 1634, for the Earl of Bridgewater, whose three children had recently been lost in Haywood Forest and who performed in the masque set in Milton's 'Wild Wood'. Sabrina's 'rushy-fringed bank, Where grow the willow and the osier dank' could equally well be by the Teme, and possibly the perfection of the scenery at Ludlow made the sober Milton put lines of such persuasiveness into the lascivious Comus's mouth that he seems by no means the villain he should be.

> Wherefore did Nature pour her bounties forth
> With such a full and unwithdrawing hand,
> Covering the earth with odours, fruits, and flocks,
> Thronging the seas with spawn innumerable,
>   If all the world
> Should in a pet of temperance feed on pulse,
> Drink the clear stream, and nothing wear but frieze . . .

But it is not scenes such as the Michaelmas night when the masque was performed that come quickly to mind when one visits the castle. Even in this council room, the atmosphere is chilly. It is not a sunny castle; you start when a pigeon clatters away from the walls; tortured figures seem about to appear through the narrow black mouths of the spiral stairways. I began walking up one of these, with my fingers in crevices, but it was too dark and dank.

The atmosphere is not surprising. It was to Ludlow castle that Edward IV sent the two young princes, his sons, who were afterwards sent to the Tower. It was in Ludlow castle that Prince Arthur, the son of Henry VII, died, after a brief few months' marriage to the young Catherine of Aragon. His apartments are in the north-west tower; a chink of light comes round a corner from the staircase; the pain of the sick, fifteen-year-old bridegroom haunts the place.

More lurid still, is the story of Marion de la Bruere, who in the reign of King Stephen let her lover, Arnold de Lisle, an enemy of the lord of the castle, in at night by means of a rope ladder. While they were amorously occupied, all her knight's men scaled the ladder also, and captured the castle. Horrified at his treachery, Marion stabbed her lover fatally with his own sword, and then leapt to her death from the Pendower Tower – which is a very nasty height indeed, and looks precipitously over river and rocks. Ludlow wasn't always peaceful.

*

To the east of Ludlow are the high Clee hills, and beyond them Cleobury Mortimer, where (most probably) William Langland, the author of *Piers Plowman*, was born. The Shropshire hills are very varied in appearance, ranging from the ancient rocky uplands such as the Stiperstones and the Long Mynd, to the gentler limestone ridge of Wenlock Edge.

Wenlock Edge, in its north easterly direction runs from the Craven Arms area towards Much Wenlock and the Wrekin. At Much Wenlock itself are the beautiful remains of Wenlock Priory, a Cluniac monastery built in the twelfth and thirteenth centuries on the site of a much earlier nunnery. The interlacing wall arcading in the chapter house is particularly lovely.

The Long Mynd, which in the distance looks like a peaceable range of calm hills, has hidden attractions and pitfalls on closer inspection. The Portway, which was still recognized as a highway in the Middle Ages, runs along its summit, and the range is about ten miles long, three or four wide. The snag is that, cutting deeply through the hill, are steep clefts and gullies, making valleys which are not only precipitous but almost indistinguishable one from another. We have often picnicked on the barren, heath-like crest of the range (and it was not until I picnicked on the Long Mynd that I realized what obtrusive creatures sheep are; they butt your car and vandalize your food and won't leave you alone for a minute). But if you are walking there, unless you intend to make a very long walk indeed, you should have a compass or take a map, to check your direction – although you can often get your bearings from a heated line of hikers doing the Portway in bursts of efficient speed. It is marvellous hill country to walk over however, and farther on above Asterton is a gliding station, where gliders swoop serenely into the air and circle back like birds.

The treacherousness of the Long Mynd was dramatically highlighted by an event in January 1865, described in a publication later that year by the Reverend E. Donald Carr, to whom the adventure occurred. He was rector of Woolstaston, about three miles across the mountain from Ratlinghope, and on Sunday afternoons he took a service at Ratlinghope. He had crossed the mountain 2,500 times, he estimated, but not for nothing were there spots named 'Dead Man's Beach' and 'Dead Men's Hollow', and the last fair before Christmas was locally known as 'Dead Man's Fair'. That January 1865, the snow was deeper than it had been for fifty-one years. After the service at Ratlinghope he had some soup and hurried off, carrying a small flask of brandy. He was walking on the Long Mynd for twenty-two hours. A furious gale had got up, 'driving clouds of snow and icy sleet before it'. He fell down a ravine. 'The pace I was going in this headlong descent must have been very great, yet it seemed to me to occupy a marvellous space of time, long enough for the events of my whole previous life to pass in review before me, as I had often before heard that they did in moments of extreme peril.' The drifts were far above his head. 'I had to face the awful fact that I was lost among the hills, should have to spend the night there, and that, humanly speaking, it was almost impossible that I should survive it.'[13]

But he did survive, after falling down another ravine, losing his fur gloves and his hat, so that his hands became numb and his hair was a solid block of ice. He was so hungry that he had wondered if he could eat one of the dogskin gloves. Then he lost his boots, but managed to find them again; they are now in the Rowley's House museum in Shrewsbury, looking very wrinkled and small. He was finally seen by some children, who were so terrified at his strange appearance that they ran away, but a little girl came back, and he was taken to the Carding Mill valley.

His adventures needn't deter holidaymakers, however. Church Stretton, at the foot of the Long Mynd, had a brief popularity as a spa in Victorian times, and was thought to be particularly healthy. Today it takes itself seriously as a holiday centre, but has not become spoilt, although unfortunately new bungalows are spreading alarmingly on the outskirts of the pleasantly laid-out town, with its avenue of trees. But there will be walking space on the Long Mynd for a good few years yet.

15 Oswestry, Ellesmere, Wem; Whitchurch; Llangollen

The inhabitants are liberal and friendly to strangers . . .
(1837)

'No, no buses. No. There's a coach to Llangollen in the summer . . .
There might be a train . . .'

'No, there's no train. Yes, to Oswestry there's a train – you change at
Gobowen. No, not on to another train. A bus. No, we don't know about
buses . . .'

It is infinitely harder to get to some parts of North Shropshire by public
transport than it is to get from Wolverhampton to London. Our car had
failed its MOT test. A garage later sent in a large bill for repairs and sent
me home with a loose fan belt. In this birthplace of British cars, where
many learn to drive as automatically as children learn to walk, standards in
garages are appalling. Perhaps with so many cars on the assembly line
they are regarded as expendable. There are legends about men taking
their cars to two old men who will spend weeks lovingly greasing everything including the mascot, but for us this solution has remained legendary.

What do people do in North Shropshire, or South, for that matter, if
they have to get somewhere in the winter and have no car? It is a bleak
prospect. Presumably relations might die while transport officials denied
all knowledge of the means of travel, or gave, as they did to me, incorrect
train times.

★

Oswestry is a garrison town, and its warlike history goes back to the
days when an early Iron Age hill fort was built at Old Oswestry. This is a
spectacular example of such forts, covering about forty acres. Watt's
Dyke later ran along its western edge.

The town derives its name from Oswald of Northumbria, who was
defeated in battle there in AD 641 by the Mercian Penda and nailed to a
tree. Later the town, like the other border towns, had its castle as defence

against the Welsh. But its history as an agricultural town goes back almost as long, and as early as the seventeenth century the area was concentrating on dairy produce. It is an important market town today, for farmers from both sides of the border. Wilfred Owen the poet was born there, a fitting birthplace for a war poet.

This North Shropshire area can be as attractive, although less obviously so, as South Shropshire. Between Oswestry and Whitchurch lie Ellesmere, and a little to the south, Wem. These two small towns are extremely pleasant, surprisingly so to those who may have read of them in guide-books as somewhat 'dilapidated', or who are not expecting elegance in deep farming country. Ellesmere lies round a square, with winding streets of timbered or brick houses. It is encircled by its meres – the large Mere and other smaller lakes – Blake Mere, Colemere, White Mere and three others. On the large mere there is boating, and it is a little like London's Serpentine in appearance in the summer, with brightly dressed crowds. People who dislike crowds of people enjoying themselves – I am not one of them, because to me the enjoyment makes up for the crowd – can shoot off back into the green dairy lands in seconds.

Wem has the same slightly unpainted, unrepaired look, infinitely preferable to an over-painted town. A petty sessions court has its offices there and it is the seat of the North Salop Rural District Council; in some respects it seems more flourishing than Whitchurch or Ellesmere, with a few very good shops. There are streets of those tall 'shoebox' houses, one with a double-bow frontage, many with fanlights. In Noble Street William Hazlitt spent much of his time until he was thirty – he was writing letters to the *Shrewsbury Chronicle* in his early teens.

Wem is famous for cheese and brewing. Wem draught bitter is delicious (the brewery is now owned by Greenall Whitley). You can see the cheese in the market, a hall overflowing with farm produce, fish, tough woollens and socks. Outsize corsets jostle the Cox's Pippins in cosy informality. Across the street is an ironmonger selling everything, including earthenware flowerpots, which are as rare as porcelain now. There is nothing plastic about this town.

Nor about Whitchurch.

*

I stayed with friends in Whitchurch. Their house looks out on a garden so English that it breathes contentment: predominantly pink flowers, roses, no stiffness; a hanging flower-basket; a sloping orchard; neat rows of vegetables on friendly terms with the flowers.

We ate roast pheasant, which my host had shot on an estate towards Llangollen. On the sideboard were apples from the orchard and Cheshire blue cheese.

'Llangollen – Wales – is so different,' I said. 'The painted woodwork on the houses. The Welsh seem such a colour-loving race.'

'Oh they were a colourful, randy lot until Wesley's time. He put an end to all that jolliness and fornication. They used to wear blue coats and coloured breeches, marvellous.'

Later they showed me on a map where, to the west of Whitchurch, the Red Brook and Grindley Brook join, to form the Wych Brook. At this point, there meet three dioceses (Chester, Lichfield, St Asaph), two provinces (Canterbury, York), three counties (Salop, Cheshire, Clwyd or Flintshire), and two countries (England and Wales).

Whitchurch has an imposingness worthy of its position at this meeting of three counties. Round about, the countryside is flat and very green, the rich dairy country that continues in Cheshire, and is some of the best in Britain. (There is virtually no arable farming until four miles below Whitchurch.) Hedges are beautifully kept; the scenery is not dramatic as in Shropshire hill country, and can look bleak in parts, but its watery greenness predominates. There is often a high wind. The town stands on a hill, with its tall eighteenth-century church looking out towards the fields. When the sun catches its pale pink sandstone it is a fine sight. Down the hill are streets with many Georgian houses, and two magnificent banks, one timbered, one the old pillared Town Hall. Also a cast-iron shopfront with arcaded windows – now Sid's Bargain Store, New and Old, Bought and Sold. Many pubs, and coaching archways into yards. Sid's may do brisk business, because on the whole the shops are meagre and tasteless. But this doesn't matter too much because you can buy everything in the Friday market, including books, although the bookstall wasn't doing too well when I visited it. There is also a noteworthy congregational chapel, and Joyce's clock factory (now owned by Smith's of Derby), which has the right appearance for specialists in turret clocks.

Traffic moves slowly in Whitchurch. Cars park all over pavements and traffic wardens are on friendly terms and enquire about your state of health and that of your family. A history of Shropshire of 1837 remarked that

The inns, tradesman's shops and private dwellings bespeak the presence of moderate wealth, good trade, quiet and contentment. The inhabitants are liberal and friendly to strangers, hospitable and polite in their manners. The trade is chiefly in malt and hops; shoes are also manufactured here for the Manchester market.[1]

The friendliness and hospitality are still evident.

The name Whitchurch comes from White Church, and earlier the name was Blancminster. In Roman times, the town, Mediolanum, was half-way between Viroconium (Wroxeter) and Deva (Chester), on the Penkridge–Chester road. Before Domesday, the town (then called Westune or Weston), belonged to the Harold who was killed at Hastings. The beautiful white church was built in about 1087, on the site of one of the many churches built by Ethelfleda. But in 1350 yet another church replaced the white one, until in 1711 the whole tower collapsed one July night, the sound being heard six miles away. The present, Queen Anne, church was speedily put up with funds which poured in (unlike today) from parishioners and from a levy made on strangers stopping in the town for a night, and from country wide subscriptions.

*

'A French mouse?'

My conversation in the church, St Alkmund's, with the rector and verger, was a little like that at the Mad Hatter's teaparty in *Alice in Wonderland*. Mr Jenkins was no exception to the breed of vicars who speak so knowledgeably about their towns, and who are amazingly forbearing towards visitors who may only drop small coins in their church boxes. But he was, rightly, more concerned with the present than the past. A service had just finished, and a pram service, which I had never encountered before and which entails, naturally enough, scores of prams with red-faced infants, was about to begin. He, the verger and myself, talked slightly frantically by the font.

'Harry Hotspur was interred here after the Battle of Shrewsbury, wasn't he?' I said.

'Who?'

'Harry Percy. And then Talbot . . .'

'Ah, Talbot. He's over there. The book's with him . . .' The verger kindly snapped on the lights for me to see the chancel. ('They will sit at the back. I don't put on the lights for them there.')

The book was lying on the nose of the recumbent figure of John Talbot, Earl of Shrewsbury. 'You can see the mark where the blow fractured his skull . . . when they re-interred the skull they found a mouse inside, with its nest.'

The mark in question was visible in a photograph on the wall. I peered at it. Picked up a spectacle box which lay near by. 'Are these your glasses?'

'Ah yes, how kind.' The verger opened the box and it was empty. He looked sad.

'The young mice were mummified,' he said, 'and there were bits of prayer book . . . You'll find it all there.' He thoughtfully left me to make my notes from the leaflet.

The rector said, 'I keep meaning to write a history of the church. You wouldn't like to do it?'

The first pram was arriving, with its lusty occupant. Soon other prams converged and mounted the steps like over-large ants. I thought it was time to go.

'If I ever had time . . .' I said.

'Yes.' And frowning, 'Harry Hotspur?'

The mouse must have been English. John Talbot, Shakespeare's 'scourge of France',[2] whose name, as late as the nineteenth century, was used to frighten naughty children with in Castillon in France, fought for Henry VI against Joan of Arc, and fell in battle at Castillon near Bordeaux in July 1453. A tablet in the church porch says 'Beneath the Stone in this Porch rests the embalmed heart of John Talbot 1st Earl of Salop . . . when lying wounded on the field he charged his faithful guard of Whitchurch men that "in memory of their courage and devotion his body should be buried in the Porch of their Church that as they had fought and strode over it while living, so should they and their children for ever pass over it and guard it when dead".'

The prams mount the steps.

Talbot's body was first buried in France. In a small valley between the Dordogne and the Lidoire to the east of Castillon is a tumulus, once a chapel, to which local tradition has given the name 'Tomb of Talbot'. He was reinterred in Whitchurch in the sixteenth century, but the mouse was found later. His body had been wrapped in 'rare cloth', but the mouse had taken some of this for its nest, and the fracture on the skull was thus revealed, showing how he died. A clergyman of 1874 wrote: 'This mouse has proved a veritable benefactor to history.'

Another John Talbot bequeathed money for the founding of the grammar school in Whitchurch, in 1550 – 'deeply considering and thoroughly perceiving what vice has increased . . . what damage hath ensued to the Realm by want of good education of the youths of the same, which being of nature prone and proclive to Sloth and idleness, the causes of all vice, having loose in their first years the reins of licentious liberty, forthwith receive and imbibe voluptuousness, carnal pleasure, and generally the swarm of all other vices'. As redress, he wanted 'one Free Schoole'. It still exists. As in his day, schooldays can occasionally be tough in the country for some children; urban comprehensives do not have a monopoly on brutal incidents.

There is an excellent library in Whitchurch, the Caldecott library – Randolph Caldecott worked for a time in the town. It has on display mementoes of Edward German the composer, who was also of this town. There are Caldecott picture-books, but there is now no home for his paintings and drawings, because the museum was shut when the old Town Hall was pulled down. 'There's nowhere for it to be.' Instead you have 'the Civic' – the civic centre with its library, cinema and restaurant. Much concrete is in evidence, but there was no cinema at all before, and the auditorium makes an un-harsh setting for concerts. We recently heard the London Mozart Players there.

Past and present meet harmoniously at Hutchinson's Blue Cheshire Cheese factory in Alkington Road. This is not a factory, but maturing cellars, where Cheshire cheeses traditionally developed a blue mould growth to become the blue variety. Mr Hassall, the present manager, can remember the cheese fairs at Whitchurch before the war, and showed me a treasured book with photographs of such fairs – the great barrel-like cheeses spread out on display. There were also photographs of landowners such as the Marquis of Cholmondeley and the Duke of Westminster, in rustic pose with dog or stick, and notes on the important Cheshire families and the places named after them:

> As many Leighs as fleas, Massies as asses,
> Crewes as crows, and Davenports as dog-tails.[3]

Mr Hassall was busy with the Christmas rush (most of the trade is with London), but gave me much information nevertheless. His father was in the business before him. 'I'm no good on theory . . . I like the practical work.' But he gave cheese an exciting aura. Cheshire cheese comes from land where there is salt; that is its basic definition. (Stilton comes from land with lime.) Salt and cheese were the staple products of the area; salt was worked in Cheshire before Domesday. There are nine main varieties of cheese in Britain, Cheshire being the richest, the product of the most fertile pastures. There are not as many farms in cheese now. Some are going over to beef; it takes seven years to get back to milk.

'You should see the farm where our cheese comes from,' I was told.

I did. Hinton Bank Farm has a distant view of the Llangollen hills, which in a warm light make a soft backdrop to the long lie of fields. I was wrapped in an equally warm welcome as soon as I arrived there. Mrs Hutchinson-Smith told me there was coffee on the stove – 'Come in when my husband has his breakfast.' (Cheese-making starts early.) She has a smile of tremendous, immediate friendliness, and seemed to be at one and the same time handing out eggs through the kitchen window to helpers on their way home, offering tea, boiling her husband's egg, seeing her son off for a day's hunting, telling me the intricacies of 'good farming practice' (she was at Edinburgh University and then won a Nuffield Scholarship, studied dairying abroad). Her vocabulary was vivid – 'Too much fertilizer produces dough instead of a good crumb structure for the soil.' 'Everything in moderation for land in good heart. The cultivation of land and the grasses you grow will affect the texture and flavour of the milk. The whey goes to pigs, which make manure, which goes in the grass, and so back to cows, milk, cheese. It's a continuous cycle. Remember that – pigs, manure, cheese.' (I didn't think I'd forget.)

All cheese farms have pigs. I saw the whey in the dairy when I watched Mr Hutchinson-Smith making the cheese. (Harry Hanlin the head cheese-maker was away.) He was inclined to an appealing air of rustiness – 'I think that's right' – but the process is highly complicated, and the dairy had the mixture of spotless scrubbed wood and chemical precision which one associates with a brewery. (Recently the farm was shown on television. 'They were horrified when I plunged my hands (clean) into the curds,' said Mrs Hutchinson-Smith. 'I explained cheese has its own way of dealing with bacteria.') The milk is cooled and lactic acid is added as the 'starter' (in the old days each small farm would just tip yesterday's whey into a bucket of milk to turn it sour overnight). The milk is now in huge stainless-steel vats, with small blobs of butter floating on top. Rennet is added in the right proportion to solidify it. After forty minutes the cheese has the appearance of junket, or white plastic blanc-mange. It is cut into small cubes and stirred with a paddle to release the whey, which is run off, to the pigs. The curds coagulate to form cheese: salt is added; it is all milled, and then pressed into moulds lined with cloths. (Dennis was busy lining moulds with cloths in another room.) After a change of cloths (operated by Pip, the other helper), and three days in the press, the 45-lb. cheeses are bandaged in calico and waxed with cheese-makers' wax.

This (briefly) is the process for standard Cheshire cheese. Mr Hutchinson-Smith was in the Air Force until four years ago. His wife was also in the Air Force until she came back to the farm. She then had the inspiration that if some Cheshire cheeses could turn blue naturally, there must be a way of reproducing the conditions in which they would do so. Hence the farm's success. Blue cheese is more digestible, because the mould breaks down the bacteria. But there must be nothing phoney. Apparently one man in Scotland has tried colouring 'Wensleydale yellow and calling it Blue Cheshire', but a London store promptly sent it back.

I learnt more while Mr Hutchinson-Smith had his breakfast, sitting on a polished oak settle, with a print of the 'Lincolnshire Ox' behind him.

There used to be more cheese farms (there are about 600 farms in the Whitchurch, Nantwich, Wrexham, Chester area). A few are creameries, which do a milk round (you can buy real farm milk with the farm's name on the bottle). Cows couldn't be milked through the winter. They calved in April and were flush with milk in the summer, when cheese was made from the surplus, and dry in the winter when they ate less. On the Continent, one-man farms still produce summer milk only and make farmhouse cheese. ('They are living in the Middle Ages still – not the large creameries, of course.') Cheshire dairy farmers suffered less than beef farmers in other parts of the country during the recent beef crisis, although barley still has to be bought to feed the cows in winter, and as I write, presumably the milk-price depression is affecting them.

However, 'It's a nice life. Farmers can still hunt.'

Their son Rupert had come in in gleaming white stock, about to set off to the meet of the Wynnstay Hunt (Sir Watkin Williams Wynn's Hounds).

'Hunting is marvellous. It's the fear . . . and meeting your friends,' said Mrs Hutchinson-Smith. 'We had the anti-bloodsports lot . . . A day's hunting makes me feel ten years younger.'

(Presumably the fox, if he escapes, feels ten years older.)

I said, 'I can't feel very sentimental about animals while there are still children suffering.' (I am aware that there is a flaw of logic in this argument.)

Mrs Hutchinson-Smith said, 'Yes. You're the first person to mention that.'

Mr Hutchinson-Smith said, 'Well, I'm leaving my money to the cats' home.' The horse box moved off. Pigs, manure, cheese. Foxes, hunts, horses, farms, land – foxes?

*

Out of Whitchurch on the Alkington Road, you pass a small but perfect Elizabethan house, Alkington Hall, once the home of the Mayor of Whitchurch. Farther on towards Wem lies Edstaston, a village with a small church, St Mary the Virgin, divided from fields only by a low stone wall. The gravestones lean, as if in the cold wind that blows here. Inside are faint traces of an ancient fresco, hanging lamps. But it is the doors which astound one. Surrounded by zig-zag Norman arches supported on small stone heads, the doors are the original Norman doors, with the original ironwork. The ironwork is curled, patterned, with branch sprays, stars, scimitar-like Turkish curves, little trees, holding the rough old wood together. The metalsmith's happy choice, and his art, tough as a crusader's sword, seem to dispel some of the loss of our age.

John had driven up to photograph these doors. It was a cold winter afternoon. The vicar and his small son were in and out, emptying vases, working. It was not surprising we got a slightly abrupt reply to our request to take photographs, because we were striding about trying to catch the last of the daylight, trailing flashlights and equipment unquietly. Perhaps the photographs will make some small amends. The church (its doors considered the richest in Shropshire) is in need of public attention.

'I don't know how much longer it will be open,' said the vicar.

'Don't people come to it?'

A wry smile. 'Yes, they come to services, but it's the upkeep of the building.'

We all looked at the little church, which had withstood so many centuries. One could imagine how much any necessary repairs or even ordinary maintenance would cost. But if ever a building should be preserved, this one should.

*

Near by is Whixall Moss. Most open fires round Whitchurch burn brown peat slabs (or turf as the cutters call it), and these you buy at Whixall Moss. There were originally several moss districts in the area, for example Deer Moss to which Deermoss Lane led. Now there are Brown Moss and Whixall. The latter is a largish, but inbred community, with its own church. You reach the moss by a white-wooden pulley bridge over the Shropshire Union Canal, which is pulled up by a chain to let boats through.

It is a desolate, boggy district. You could be in Ireland. Until recently people washed in the ponds that lie in the scrubby grass, among silver birch trees. Now they have a pump, and the small brick cottages have been renovated. They used to have tiny windows opening out of each ordinary window, like one pane opening to let in the air, but the council have banned these little openings. One man, who works for a firm in Wolverhampton, was doing up his own house when we were there and replacing a bigger opening area within the window.

Fat magpies fly up from the grass. There are also rare butterflies in summer, and many other birds. The ground sucks at your feet. There are bulrushes, and red sorrel roots that seep up the reddish water. The turf is cut in trenches, and these stretch out into the flat distance of this land like a blasted heath, cutting through grass which in winter is like sheets of pale blond hair. The narrow cuts of water make silver channels through this pale mistiness; above is the colourless winter sky. You can breathe in deeply the icy air and your eyes hold the scene like a painting.

In the summer the cotton-grass, standing in clumps in the channels, flowers in soft hare's tail tufts, blowing in white sprays against the dark water. Cuckoos sing on and on, and there are cuckoo-spit flowers.

We talked to Mr Tinsley, who was cutting turf there, and he told us that it is now mostly used for fertilizer, horticultural uses. 'Percy Thrower uses it.' He showed us how you cut the 'benches', cutting the turf and piling it in a row along the cut (it looked like walls of chocolate fudge in the distance). It is then left for about three weeks to dry out. The next year the bench is cut deeper, and then another bench is started. The slabs used to be longer, for burning, but are now squarish. They are marked out and cut with a sharp mattock-like cutter, and then lifted with a square spade.

Mr Tinsley told us that one person can cut about 300 turfs an hour, but a German machine has been introduced in another part of the moss which can cut 1,500 turfs an hour. He didn't seem to begrudge this. There are about 5,000 acres in all. 'It will come to an end in time, but not in our time.' 'The young ones won't touch it – too much hard work,' he said, piling up the mounds deftly and seemingly without effort although it must be heavy work lifting the slabs. He isn't a hefty man, and has a very cheerful, quickly smiling face, with a country openness about it. He wears overalls and a soft canvas hat.

We left him to walk down by the canal, where there are small farms. Horses were tethered along the canalside. Three dogs and a man were driving two cows home. If you can see the Welsh mountains from Whixall it means it will rain, he had told us. If you can't see them it is a sign of good weather.

*

To the west of Whitchurch and Ellesmere lies Llangollen, in its valley. You can reach it through the small town of Ruabon, or through Chirk, with its castle and famous aqueduct crossing the valley at a height of seventy feet. An even more spectacular sight is Telford's aqueduct at Pontcysyllte, which carries the Llangollen Canal over the River Dee. A superb monument of canal engineering, it is over 1,000 feet long and spans the river at a height of 121 feet on eighteen slender masonry piers. Its finely tapering shape makes a striking contrast to a solid early stone bridge which crosses the river near by. Navigating the aqueduct in a narrow boat at this height must be a little nerve-shattering .

At the wharf in Llangollen is an exhibition of canal history, and there are horse-drawn narrow-boat trips. The Llangollen Canal is one of the most popular for holidaymakers, running through this unspoilt area.

Why is Wales so different to the eye? I travelled to the Eisteddfod at Llangollen through fields scattered with daisies. Purple and blue flowers ramped up the banks. (Do conservationists need to be quite so doom filled? Flowers seem to be creeping back, if they ever vanished here.) A pigeon flew across the trees; by the river Tern between Wellington and Shrewsbury a massed hedge of wild roses hung down to the water. The sun shone.

The sun shone in Wales, too, but there was a difference. I came to the conclusion that it was something flinty in the light, a greyness that was nothing to do with gloom but possibly something to do with reflections from grey stone cottages and walls, from flints and slates and the thin grey spires of churches. Everything seemed edged with black, and everywhere there was the silver of splashing water, in the deep valleys. The trees are scrubbier, too. Wales is pretty or spectacular, rarely lush. One doesn't look for calm Georgian mansions, but for pinnacled follies or hidden castles, or for houses such as that in which the generous and eccentric Ladies of Llangollen entertained their famous guests a century and a half ago.

Llangollen itself, even during the Eisteddfod, or perhaps particularly, is ridiculously pretty. There is the cream-and-brown, frilled railway station, now disused; the pinnacled Royal Hotel by the bridge; countless little timbered houses; the squat stone church. And yet it doesn't look prettified; possibly the wide River Dee splashing over its flat slabs of rock and flowing under the arched fourteenth-century bridge (one of the seven wonders of Wales) gives a sense of space and grandeur that saves the situation. Certainly with the flags and pennants flying across the streets for the festival, one feels that for once foreign visitors will get what they expected, and more.

The crowds are carried along on an intoxicating wave of exuberance to the Eisteddfod ground in a large field, ringed round with green hills on which perch white farm cottages; on one of the hills stand the ruins of Castell Dinas Brân in solitary ruggedness. From this bowl the music rises up, relayed by microphones from the marquee, so that you can stand in the sun and look up to the castle where Myfanwy spurned her suitor, poor Hywel ap Einion, and to the other green Welsh hills, while a Welsh tenor voice or a joyful Austrian choir literally transports you with music so soaring that you could be in the fourteenth century of Hywel, or another century; any time, but one place, Wales.

*

I left my neighbour of bus and train, a bright-eyed grandmother just retired from working in Aberystwyth, who had travelled from there each day to the Eisteddfod, because she sang in a choir herself, and was lonely at home now her daughters were away, and sometimes she thought she'd be better off without them anyway, her daughters. Travelling took you out of yourself, and so did music. She liked reading too – but reading didn't get you anywhere, did it? I suggested it could be heartening, and she agreed it could.

Inside the tent, flowers are tiered up behind the stage to make a cottage border, with lupins and stocks and marigolds and trailing creepers, arranged more artistically than any border and fresh scented. The competitions progress briskly – three finalists in each class, and then the 'adjudication', which resembles a school report; the judge doesn't mince matters and uses phrases such as 'less effective in the lower regions', or 'the Almighty has given her a tremendous instrument', or even, searchingly, 'Is Mrs Jones a true mezzo-soprano? . . . Is she not a soprano?' But he can be equally lyrical when the occasion arises, praising the most lovely rendering of a Welsh lyric by a soprano, or the faultless tone and expression of a tenor. There is impartiality, but still it is clear that this is a very local occasion too. There is added warmth in the voice in announcing Marion Jones from a Welsh village and it is clear where the audience's sympathies lie. 'Isn't she little?' 'She's got it . . .' But then, no singing could be more lovely than a Welsh voice singing in Welsh? Certainly that day there were two voices that in the hot marquee with its rattling guy ropes, restless children, long programme, forced the audience to listen tensely to every note.

Outside the tent there are young people from every country wandering across the field, being photographed, dancing in national costume for the television crew who sit like bored Roman emperors at their cameras, while a team of Basque dancers still manage to perform a courting dance with stylized bashfulness as the sweat trickles down their necks on to white lace scarves.

The choirs talk to each other spontaneously; after all there is common ground to talk about, and so the occasion has nothing forced about it; I am sure the organizers are right in their claim that immense international goodwill is engendered here. In spite of the ice-cream vans and souvenirs there is something purposeful and un-flashy about the scene. It is genuine.

I asked an entrepreneurial postcard-seller what the place was like in the winter, and he used that emphatic phrase – 'A cemetery with lights on'. Visitors from abroad had usually read *How Green Was My Valley* and knew little else about Wales, he said, but visitors to the festival can stay in private homes to get to know a little more about the district.

I also talked to the publisher John Jones from Cardiff, who had a stand in the Eisteddfod grounds, and who is producing imaginatively designed books about Wales. He said that tourism was 'only just beginning' in Wales. Certainly you get the feeling here that you can still get the best of both worlds, or as the postcard-seller put it, you can still hear Welsh singing in pubs after time if you know where to go, although a bit of this is put on for the tourists too.

> Forty to the gallon; into the green
> Fields in the past of English history;
> Louis MacNeice, *Autumn Journal* viii[1]

In visiting Chester, we had come full cycle, to our starting point, for it was while driving up to the Chester festival in 1973 that we first thought of attempting this book. We were going there to meet Dom Hubert van Zeller, who had an exhibition of sculpture at the festival; we drove through a region that was for the most part new to us, in this centre of the country, and were amazed at what we had been missing, at the powerful and changing landscape. We wanted to get to know it, more thoroughly than one could do on a short visit; to try to crack its gritty kernel.

Chester, the Roman Deva, part of the ancient kingdom of Mercia, with two churches restored by Leofric and Godiva; a city which held out longer than any other city against William the Conqueror; a leading Marcher stronghold against Wales; a large diocese in Tudor times; later firmly part of the Midland canal network – I make no apology for including it in this book. Spiritually it seems both a part of, and apart from, the Western Midlands, like a rich crown, a grail, an apogee lending the area borrowed glamour, but in essentials, the same territory.

*

We were to meet Dom Hubert for a picnic by the cathedral before seeing his sculpture. It was torrid, un-British July weather.

'Just shortbread and port,' he had said with typical panache. He has great style; has a penchant for telegrams and desert boots (he was wearing beatle boots long before the Beatles), and often sweeps a long scarf round his neck as he is cold almost anywhere but the equator. Preacher, leader of retreats, writer and sculptor, Dom Hubert tells in his autobiography *One Foot in the Cradle*[2] how, as a young man, his friends saw him off to become a Benedictine monk wearing gardenias in their buttonholes. If he is not a saint, you will not meet one here on earth. In spite of almost constant migraine, his vitality, wit and gentleness are boundless. His short stories, laced with astringent and zany humour, give an insight into his personality, his witty compassionateness, love of children. At present he is in Colorado, which he loves, at St Walburga's Convent; he is often at Downside where he took his vows, and has been for long spells in Wales, where the perpetual rain does not seem his proper element.

I once got a postcard from him, saying:

> Somewhere in the throbbing heart of Rhyl
> Am I. . .
> Untroubled by the chips, the bingo and the pill
> Which pass me by.
> But soon the summer season comes to fill
> The streets with accents strange and shrill.
> One wonders why. . .

We walked to St John's Church, where the exhibition was, with Hubert waving to émigré princes, festival organizers and half the aristocracy of several counties (Roman Catholics always seem to know everyone). The church, with a nineteenth-century exterior, is believed to have been the eleventh-century cathedral, and has a Norman nave, medieval ruins outside. Hubert van Zeller's sculpture, much of it in Chester sandstone, is strong, chiselled, reminiscent of Epstein's *Ecce Homo*; although my favourite piece, of a mother and child, is formed of the minimum of naïve curves. This is now at the convent where Dom Hubert was chaplain, at Craigside, near Llandudno.

We saw other exhibitions, which at the Chester festival are not in the least parochial. It was Hubert who told me about St Werburgh, daughter of King Wulfhere of Mercia, to whom the church of that name was dedicated, before it was rebuilt as a Benedictine Abbey in 1093 and later still enlarged to become the present cathedral.

*

The central event of the Chester festival is the Mystery Plays, performed approximately every three years. In 1973 the producer was James Roose-Evans. John and I had not managed to get tickets; we stood unhappily in the flap of the tent in which the plays were performed, feeling we couldn't miss this whole point of the festival. 'Are you inside or out,' a bearded organizer asked us. 'You look as though you're in,' and he firmly dropped the flap behind us.

This is typical of the spirit of the plays. They are not just a performance, but an event in which the whole town takes part. Auditions and rehearsals begin long in advance; you meet people whose daughters have narrowly missed a part, or those who are performing. In the production we saw, the plays were in modern dress, and the first shock of seeing Mary Magdalene or Martha in un-streamlined trousers gave place to a feeling of reality until with the Passion of Christ, performed round a central, real tree, used as a cross and then as a living tree of people climbing up to share the agony, one became a sweating, tensely stretched part of what one so often reads about and so rarely experiences – audience participation. Afterwards the performers and much of the audience flocked off to the pub, or walked round the walls.

Possibly it is Chester's compact size, as well as events such as the plays, which enable it to be a community still, not just a tourist trap. The walls form a complete circuit of two miles – the only city in England still with a perfect ring of walls.

They were rebuilt by Ethelfleda, as a fortress, on the ruins of the old Roman fortifications. The Romans knew how to pick their sites, as the archaeologist at Letocetum had said. Here at Chester on the River Dee, at Wroxeter overlooking the wide curve of the Severn; two of the loveliest as well as most convenient places one could choose. Deva was from about AD 86 the headquarters of the famous XXth Legion, and a port as well as a fortress, as the river then curved much farther towards the town, over the area which is now the Roodee, or racecourse (maps of 1580 show the river still coming up to the Watergate). Until the seventeenth century and later, Chester was the second port to Bristol in the west.

In the Grosvenor Museum are inscribed Roman gravestones, mostly found in the north wall when it was repaired. Reliefs, roof tiles, water pipes and museum maps showing the movements of the legions in the conquest of Britain, bring the period close. An army payslip shows compulsory deductions for bedding, food, boots, clothing and equipment, annual dinner, and burial club.

Other treasures in this museum are Hepplewhite furniture, and dolls' houses, with a little tin model of the London–Bath coach-and-four made for a nursery at Broughton Hall.

There is almost too much history in Chester, and some of the renovated black-and-white becomes cloying. But the finest houses, such as Bishop Lloyd's house or the Bear and Billet Inn, once the town house of the earls of Shrewsbury, are outstanding. From the walls you can also see the small Nine Houses, restored by the corporation in 1969, each with a lion doorknocker; and, across the broad river, enviable modern flats. The rows, the historical two-storey shopping arcades, which are genuinely attractive, house luxury shops, pubs, jewellers. At one point they cross the road via a decorative ironwork clock bridge of 1897, erected by Richard Lord Grosvenor to celebrate sixty years of Victoria's reign, 'at his own expence'. This is hard by the Grosvenor Hotel, whose wheatsheaf insignia heralds the wealth within – full evening dress in the bars and a dining room which has rather the air of London's Connaught Hotel. This is Cheshire, oor kid, unmistakably. 'Have you booked?' said the head waiter nervously, eyeing my travel-worn clothes. We reassured him that we had no intention of eating there.

The cathedral is less packed, perhaps 200 of the 600 or so seats filled at the Trinity Sunday service we went to on our second visit to Chester. Blond Cheshire children, moneyed Cheshire parents. Choirboys whose voices rise up chanting to the traditional tunes, past the lace-like screen with its tapering points, the sandstone pillars, roof ribs, the organ high on the wall with its filigree work and resonant trumpet notes rising from golden pipes; past the pointed arch of the luminously, cloudily-green stained-glass of the window, to circle round in the roof and soar on triumphantly. Stone, glass, voices, effortlessly meeting. This is the core of Chester.

Outside they have built a new green bell tower, which at first glance seems inappropriate. But it grows on you, and in the distance makes a good silhouette, beside the flag flying from the cathedral's square tower. There is something almost toylike about Chester, in its perfection.

*

'When we first came to Chester we used to go on mystery tours, and we always hoped we would end up at Eaton Hall,' we were told by someone who has lived in the city some time. 'It was marvellous, with the setting sun on it . . . And they're very good to their tenants, you know, you should have seen the wreaths when the old duke died . . . mind you, that earl in Eccleston Church was a bit of a one if you ask me – wife of so and so, daughter of so and so, second wife . . .'

The English still love a lord, are reluctant to let feudalism go. Or the correct way of doing things. In the Grosvenor Arms – 'Oysters At the Bar' – radishes were sliced to go with Grosvenor Pie at a speed quite unsuited to the hordes descending on Eaton Hall for Rhododendron

Sunday. We joined the throng and were waved with military precision round the obelisk and into two fields which were fine for Grosvenor sheep but lethally bumpy for D registrations.

Eaton Hall lies in the flat expanse of the Dee lowlands, which with the East Cheshire plain make up the saucer of the county, only a ridge in the middle dividing them. The land is rich, buttercuppy, dotted with palace-like farms, cows, oaks, white iron fences and poplars like the ones that come with toy farm sets. In this flat expanse the perfectly-straight drive of Eaton Hall stretches for a mile and three-quarters, past a tall obelisk – an approach which is more impressive than that of any palace I have seen. Behind the obelisk the old house used to stand, with a tower matching that on the remaining chapel, we were told. Now there is a modern house, built for the present Duke of Westminster (the old house had to be demolished in 1961). It is strangely thirtyish, with rounded corners to its straight lines. The setting cries out for drama, for a swoop of glass, and has been given a mini American embassy. Could Coventry Corporation be persuaded to exchange their swimming baths for it?

'I don't know what you think of it; I *don't* think much of it myself,' said one unfeudal guide at the gate; 'but you can get a nice cup of tea round in the stables.'

The gardens are beautiful, with colour blazing round the lake. Wistaria covers walls, clematis encroaches on statues. And there are only two gardeners now, for eighty-five acres – two others having been made redundant, one of the remaining ones told us as he dashed from fountain to fountain, switching on frantically. 'Walk anywhere on the grass,' he said light-headedly. Anyone who doubts the truth of complaints about death duties can ponder on this.

To one side is a long conservatory walk lined with camellias, beyond a pretty folly parrot house. Endless walled gardens and riding schools; the gothic coach yard and chapel. There is something a little chilling about these latter, in spite of a calm painting of Constance, Duchess of Westminster, by Millais, in the coach house. The sheer size of it, its ornate orderliness and prancing bronze horses, call to mind one of those long German novels in which elderly relations live shut away in a wing somewhere, or a frustrated heir strides through the stables, with lip and whip curled. In the distance, the pinnacles are marvellous, as we had been told – like a plate from a fairytale.

The Grosvenors lie buried in Eccleston Church, across the park. Again the scene is pollarded and gothic, but it is a sunny small village, with contented feudal faces leaning over gates. In a heart-shaped plaque in the church, Christina Rossetti's poem is quoted as a particularly moving epitaph to Doramina Erskine Wemyss, wife of Henry George Grosvenor, who died at Eaton on Christmas Day 1894, aged thirty-eight.

> Remember me when I am gone away
> Gone far away into the silent land:
> When you can no more hold me by the hand.
> Nor I half turn to go yet turning stay.
> Remember me when no more day by day
> You tell me of our future that you planned:
> Only remember me; you understand
> It will be late to counsel then or pray.
> Yet if you should forget me for a while
> And afterwards remember, do not grieve:
> For if darkness and corruption leave
> A vestige of the thoughts that once I had
> Better by far you should forget and smile
> Than that you should remember and be sad.

To the south of Chester the country in the west is very different to that in the east. In fact the meeting of the three counties just to the west of Whitchurch seems the meeting of three moods, three life-styles. Hanmer, a pretty small village overlooking Hanmer mere and just inside what was Flintshire (now Clwyd), could still be in Shropshire, with its small brick cottages, and honeycombed barns. A little farther on, Overton is beginning to look Welsh, with pointed windows and an abundance of woodwork, and across the old county border at Cross Lanes, there are more pointed windows, and colourwashing, and you are definitely in Wales.

Wrexham sports turrets and woodwork, decorated with Welsh dragons. The Border Ales Brewery in Mount Street is like a castle, and there is decorative ironwork on the Wrexham Crest motel and the market gates. There is also typical Welsh greyness – the Wrexham Industrial Estate with bleak-looking houses, and barrack-like modern flats in the town. There are works such as Rubery Owen, and outside the town the Gresford Colliery, which has, behind more modern buildings, its old colliery buildings and the green Meccano-like structures at the pitheads. Farther on up the Chester road are little Welsh dolls' houses in grey and black at Marford and a huge waterwheel at Rossett on the River Alyn. Pulford has chimneys twisted and curled like barley-sugar, and the road advances into the ample, rich Cheshire plain.

The traditional industries of Cheshire were salt evaporation, cheese-making and tanning, with of course agriculture. As the county had little coal, industrial expansion did not arrive properly until the electro-technical age. In this growth of industry salt is still a prime factor, as both in the more northerly districts and here in the Middlewich Sandbach area it forms the basis of the chlorine and alkali branches of the chemical industry – making this the most important chemical region in Britain. Nantwich, once the leading town of the salt 'wiches' and the second town in Cheshire, lost its lead to the others early on, having at one time 400 salt houses, 216 salt works in the reign of Elizabeth I and in 1774 only two works. This means however that the town has stayed remarkably unspoilt, very much an old market centre in appearance.

Salt was one of our oldest industries, and was worked in Cheshire long before the coming of the Normans. At the time of the conquest the 'wiches' belonged to the crown and the earls of Chester. It was also used for one of the earliest taxes of the Romans, and as part pay for their soldiers – hence the word *salarium*. There were numerous salt springs, but also beds of rock salt, which were only discovered later on, the first pit being sunk in 1720. In the old days salt brine was evaporated in lead pans over wood fires, later in iron pans over coal. The author of *Rambles in Cheshire* (1862) tells how two salt crystal mines were opened to the public near Northwich and illuminated with candles, the roof being supported by colossal pillars of crystal. It must have been much more attractive than the usual run of tourist 'caves'.

*

Nantwich lies to the east of the range of hills which rises from the central Cheshire plain, the long ridge standing out in startling contrast to the flat ground, with an odd flat-topped mound like a pimple at the north-ernmost end. Over the hills, one is back in the lovely green grassland, with oak trees and old painted iron signposts at the edge of the road. Dorfold Hall, a fine Elizabethan house is just outside Nantwich, and in the town itself are many old buildings including one of the best examples of a framed house in the country – the Crown Hotel (which has an inset panel of wattle-and-daub walling in a showcase). There are also curved Georgian houses, and a church which contains several treasures as fine and more unsung than those in Ludlow. A window by 'Mr Kempe', made from pieces of old glass, to give a lovely patchwork effect; faintly discernible old murals; choirstalls of *c.* 1380 so knotted and rosetted and interwoven from fine filigree work that they alone proclaim the town's one-time status, and also clearly show the proper function of such stalls in warding off draughts from bald ecclesiastical heads. Misericords to prop up priests during long medieval services, carved like those at Ludlow, one of them showing a boy carrying a cock to a cockfight. A more inspired notice than most of those found in churches is posted beside a legless alabaster effigy of Sir David Cradoc, knight, who owned property in Nantwich and who during the reign of Richard II was Mayor of Bordeaux and engaged on the king's business in Gascony – Bordeaux then being the chief port for the export of wine to the port of Chester. At the time the chief local export from this end was wool, and strangely, ground alabaster was held to be the cure for sheeprot. The absence of legs on Sir David's effigy may thus not be due to the usual Civil War defacements, the notice suggests. 'Sir David's legs may have provided the medicine required to maintain the export trade of England.'

*

South of Nantwich you come back into Shropshire, and to one of Shropshire's most pleasant, unjostling towns – Market Drayton. It has wide streets, eighteenth-century houses, including one now a school with a clock over the stableyard. There are tiled shop doorways, old-fashioned cobblers' shops and saddlers. The roofs make an eventful skyline, particularly the rounded back of an 1870 Baptist chapel, which looks more like a brewery. Lilac falls over walls in Kilnbank Road and Shropshire Street is imposing. Even the housing estates look well laid out. Close to the borders of Shropshire, Cheshire and Staffordshire, the town seems to have some of the best features of all three, having a distinct whiff of the Potteries about it. The guide books do not say much about it, except to mention the usual skirmish by Prince Rupert, and a desk initialled by Robert Clive who was at school there. For industries they list a pork products firm and Corset Silhouette. (Fordhall Organic Farm is in the country near by.) So the small market town goes virtually unscathed, and there you can relax and peacefully breathe in the flavour of an English country town that is a far cry from lofty spires or medieval moats – that is nevertheless England and memorably so.

*

From here, after visiting Chester, we drove back past Hodnet Hall with its gardens, through country as enviable as the place names – Sleapford, Longdon-upon-Tern, Marsh Green – back to the area around Shrewsbury that must be some of the loveliest anywhere, the green border land to the Black Country. 'Forty to the gallon; into the green / Fields in the past of English history.'

At Atcham there is a broad curve of the Severn, placid in the evening light, but alive with fishermen (and fishing is not an esoteric pleasure in this region; men will dash from the office with the minimum of ceremony and maximum keenness, unload waders by the roadside). The area is devoid of pylons; an old bridge is reflected in perfect tennis-racquet curves in the water. The river divides in two gleaming tongues. Nowhere is Sabrina more fair. (Nor an Englishman more himself than fishing by the Severn. More himself than dancing the floral dance or beefeating beef.)

I think when we came to the area we dreamed of living somewhere like this; perhaps most people in the region do. 'Social climbers make for Shropshire,' a brisk Wulfrunian whose spiritual home is London told us. Who can blame them? English people have traditionally loved the country, have moved there when they have made their pile.

We are glad now perhaps to have been thwarted in a dream that in days of petrol shortages and demanding work hours might have proved less than substantial (we live in a home, not a second home). Glad also because it is not in the green borderland but in the black heartland itself that you can more easily begin to discern the patterns that have shaped the area, the dogged currents that wash against or with the larger national tides, criss-crossing them as in a bay, propelling them, washing back or moving onwards, truculent or inventive, dead asleep or thunderous, and as the salt is of the sea, most English of the English.

Notes

The numerals refer to footnote numbers as they appear through each chapter.

Introduction

1. John Betjeman, *English Cities and Small Towns*, 'Britain in Pictures' series, Collins, London, 1943.

Chapter 1

1. Nikolaus Pevsner and Alexandra Wedgwood, *The Buildings of England* (Warwickshire), Penguin Books, Harmondsworth, 1966.
2. George Eliot, *Mr Gilfil's Love Story*.
3. *Welcome, Birmingham Post and Mail*, 1975.
4. See also Edward D. Mills, *The National Exhibition Centre*, Crosby Lockwood Staples, London, 1976.

Chapter 2

1. R. T. Howard (Provost of Coventry, 1933–58), *Ruined and Rebuilt – The Story of Coventry Cathedral, 1939–1962*, Council of Coventry Cathedral, Coventry, 1962.
2. Frederick Smith, *Coventry: Six Hundred Years of Municipal Life*, Coventry Corporation in association with Coventry *Evening Telegraph*, Coventry, 1945.
3. Nikolaus Pevsner and Alexandra Wedgwood, op. cit.
4. Basil Spence, *Phoenix in Coventry*, Geoffrey Bles, London, 1962.
5. F. Bliss Burbidge, *Old Coventry and Lady Godiva*, Cornish Brothers, Birmingham, 1952.
6. Ibid.
7. Joan C. Lancaster, *Godiva of Coventry*, Coventry Corporation, Coventry, 1967.
8. Valerie E. Chancellor (ed.), *Master and Artisan in Victorian England*,

(the Diary of William Andrews and the Autobiography of Joseph Gutteridge), Evelyn, Adams and Mackay, London, 1969.

9. Kenneth Richardson, *Twentieth-Century Coventry*, Macmillan, London, 1972.

Chapter 3

1. W. H. Auden, *Collected Longer Poems*, Faber and Faber, London, 1968.
2. John Betjeman, op. cit.
3. W. G. Hoskins, *Chilterns to Black Country*, 'About Britain No. 5', Collins, London, 1951.
4. George T. Lawley, *A History of Bilston*, Bilston, 1893.
5. *Boscobel, or the History of His Sacred Majesties Most Miraculous Preservation After the Battle of Worcester*, London, 1660, reprinted in 1822.
6. *The Earthly Paradise* by William Morris, illustrated in stained glass at Wightwick by Kempe.
7. Gerald P. Mander and Norman W. Tildesley, *A History of Wolverhampton*, Wolverhampton Corporation, Wolverhampton, 1960.
8. Phil Drabble, *Staffordshire*, Robert Hale, London, 1948.
9. Stephen Morris, *The Revolutionary and Other Poems; The Kingfisher Catcher*, Aquila Publishing Co., Shirley, Warwickshire, 1975, 1974.
10. Stephen Morris, *Penny Farthing Madness*, Summerstar Publications, Birmingham, 1969.

Chapter 4

1. Walter Allen, *Black Country*, Paul Elek, London, 1946.
2. 'Nine Times a Night', from *Kate of Coalbrookdale*, songs from broadsheets collected by Jon Raven, Robbins Music Corporation Ltd, 1971.
3. Phil Drabble, *Black Country*, Robert Hale, London, 1952.
4. *Birmingham and the Black Country, c.* 1870.
5. From 'Brave Collier Lads', in *Kate of Coalbrookdale*, Jon Raven, 1971.
6. Jo Manton, *Sister Dora*, Methuen, London, 1971.
7. From 'The Tommy Note', in *Canal Songs*, Jon and Kate Raven, 1974.
8. 'History of Royal Brierley Crystal', Royal Brierley Crystal leaflet.
9. John Petty, *5 Fags a Day*, Martin Secker and Warburg, London, 1956.
10. F. W. Hackwood, *The Wednesbury Papers*, Wednesbury, 1884.

11. Inga Bulman, *The Communities* (Wayland Regional Studies – The Midlands), Wayland Publishers, London, 1973.
12. 'Black the Name', from *Folk Lore and Songs of the Black Country and the West Midlands*, Vol. II, by Michael and Jon Raven (Wolverhampton Folk Song Club), 1966.

Chapter 5

1. Asa Briggs, *History of Birmingham*, Vol. II, Oxford University Press, London, 1952.
2. Robert K. Dent, *Old and New Birmingham*, Birmingham, 1880.
3. Louis MacNeice, *Autumn Journal* viii, Faber and Faber, London, 1939.
4. Edward Lowbury, *Time for Sale*, Chatto and Windus, London, 1961.
5. Andre Drucker, *Little Men in a Blind Alley*, Figaro Press, Birmingham, 1973.
6. Meriol Trevor, *Light in Winter*, Macmillan, London, 1962.
7. Essay, 'The Development of Religious Error'. The case for Newman's canonization is at present being prepared.
8. Nikolaus Pevsner and Alexandra Wedgwood, op. cit.
9. *Birmingham Post*, 23 June 1955.

Chapter 6

1. Angus Wilson (with Edwin Smith and Olive Cook), *England*, Thames and Hudson, London, 1971.
2. H. W. Timperley, *Shropshire Hills*, J. M. Dent, London, 1947.
3. John Hillaby, *Journey through Britain*, Constable, London, 1968.

Chapter 7

1. Phil Drabble, *Staffordshire*, Robert Hale, London, 1948.

Chapter 8

1. M. J. C. Hodgart, *Samuel Johnson*, Batsford, London, 1962.
2. Lomax, *Guide to Lichfield*.

Chapter 9

1. Life of St Modwen, by Geoffrey, sixth Abbot of Burton, 1151.
2. Rupert Brooke, *The Great Lover*.

3. H. J. Wain, *A Walk Around Burton Upon Trent*, Burton on Trent Civic Society.
4. Shakespeare, *King John*.
5. Sir Oswald Mosley, *My Life*, Nelson, London, 1968. Reissued by Sanctuary Press, London, 1975.
6. Izaak Walton, *The Compleat Angler*.

Chapter 10

1. Arnold Bennett, *These Twain*, Methuen, London, 1916.
2. Henry Allen Wedgwood, *People of the Potteries*, Adams and Dart, Bath, 1970.
3. Mervyn Jones, *Potbank*, Martin Secker and Warburg, London, 1961.
4. C. Shaw, *When I Was a Child*, Methuen, 1903, republished by S. R. Publishers, Yorkshire, 1969.
5. Arnold Bennett, 'The Death of Simon Fugue', in *Tales of the Five Towns*, Chatto and Windus, London, 1905.
6. John Wain, *Sprightly Running*, Macmillan, London, 1962.
7. Margaret Drabble, *Arnold Bennett*, Weidenfeld and Nicolson, London, 1974.
8. Jack Ashley, *Journey into Silence*, The Bodley Head, London, 1973.

Chapter 12

1. Letter to Sidney Colvin.
2. Letter, Elgar Birthplace, Lower Broadheath.
3. W. H. Reed, *Elgar As I Knew Him*, Victor Gollancz, London, 1936.
4. Letter to Walford Davies quoted in *Edward Elgar* by D. McVeagh, J. M. Dent, London, 1955.
5. This photograph and the quotations above are in the beautiful study by Jerrold Northrop Moore, *Elgar: A Life in Photographs*, Oxford University Press, London, 1972.

Chapter 13

1. From *A Shropshire Lad*, in *The Collected Poems of A. E. Housman*, Jonathan Cape, London, 1939.
2. John Hillaby, op. cit.
3. Jean Hughes, *Shropshire Folklore, Ghosts and Witchcraft*, Wilding and Son, Shrewsbury.

Chapter 14

1. John Betjeman, *English Cities and Small Towns*, 'Britain in Pictures' series, Collins, London, 1943.
2. Not to its friends. Last time we were there, a new bench spoilt the view, the desolate dignity of the place.
3. *The Journeys of Celia Fiennes*, edited by Christopher Morris, Cresset Press, 1947.
4. Vincent Waite, *Shropshire Hill Country*, J. M. Dent, London, 1970.
5. Mary Webb, *Precious Bane*, Jonathan Cape, London, 1924.
6. W. Reid Chappell, *The Shropshire of Mary Webb*, Palmer, London, 1930.
7. W. Byford-Jones, *The Shropshire Haunts of Mary Webb*, Wilding and Son, Shrewsbury, 1948.
8. Thomas Moult, *Mary Webb: Her Life and Work*, Jonathan Cape, London, 1932.
9. Nikolaus Pevsner, *The Buildings of England* (Shropshire), Penguin Books, Harmondsworth, 1958.
10. John Betjeman, op. cit.
11. From *A Shropshire Lad*, in *The Collected Poems of A. E. Housman*, Jonathan Cape, London, 1939.
12. *Parta Quies*, in *The Collected Poems of A. E. Housman*, Jonathan Cape, London, 1939.
13. Rev. E. Donald Carr, *A Night in the Snow*, Onny Press, Craven Arms, 1960; first published 1865.

Chapter 15

1. T. C. Duggan, *The History of Whitchurch, Shropshire*, Whitchurch Herald Ltd, Shropshire, 1935.
2. *Henry VI*, pt. I, Act 2.
3. Edmund Driver, *Cheshire – its Cheese-makers, Their Homes, Landlords and Supporters*, 1902.

Chapter 16

1. Louis MacNeice, *Autumn Journal* viii, Faber and Faber, London, 1939.
2. Hubert van Zeller, *One Foot in the Cradle*, John Murray, London, 1965.

Select Bibliography

ALLEN, WALTER, *Black Country*, Paul Elek, London, 1946.

BENNETT, JOAN, *George Eliot*, Cambridge University Press, Cambridge, 1962.

BETJEMAN, JOHN, *English Cities and Small Towns*, 'Britain in Pictures' series, Collins, London, 1943.

BIRD, VIVIAN, *Staffordshire*, Batsford, London, 1974.

—— *Warwickshire*, Batsford, London, 1973.

BOTTRALL, MARGARET, *Izaak Walton*, Longmans, London, 1955.

BRIGGS, ASA, *History of Birmingham*, Vol. II, Oxford University Press, London, 1952.

BULLETT, GERALD, *George Eliot: Her Life and Books*, Collins, London, 1947.

BULMAN, INGA, *The Communities* (Wayland Regional Studies: The Midlands), Wayland, London, 1973.

BURBIDGE, F. BLISS, *Old Coventry and Lady Godiva*, Cornish Brothers, Birmingham, 1952.

BURRITT, ELIHU, *Walks in the Black Country and its Green Border-Land*, Sampson Low Son and Marston, London, 1868.

BURTON, ANTHONY, *Remains of a Revolution*, Andre Deutsch, London, 1974.

BYFORD-JONES, W., *The Shropshire Haunts of Mary Webb*, Wilding and Sons, Shrewsbury, 1948.

CHANCELLOR, VALERIE E. (ed.), *Master and Artisan in Victorian England* (*The Diary of William Andrews and the Autobiography of Joseph Gutteridge*), Evelyn, Adams and Mackay, London, 1969.

CHAPMAN, HESTER W., *The Tragedy of Charles II in the Years 1630–1660*, Jonathan Cape, London, 1964.

CHAPPELL, W. REID, *The Shropshire of Mary Webb*, Palmer, London, 1930.

CHITHAM, EDWARD, *The Black Country*, Longman, London, 1972.

CLAYTON, HOWARD, *Coaching City*, Dragon Books, Bala, N. Wales, n.d.

DENT, ROBERT K., *Old and New Birmingham*, Birmingham, 1880.

DERRY, T. K. and JARMAN, T. L., *The Making of Modern Britain*, John Murray, London, 1962.

DOMESDAY BOOK FOR STAFFORDSHIRE, Staffordshire Local Education Committee Edition, 1970.

DRABBLE, MARGARET, *Arnold Bennett, a biography*, Weidenfeld and Nicolson, London, 1974.

DRABBLE, PHIL, *Staffordshire*, Robert Hale, London, 1948.

—— *Black Country*, Robert Hale, London, 1952.

DUGGAN, T. C., *History of Whitchurch, Shropshire*, Whitchurch Herald, Shropshire, 1935.

FORREST, H. EDWARD, *Shropshire in English History*, Wilding and Son, Shrewsbury, 1923.

FRASER, ANTONIA, *Mary, Queen of Scots*, Weidenfeld and Nicolson, London, 1969.

FRASER, MAXWELL, *Welsh Border Country*, Batsford, London, 1972.

GILL, CONRAD, *History of Birmingham*, Vol. I, Oxford University Press, London, 1952.

HACKWOOD, F. W., *The Wednesbury Papers*, Wednesbury, 1884.

HADFIELD, CHARLES, *Introducing Inland Waterways*, David and Charles, Newton Abbot, 1973.

HANKINSON, JOHN, *Canal Cruising*, Ward Lock, London, 1967.

HILLABY, JOHN, *Journey through Britain*, Constable, London, 1968.

HODGART, M. J. C., *Samuel Johnson*, Batsford, London, 1962.

HOSKINS, W. G., *Chilterns to Black Country*, 'About Britain No. 5', Collins, London, 1951.

—— *The Making of the English Landscape*, Hodder and Stoughton, London, 1955.

HUGHES, JEAN, *Shropshire Folklore, Ghosts and Witchcraft*, Wilding and Sons, Shrewsbury, n.d.

HUTTON, WILLIAM, *The Life of William Hutton, Stationer, of Birmingham*. First published 1816. Facsimile edition from 1841 edition by Templar Books, Easingwold, Yorks.

JONES, EDGAR YOXALL, *Father of Art Photography: O. G. Rejlander*, David and Charles, Newton Abbot, 1973.

JONES, MERVYN, *Potbank*, Secker and Warburg, London, 1961.

LANCASTER, JOAN C., *Godiva of Coventry*, Coventry Corporation, Coventry, 1967.

LAWLEY, GEORGE T., *A History of Bilston*, Bilston, 1893.

LEES-MILNE, J., *Worcestershire* (Shell Guide), Faber and Faber, London, 1964.

LORD, PETER, *Portra it of the River Trent*, Robert Hale, London, 1968.

MANDER, GERALD P. and TILDESLEY, NORMAN, *A History of Wolverhampton*, Wolverhampton C.B. Corporation, Wolverhampton, 1960.

MANTON, JO, *Sister Dora – The Life of Dorothy Pattison*, Methuen, London, 1971.

MEE, ARTHUR, *The King's England. Herefordshire and Worcestershire* (revised edition), Hodder and Stoughton, London, 1968.

—— *The King's England. Shropshire* (revised edition), Hodder and Stoughton, London, 1968.

—— *The King's England. Staffordshire* (revised edition), Hodder and Stoughton, London, 1971.

—— *The King's England. Warwickshire* (revised edition), Hodder and Stoughton, London, 1966.

—— *The King's England. Worcestershire* (revised edition), Hodder and Stoughton, London, 1968.

METEYARD, ELIZA, *The Life of Josiah Wedgwood*, Hurst and Blacket, London, 1865.

MEYNELL, LAURENCE, *Great Men of Staffordshire*, The Bodley Head, London, 1955.

MOORE, JERROLD NORTHROP, *Elgar : A Life in Photographs*, Oxford University Press, London, 1972.

MORRIS, CHRISTOPHER (ed.), *The Journeys of Celia Fiennes*, Cresset Press, London, 1947.

MOULDER, MICHAEL, *Shropshire* (A Shell Guide), Faber and Faber, London, 1951.

NOBLE, FRANK, *The Shell Book of Offa's Dyke Path*, The Queen Anne Press, London, 1969.

PEVSNER, NIKOLAUS, *The Buildings of England* (Shropshire), Penguin Books, Harmondsworth, 1958.

—— *The Buildings of England* (Staffordshire), Penguin Books, Harmondsworth, 1974.

—— *The Buildings of England* (Worcestershire), Penguin Books, Harmondsworth, 1968.

PEVSNER, NIKOLAUS and WEDGWOOD, ALEXANDRA, *The Buildings of England* (Warwickshire), Penguin Books, Harmondsworth, 1966.

RICHARDSON, KENNETH, *Twentieth-Century Coventry*, Macmillan, London, 1972.

ROWLEY, TREVOR, *The Shropshire Landscape*, Hodder and Stoughton, London, 1972.

SEWARD, ANNA, *Memoirs of the Life of Dr Darwin*, London, 1804.

SHAW, C., *When I Was a Child*, Methuen, 1903. Re-published by S. R. Publishers, East Ardsley, Yorkshire, 1969.

SHAW, REV. STEBBING, *The History and Antiquities of Staffordshire*, London, 1798.

SMITH, FREDERICK, *Coventry: Six Hundred Years of Municipal Life*, Coventry Corporation in association with Coventry *Evening Telegraph*, 1945.

SUTCLIFFE, ANTHONY and SMITH, ROGER, *History of Birmingham*, Vol. III, Oxford University Press, London, 1974.

SYLVESTER, DOROTHY, *A History of Cheshire*, Darwen Finlayson, Henley-on-Thames, 1971.

TREVOR, MERIOL, *Light in Winter*, Vol. II of Newman, Macmillan, London, 1962.

UNDERHILL, CHARLES HAYWARD, *History of Burton Upon Trent*, Tresises, Burton, 1941.

—— *History of Tutbury and Rolleston*, Tresises, Burton, n.d.

VINCE, JOHN, *Canals and Canal Architecture*, Shire Publications, Aylesbury, 1973.

WAITE, VINCENT, *Shropshire Hill Country*, J. M. Dent, London, 1970.

WALTON, IZAAK, *The Compleat Angler*, Everyman's Library, J. M. Dent, London, 1906.

WEDGWOOD, HENRY ALLEN, *People of the Potteries*, Adams and Dart, Bath, 1970.

WEDGWOOD, JOSIAH, *Letters to Thomas Bentley, Friend and Partner*, London, 1903.

WHITELOCK, DOROTHY, with DOUGLAS, DAVID C. and TUCKER, SUSIE I., *The Anglo-Saxon Chronicle, a revised translation*, Eyre and Spottiswoode, London, 1961.

WRIGHT, THOMAS, *The History and Antiquities of Ludlow*, E. J. Morton, Didsbury, Manchester, 1826. Re-published 1972.

Index

Michael Gordon

BP = Birthplace

Abbots Bromley, 134
Aethelflaed (Ethelfleda), 125–6, 144
Alfred, King, 183, 186
almshouses, Trinity Hospital, Clun, 196–7
Alkington Hall, 228
Alstonefield church, 158
Anson, Admiral, 131
Arbury Hall, and George Eliot, 26
Arden, forest of, 19–22
Arthur, Prince, 179, 185, 218
Ashley, Jack, MP, 173–5
Ashmole, Elias, 138
Atherstone, oaks at, 19
Auden, W. H., 45, 96–7
Aylesford, Earl of, and ancestors, 27–30

Badger, 60
Baldwin, Sir Stanley, *BP*, 179; 213–14
Barlaston, Wedgwood works at, 166–8
Barnfield, Richard, *BP*, 129
Baskerville, John, 94, 99
basket making, 110–11
baths, brine, at Droitwich, 189–90
Beckbury, 60
Beecham, Sir Thomas, 101–2
Bennett, Arnold, *BP*, 168; 161, 162, 164, 165, 168
Berrington Hall, 189
Betjeman, Sir John, 48, 216
Bewdley, 177, 179–80
Bickenhill, National Exhibition Centre at, 20, 30–33, 62, 106
Biddulph Moor, 124
Bilston, 53–8; steel works at, 53–6; Museum, 56–7
Birmingham: jewellery quarter, 91–3; the Bull Ring, 93, 99–100; history, 93–6; Museums and Art Galleries, 94, 98–100; University, 96, 103–4; literary centre, 97–9; cathedral, 99–100; theatres, 100–

1; music, 101–2; *The Birmingham Post* 102–3; new architecture, 104–6; industry, 105–7; Edgbaston, 103–6; Oratory Church, 104; Bournville, 104
Bishops Castle, 195–6
Black Country, the, 67–70 *et seq.*; Open-Air Museum, 67–8
Bomere Pool, 213–14
Bonomi, Joseph, 27
Borrow, George, 126
Boswell, James, 137
Boulton, Matthew, 94
brewing beer, 151–3
Bridgnorth, 108–13; the Severn at, 108–10; industries, 110–11; railway, 111–12
Brierley Hill, glass making at, 82–3
Brindley, James, 166, 177, 179–80
Brocton Coppice, oaks at, 133
Bromsgrove, Avoncroft Open-Air Museum at, 179
Brown, Capability, 27, 189
Buildwas Abbey, 113
Bumble Hole, 78
Burne-Jones, Sir Edward, 60, 100
Burritt, Elihu, *Walks in the Black Country . . .* by, 60; 74
Burslem, 165–9
Burton-upon-Trent, 147–53; Andressey Island at, 149–50; beer brewing, 151–3

Caer Caradoc, 194
Caldecott, Randolph, 226
Caldecott Library, Whitchurch, 226
canals: tunnels, 77–9; *The Canal Show*, 79–80; at Birmingham, 94; history of, 110, 166, 179–80, 231; at Burton, 147; at Stourport, 176–8; boatmen on, 180–2; Telford's aqueduct, Pontcysyllte, 231; at Chester, 234; *also* 46, 77, 121, 129, 229

Cannock Chase, 124, 129–36
car industry, 106–7; (Coventry), 41–4; (Tamworth), 144–6; (Wolverhampton), 51
Carroll, Madeleine, 97
Casson, Sir Hugh, 104
Castell Dinas Brân, 232
castles, Welsh border, 202–4
Chad, St, Bishop of Mercia, 128, 140
chainmaking, 74–6, 81, 82
Chamberlain, Joseph, 89, 95
Chantrey, Sir Francis, 128, 141
Charles I, King, 112
Charles II, King, 58, 72
Chartley Park, 61
cheese-making, Cheshire, 226–8
Chester, 234–9; cathedral, 128, 235, 237; St John's Church, 235; Grosvenor Museum, 236
Chirk, 230
Church Eaton, 124
Church Stretton, 195, 220
Churchill, Lord Randolph and Lady (Jennie), 28–9
Claverley, 60
Clee Hills, 218
Cleobury Mortimer, 218
Clive, Sir Robert, 195, 241
Clive House (museum), 207–8
Clun, 193, 196; Museum at, 196; Trinity Hospital (almshouses) at, 196–7
Clun-Clee Ridgeway, 197–8, 199
Clun Forest, 199
Clunbury, Clungunford, Clunton, 194, 200
Cnut, King, 134
Coalbrookdale, 113–14
Coalport China works, 114
Cotman, John Sell, 108
Cotton, Charles, 158–9
Coventry, 34–44; Herbert Museum and Art Gallery, 37, 41–2; Lady Godiva, 37–8; theatre, 38; architecture, 35–6, 38–9; industry, 40–4
Cox, David, 50, 100, 210
Cradley, 76–7, 82
Craven Arms, 194
Cromwell, Oliver, 112
Cross Lanes, 239
Croxen Abbey, 157

Darby, Abraham, and coked coal, 72, 113
Darby's Hill, 78

Darwin, Charles, 166, 208
Darwin, Erasmus, 138, 166
Dee, River, 231–2
Deritend, 94
de Wint, Peter, BP, 129; 210, 212
dialects, 61, 86
Dickens, Charles, Old Curiosity Shop by, 73, 123
Digbeth, 93, 94
Disraeli, Benjamin, Sybil Lothair by, 73, 157
Donne, John, 202
Dovedale, 158–9
Drabble, Margaret, 169
Drabble, Phil, 61, 65, 71, 124, 134–5
Droitwich, 189–90
Drucker, Andre, 102
Dudley, Dud, and iron smelting, 72, 113
Dudley, 71–2, 82; Museum, 67–8
Dudley Port, Dudley Wood, 80
Dugdale, William, BP, 26
Dvořák, Antonin, 101

Eaton Hall and gardens, 237–9
Eaton Hall (home of Hakluyts), 189
Edgbaston, 103–4, 105
Edgeworth, Maria, 140
Edric and Godda, 199–200, 204
Edgbaston, village and church, 228–9
Edward VII, King, 28–9, 152
Elgar, Sir Edward, OM, 185; BP, 188–9
Eliot, George, BP, 26–7; 40, 73, 102, 141, 157–8
Elizabeth I, Queen, 125
Ellesmere, 222
Enright, D. J., 97
Etruria Hall and works (Wedgwood), 162, 165
Evans, Roy, 114–16

Farquhar, George, The Beaux' Stratagem by, and Lichfield, 139
Fenton, 171–2
Fidler, A. G. Sheppard, 105–6
Fisher, Roy, 98
Flaxman, John, 163
Forseth, Einar, mosaics by, 35

Gardner, Prof. Dame Helen, 96
Garrick, David, 138
Gaunt, John of, 154
German, Edward, 226
German War Cemetery, 133–4

glass making, 82–4, 135
Godiva, Lady, 22, 37–8, 58–9, 234
Gornal, 87–8
Gorton, Bishop Neville, 36
Greville, Fulke, 209
gun making, 93–4
Guy, Thomas, 143

Hakluyt, Richard, 189
Hampton in Arden, 19–22
Handel, George Frederic, 27
Hanley (Stoke), 161, 169–71; Museum and Art Gallery, 170
Hanmer, 239
Hazlitt, William, 222
Henry IV, King, 205–6
Henry VII, King, 125
Herbert, Sir Alfred, 41
Herbert, George, 202
Holland, Henry, 129
Hotspur, Harry, 204, 205–6, 224–5
Housman, A. E., 193–4, 217
Howard, Henry, Earl of Northampton, 196
Hutton, William, *History of Birmingham* by, 98–9

Ironbridge, 114–16; Ironbridge Gorge Museum, 114

jewellery making, 91–2
John, King, 185
Johnson, Dr Samuel, *BP*, 137–39; 156
Jones, Mervyn, *Potbank* by, 164

Kemble, John Philip, 51
Kempe, Charles, 59, 141, 155
Kidderminster, 176

Langland, William, *BP*, 218–19
leather workers, 83–86
Leofric of Mercia, Earl, 37–8, 59, 191 234
Leominster, 181, 190–2; Priory Church, 190–1
Lichfield, Patrick, Earl of, and ancestors (Anson family), 129–33
Lichfield, 137–45; St Chad's Church and Cathedral, 140–2; Cathedral library, 141–2
Ling, Arthur, 39
Llangollen, 230–3
Long Mynd, the, 194, 219–20

Longton, 171–2
Lowbury, Dr Edward, 97, 98–9
Lower Spoad (farm), 201
Ludlow, 193, 207, 214–18; St Laurence Church, 210, 216–18
Ludlow Castle, 185, 204, 217–18

MacNeice, Louis, 96, 234
Madeley, 115–16
Madin, John, Design Group, 89, 105
Manifold valley, 158–60
Manzoni, Sir Herbert, 105
Marion de la Bruere, 218
Mary, Queen of Scots, 133, 154
Market Drayton, 241
Mendelssohn, Felix, 101
Meriden, 23–4; Triumph works at, 23–6
Milldale, 158
Mills, Edward D., 31–3
Milton, John, and *Comus* at Ludlow Castle, 217–18
Molesworth, Mrs: *The Cuckoo Clock* and Ludlow, 216
Montgomery, 202–3
Morgan, Barbara (Barbara Foxall), 100–1
Morris, Stephen, 63–4
Morris, William, 59–60, 100
Moseley Old Hall, 58
Moseley family, 154–6
Much Wenlock, 219
Murdock, William, 94
Mushroom Green, 80–2
Mystery Plays at Chester, 235–6

Nantwich, 240–1; Dorfold Hall at, 240
National Exhibition Centre, *see* Bickenhill
Nelson, Horatio, Lord, 216
Nesfield, William, 21
Netherton, 69–71, 77–8
Newman, Cardinal John, 104–5
Newtown, 201–2

Offa, King, 143–4
Offa's Dyke, 198–200
Oldbury, 82
Oswestry, 221–2
Overton, 139
Owen, Gareth, 97
Owen, Robert, *BP*, 202
Owen, Wilfred, *BP*, 222

Packington, Little, 26
Packington Hall, 27–9

Pattingham, 60
Pearson, Joseph, 65
peat (turf) cutting, 229–30
Peel, Sir Robert, 143
Penn, 58–9
Percy, Bishop, *BP*, 109
Pevsner, Sir Nikolaus, 20, 21–2, 35, 105, 215
pigeon racing, 135
Portway, the (Long Mynd), 219
pottery making: 114–16; Wedgwood, 166–7; bottle ovens, 169–70; Worcester, 186–7
Priestley, Dr Joseph, 94
Pryce-Jones, Sir Pryce, 201
Pugin, Augustus, 97

Raven, Jon, 79
Raymond, Carole, *embroidery* by, 100
Reed, Henry, 96
Rejlander, Oscar Gustav, 52
Reliant works at Tamworth, 144–6
Robert, James, 105
Rolleston, 154–6
Rossetti, Dante Gabriel, 60
Rupert, Prince, 45, 241

saddlers, 84–6
Salt, William, libary of, 127
salt industry, 226, 239–40
Scott, Sir Walter, *The Betrothed* by, and Clun, 196
Sedgley, 81
Sentinel, The (Stoke), 174
Severn, River, 108–10, 121–2, 177–8, 201, 208, 242
Severn Valley Railway, 11–12
Seward, Anna ('The Swan of Lichfield'), 138
Shakespeare, William, 19, 102, 205
Shaw, C., *When I was a Child* by, 164–5, 172
sheep sales, 194–5; farming, 198
Shenstone, Roman farmstead at, 143
Shenstone, William, 98
Sheridan, R. B., MP for Stafford, 126
Shire horses, 211–12
Shrewsbury, 204–14; Battlefield and church at, 204–6; Clive House (porcelain and military museum), 206–8; Rowley's House (museum), 207–8; Shrewsbury School, 208–10; St Mary's Church, 210–11

Shugborough, 129–33; museum at, 132
Shustoke, 26
Siddons, Sarah, 51, 216
Sidney, Sir Philip, 179, 208, 209–10, 217
Smith, R. D., 97
Soho works, Birmingham, 94
Spence, Sir Basil, 35–6
Spodes, Josiah, 171
Stafford, 124–8; Salt Library at, 65, 127; St Mary's Church, 127; Museum and Halfhead Farm (Izaak Walton), 127
Staffordshire Way, 135
steelworks at Bilston, 53–6
Stiperstones, the, 199, 219
Stoke-on-Trent, 161–75; Gladstone Pottery Museum, 171–2; City Museum and Art Gallery, 162, 170; St Peter's Church, 163
Stokesay Castle, 194
Stone, 128–9
Stourbridge, 82
Stourport, 176–9
Stubbs, George, 166
Sudbury *and* Sudbury Hall, 156
Sutherland, Graham, 36
Sutton Park, 19, 103

Talbot, John, Earl of Shrewsbury, 224–5
Tamworth, 143–6; Castle, 144; Reliant works, 144–6
Telford, Thomas, 112, 179, 231
Telford New Town, 116–19
Teme, River, 214
Terry, Dame Ellen, *BP*, 38
Tettenhall, 59–60
Thornycroft, Thomas, 52
Tipton, 80
Tividale, 80
Toft, Ralph and Thomas, 171
Tolkien, Prof. John, 97
Tong church, 122–4
Treece, Henry, 97
Tunstall, 164–5
Turner, Joseph Mallord William, 108
turf (peat) cutting, 229–30
Tutbury, 153–4

Uttoxeter, 156–7

Victoria, Queen, 52
vinegar making, 178–9

Walcot Hall, 195
Wall (Letocetum), 142
Walsall, 83–6 181; Sister Dora, 73; leather works at, 82, 83–6
Walters, Bryan, 98
Walton, Izaak, *BP*, 127; 153, 155, 158 159
Watling Street, 121, 142
Watt, James, 94
Watt's Dyke, 221
Wayfarer (W. M. Robinson), 22
Weald Moors, the, 119, 121
Webb, Mary, 212–15
Wedgwood, Josiah, *BP*, 165–6; 131, 162, 163, 170, 171, 180
Wednesbury, 82
Wednesfield, 59
Wellington, 116, 120–21
Welshpool, 202
Wem, 222
Wenlock Edge, 193–4, 219
Wenlock Priory, 219
Wesley, John, 61, 223
Weston Park, 120–1
whippet racing, 79–80, 135
Whitchurch, 222–30; church, 224–6; Caldecott Library, 226; cheese-making, 226–8

Whixall Moss (peat), 229–30
Wightwick Manor, 59–60
Wild Edric, 199–200, 204
Willenhall, 82
Willetts, Prof. R. F., 96
William I, King, 61, 134, 196, 234
Wolverhampton, 45–53, 62–6; history, 46–8, 51–3, 65; St Peter's Church, 45, 46–8; Art Gallery, 49–50, 57; Bantock House Museum, 56–7; *see also* Bilston
Womere, 133
Wood, Ralph, 170
Worcester, 183–8; history, 183–4, 185–6; Three Choirs Festival, 184; Tudor House Museum, 184; Cathedral, 185; Royal Porcelain Co. and Dyson Perrins museum, 186–8
Wotton, Sir Henry, 155
Wrekin, the, 113, 117, 119–20, 194; 'Forest Glen' pavilion at, 120
Wrexham, 239–40
Wroxeter (Viroconium), 121–2, 142, 236
Wulfrun, The Lady, 48
Wulfstan, St, 185
Wyatt, Samuel, 94, 129–30

Zeller, Dom Hubert van, 234–5